Democratic Transformation and Obstruction

I0084493

Although "democracy promotion" has become a popular term for policy makers and scholars, democratization is rarely a smooth or linear transition. While some countries quickly democratize, others lag behind despite a long period of democracy promotion activities. Furthermore, while democracy promotion itself has been widely studied, there is a paucity of literature available assessing the outcome or the impact of democracy promotion.

This book investigates democracy promotion by the European Union and the United States of America, and seeks to uncover why intensive democracy promotion has resulted in limited democratic progress. Exploring case studies of Armenia, Azerbaijan, and Georgia, this book examines the conditions in which democracy promotion is more likely to result in democratic transformation. In addition, it introduces the concept of the "democracy blocker," a powerful authoritarian regional actor that is capable of blocking democratization in other countries.

This book will be of interest to students and scholars of Political Science, Democracy, Democratization, EU Studies, US Politics, Comparative Politics, and Foreign Policy.

Nelli Babayan is a Senior Researcher in the Otto Suhr Institute of Political Science at the Freie Universität Berlin, Germany.

Democratization Studies
(Formerly Democratization Studies, Frank Cass)

Democratization Studies combines theoretical and comparative studies with detailed analysis of issues central to democratic progress and its performance, all over the world.

The books in this series aim to encourage debate on the many aspects of democratization that are of interest to policy makers, administrators, journalists, and aid and development personnel, as well as to all those involved in education.

Democratic Transformation and Obstruction

EU, US, and Russia in the South Caucasus

Nelli Babayan

Routledge
Taylor & Francis Group

LONDON AND NEW YORK

First published 2015
by Routledge
2 Park Square, Milton Park, Abingdon, Oxfordshire OX14 4RN

and by Routledge
711 Third Avenue, New York, NY 10017

First issued in paperback 2016

Routledge is an imprint of the Taylor & Francis Group, an informa business

British Library Cataloguing in Publication Data
A catalogue record for this book is available from the British Library

Library of Congress Cataloging in Publication Data
Babayan, Nelli.
Democratic transformation and obstruction : EU, US and Russia in the South Caucasus / Nelli Babayan.
  pages cm. – (Democratization studies ; 28)
  Includes bibliographical references and index.
  1. Democratization–Government policy–United States.
  2. Democratization–Government policy–European Union countries.
  3. Democracy–Armenia (Republic) 4. Democracy–Azerbaijan.
  5. Democracy–Georgia (Republic) 6. New democracies–Caucasus, South. 7. United States–Foreign relations–1989– 8. European Union countries–Foreign relations. 9. Russia (Federation)–Foreign relations.
  I. Title.
  JZ1480.B29 2014
  320.9475–dc23   2014010146

ISBN 13: 978-1-138-23821-3 (pbk)
ISBN 13: 978-0-415-74866-7 (hbk)

Typeset in Times New Roman
by Wearset Ltd, Boldon, Tyne and Wear

To you, who chose this over another dragons and zombies book

Contents

About the author

Nelli Babayan has a PhD from the University of Trento and is a Senior Researcher at the Freie Universität Berlin, where she has also taught on democratization and the role of information technologies in democracy. Her research includes democracy promotion/democratization, EU and US foreign policies and transatlantic relations, the politics of the South Caucasus, and the role of information technologies in democracy. In 2005–2008, prior to doctoral studies, she worked for a USAID-funded project, where she was Training Department Manager in 2006–2008. In 2010 she was visiting researcher at the Center for Comparative and International Studies, ETH Zürich and the think-tank FRIDE, Madrid.

Preface and acknowledgments

In April 2002 I received a call from the American Councils' director in Armenia telling me that I was in a small group of those selected in a nationwide competition for a US State Department scholarship to spend an academic year at a US university. Through the jumpy excitement of an 18 year old getting ready for a major trip, little did I know that this experience would define my career and my friendships. My scholarship was part of a US democracy-promotion policy, and later I spent three years working for a USAID-funded project, writing my doctoral dissertation on the very policy that I was a lucky part of.

I am preparing this manuscript amidst the crisis in Ukraine, which in early March 2014 is characterized by polarized coverage in English- and Russian-language media, EU and US confusion over next steps, and Russia's conviction of its righteous cause. While in this book I discuss a different region, the main argument also applies to Ukraine. Similar to the cases I discuss, Ukraine is also caught between different strategic interests, domestic disagreements, and less-than-democratic authorities on its way to democracy. Even if the prospects for speedy democratizations seem unrealistic, I am submitting this manuscript looking forward to more active, coordinated, and peaceful efforts at advancing democracy.

This book is based on my doctoral dissertation, which greatly benefited from invaluable advice by Sergio Fabbrini, Roberto Belloni, Frank Schimmelfennig, and Peter Burnell. Thomas Risse's pointed recommendations and constructive criticism helped me address initial shortcomings.

No academic endeavor, however, would be full without exciting extracurricular life. I want to thank my parents, who were not afraid of sending their teenage daughter over the Atlantic. For contributing to the adventure and the excitement in my life I want to thank my best friends who I met thanks to that scholarship: Ella, Tatev, Meri, Ruzanna, and Rebecca. I want to thank Kevin for telling me to stay focused on writing the book every time I tried to sneak-read another chapter of a book.

Last but not least, I want to thank the reader who will pick up this book and hopefully stay interested beyond the introduction.

Introduction

Democracy is not a free ride. It demands more of each of us than any other arrangement.

Eric Sevareid, CBS 1972

The eighth year of decline in political liberties (Puddington 2014) has yet again demonstrated that democratization is a distance event with hurdles rather than a sprint. Yet, democracy promotion[1] has become the buzzterm for policy makers and scholars, even if the euphoria of post-communist transitions has long passed (Diamond 2008; Carothers 2009; Burnell 2010; Youngs 2011). While some post-communist or authoritarian countries quickly democratized and even launched their own democracy-promotion programs (e.g. the Baltic States, Poland, and the Czech Republic), others are democratic laggards despite almost two decades of democracy-promotion activities—e.g. Armenia and Azerbaijan. Though on a law-making level some countries have at least embraced democratic principles, others have not even bothered with democratic pretense. Other countries pledging their loyalty to democratic principles have either fallen back into autocracy or have stalled between autocracy and democracy, generating the puzzle behind this book: *extensive democracy promotion but limited democratic transformation.*[1]

Labeling democracy promotion as a grand failure of the Western world would be an easy way out for pundits analyzing the struggling multi-billion dollar industry. However, distinguishing the outcome of specific democracy-promotion projects and deciphering their mechanisms provides improved evaluation of the policies, rather than merely turning to a democracy index. The purpose of this book is to analyze democracy promotion and to explain why democracy has not become "the only game in town," even in countries where democracy promotion is welcome. More specifically, *under what conditions is democracy promotion more likely to result in democratic transformation?*

Several factors have undermined the previous view of democracy as a "universal value" (Sen 1999), among them China's blistering economic growth without democratization, and Russia's bullying authoritarianism with accelerating plans of building a Eurasian Customs Union (Putin 2011). Pressure exercised by Russia on Armenia and Ukraine in 2013 further fuelled concerns about

Russia's authoritarian ambitions and its role as a powerful democracy blocker. The issue of a democracy-blocking regional power is one of the underlying themes of this book, which argues that democratic stagnations or setbacks into authoritarianism are often the result of democracy-blocking activities. US intervention in Iraq under the banner of democracy promotion, its global surveillance through the National Security Agency (Human Rights Watch 2014), and the double-standards of Western approaches to friendly but "oily" autocrats, have also cast a dark shadow over the legitimacy and credibility of democracy promotion and the observation of human rights. Despite their dubious long-term democratization effects, the 2011 events in the Middle East and North Africa (MENA) have refocused attention on the issue of democratization and re-inspired supporters of democracy. Yet, the cry for democracy in MENA seems to have been home-grown, casting further doubts about the value of external democracy promotion and raising questions on its impact. Despite the obstacles, the democratic rhetoric of both democracy promoters and democracy targets continue, and billions are spent on democracy-promotion projects. This book explores the interaction between external democracy promotion and domestic democratization that has produced varying outcomes in different countries and, likely, also different sectors—elections, political parties, and the media.

Given that "never in human history had international forces—political, economic, and cultural—been so supportive of democratic ideas and institutions" (Dahl 1998), the limited progress of democracy has been even more surprising. Since the early 1990s, states and organizations have targeted virtually every corner of the world with democracy-promotion activities. However, after the "third wave of democratization" (Huntington 1993), liberal democracy has made little progress or has even broken down (Diamond 2008), arguably pointing to a third reverse-wave of democratization. However, policies of democracy promotion have also lacked consistency and well-defined strategies, leaving practitioners and academics wondering how democracy promotion would proceed (Cox *et al.* 2000; Smith 2008; Youngs 2002). To shed light on these issues, the book investigates democracy promotion by the European Union (EU) and the United States of America (US) in Armenia, Azerbaijan, and Georgia against the backdrop of Russia's regional interests.

Numerous studies have emerged giving their evaluation (ex-post) but not appraisal (ex-ante) of democracy promotion by individual countries and organizations (Burnell 2007, 2008a; Carothers 2004). The analyses available on democracy-promotion strategies of the most influential international actors (Burnell and Youngs 2009; Carothers 1999; Youngs 2002) without doubt shed light on the causes, and even strategies, of democracy promotion. The praiseworthy effort of finally comparing two most prominent democracy promoters in a full volume (Magen *et al.* 2009) has contributed to the understanding of similarities and differences between the strategies of the EU and the US. However, scarce literature is available assessing the outcome or the impact of democracy promotion, including recent practitioner endeavors (Kumar 2012). As Magen *et al.* mention (2009, p. 20 and p. 268), they do "not venture to evaluate their [strategies'] impact," and "this task has to wait for another book." The book aims to evaluate the outcomes of democracy promotion and democratization processes to produce usable information for democracy promoters and democracy advocates.

The goal of this book is to evaluate the outcome of democracy promotion by juxtaposing the strategies of promoters and domestic conditions provided by targets. It offers a simultaneous analyses of three different target-sectors of democracy promotion—elections, parties, and the media—in three countries. It demonstrates democratic transformation on the macro level of a country and on micro levels of specific sectors. Thus, this book offers a tridimensional comparison of promoters and their strategies, of country-specific democratic transformations, and of sectors within and across country-cases. Unlike many voices in democracy promotion analysis, this book does not blame international actors in the failures of democracy promotion. It rather emphasizes that democracy promotion cannot be viewed in isolation from domestic actors and processes, and it endeavors to understand what has been done, and how to make democracy promotion more effective and democratization more efficient. In addition, this book poses an overarching aim to understand whether democracy can be achieved from outside, and what would be the advantages and the obstacles of such an endeavor.

Democracy promotion and democratization: the hybrid

Speaking of democratization or democracy promotion as separate processes has become obsolete. Thus, while these two processes should be viewed as partially simultaneous and complementary, it is also more effective to speak of democratic transformations as the outcome of these two processes. Consequently, this book analyzes the outcome of democracy-promotion policies and strategies juxtaposed with domestic conditions. Without a clear understanding of the mechanisms of democracy-promotion strategies and their possible outcomes, democracy-promotion studies will continue to lack clarity and applicability to in-field democracy promotion. Democracy promotion runs the risk of wasting billions, and due to its notorious underperformance may also diminish the credibility and leverage of democracy promoters in other policy areas. The objective of this book has required an analytical framework that would provide an advantage of a prognostic value for academic studies and policy recommendations for practitioners. However, democracy-promotion studies have so far suffered from a lack of such a framework.

Although useful in identifying the causes of democracy promotion, international relations theories are of little assistance in identifying the strategies of democracy promotion that may result in positive outcome or democratic transformation because of their neglect of domestic realities of target countries. Theoretical frameworks of democratization from comparative politics do not take into consideration international actors and factors, focusing exclusively on elite behavior, economic development, or political culture. However, due to the increased interconnectedness of international and domestic political and economic realities, a highly hybrid phenomena such as democracy promotion and democratization require an analytical framework that equally takes into account international and domestic actors and processes. Thus, by developing an analytical framework applicable to policy development and implementation, this book has identified the mechanisms and conditions of democracy-promotion policies that result in certain types of democratic transformation.

The quest for an analytical framework did not begin from scratch. Instead of re-inventing the bicycle, this book employs a tested theoretical framework of international socialization (Schimmelfennig *et al.* 2006). This account of international socialization has been useful for the objective of this book particularly since it allows capturing and analyzing the interaction between international and domestic factors that lead to democratic transformations. This framework is also adapted to democracy promotion by expanding its structural and geographical scopes and the range of variables it analyzes. The original international socialization framework focused on EU promotion of democratic norms in Central and Eastern Europe (CEE). This book broadens the initial geographic scope by adding a new promoter (the US) and three countries (Armenia, Azerbaijan, and Georgia) which do not have an EU membership perspective. It broadens the analytical scope by analyzing a larger variety of external and internal conditions to provide a better account of the interaction between the promoter and the target. The book also broadens the original explanatory logic by analyzing different types of democratic transformations (formal, behavioral, and unintended), thus providing more nuanced understanding of democratic transformation.

International socialization has been defined "as a process in which states are induced to adopt constitutive rules of an international community" (Schimmelfennig *et al.* 2006, p. 2). While this understanding can to some extent be applied to democracy promotion, the scope adopted by this book requires further clarifications and adaptations. International socialization has been mainly understood as socialization of individuals and has been viewed as a process, not an outcome. Thus, "a failed socialization process would not count as a socialization at all" (Schimmelfennig *et al.* 2006, p. 2). Such an approach to democracy promotion would be problematic because—regardless of whether the outcome is positive or negative—democracy promotion has happened and most likely some type of an outcome has followed. In addition, taking "compliance" as the outcome of international socialization, Schimmelfennig *et al.* are only interested in whether the country complies with the rule of the international organization or not, having as an indicator "legal rule adoption" (Schimmelfennig *et al.* 2006, p. 58). They do not investigate further to see whether the new rule or law is actually enforced because "the Western organizations were generally content with legal adoption and greeted the passing of norm-conforming laws as indications that their demands were fulfilled" (Schimmelfennig *et al.* 2006, p. 58). However, the examples of many post-Soviet countries show that mere legal adoption of a rule does not guarantee rule-based behavior within any of the sectors of democracy promotion or democratization. In addition, the assessments of democracy-promotion projects acknowledge that, even if the rule has been legally adopted, "the challenge … lies in converting new formal rules into working rules" (ARD 2002, p. 24). Moreover, the formal adoption of the rule on a civil society level does not also guarantee its prevalence on political or state levels, often due to the weakness of the civil society in democratizing countries. Thus, while "compliance" is useful to understand short-term effects of rule promotion, democratic transformation within domestic political and societal systems is more useful for understanding the potential overall outcome of democracy promotion, *inter alia* providing a better understanding of its impact.

Democratic transformation: the analytical framework

The components of international socialization are used solely as a starting point for further development of the democratic transformation framework. Democratic transformation of the target is defined as the outcome of a multifaceted interaction between external conditions of democracy promotion and internal conditions of local democratization. This definition implies several conceptual decisions, resulting in theoretical and methodological implications, and, while it would be folly to attempt to unveil all possible influencing conditions, the ones presented here are the ones proven to have the greatest importance.

Within democracy-promotion studies, states have been generally understood as the targets of democracy promotion, with progress towards democracy having been measured on state level. However, successful democratization encompasses the interaction of several elements building up towards the desired advancement in democracy. In addition, democracy promotion varies not only in its implementation strategies but also in its targets and sectors. The democratic machinery properly functions only when the behavior of state institutions, political parties, and the civil society comprised of citizens and various organizations is in line with democratic rules. Based on the adopted definition of democracy as a system that ensures participation and contestation (Dahl 1972; Diamond *et al.* 1989; Munck and Verkuilen 2002), democracy-promotion activities are classified according to the levels of state, political society, civil society, and individual citizens (Carothers 1999; Schmitter and Brouwer 1999). Thus, going beyond the traditional statist approach to democracy promotion, this analytical framework encompasses the analysis of democratic transformation within three target-sectors: elections, political parties, and the media as part of civil society. This approach allows for a more nuanced understanding of democratic transformation both on the macro level of states and micro level of target-sectors.

The outcome of democracy promotion and democratization is studied by the analysis of elections projects, which encompass all three levels of targets; party development projects, which encompass the political parties' level; and media development projects, which encompass the civil society level. These types of projects not only reflect the theoretical requirements of democracy—participation and contestation—but also represent the conventional democracy-promotion package of many promoters. The analysis of these projects aims to reveal the general pattern of strategies and implementation rather than presenting the outputs such as the number of people trained. Thus, instead of following the beaten track of "success story" templates (Bryson and Eley 2007), the book aims to provide a comprehensive picture of democracy-promotion strategies provided in response to the domestic democratization environment.

The variation within democratic transformation, as the outcome of democracy promotion and democratization—formal, behavioral, and unintended (Schimmelfennig 2002, p. 9)—is based on the discussion on conceptions of norms (Finnemore and Sikkink 1998) and is often used in the norm diffusion literature (Raymond 1997; Risse *et al.* 1999; Cortell and Davis Jr. 2000). Behavioral democratic transformation is also the most difficult one to achieve because it would mean that democracy has become "the only game in town." In addition, behavioral democratic transformation is considered within each analyzed sector of democracy promotion (elections, party politics, and media freedom) and entails fulfillment of specific functions ascribed by democratic rules. While the international socialization framework uses a dichotomous categorization for rule adoption (compliance versus non-compliance), to fully account for possible outcomes a trichotomous categorization is more fitting. At the same time, taking into consideration the implementation process of a policy and customary monitoring and evaluation strategies of promoters, the measurement of democratic transformation involves indicators from two dimensions: promoter and target. This is justified by the fact that often promoters measure the effectiveness of their projects not by domestic political dynamics, but according to their checklists of completed activities. In addition, it is important because the outcome of democracy promotion occurs as a result of the interaction between promoters and targets.

A broad term of multifaceted interaction allows for various mechanisms and strategies of democracy promotion, ranging from normative persuasion to conditionality and material incentives. However, specific interactions in different country- and sector-cases are not predetermined by the theoretical understanding of interaction but by the actual interacting conditions. Coming from both rational and constructivist perspectives, these conditions include but are not limited to cooperation between promoters, local ownership, democracy blockers, consistency of strategies, involvement of promoters in other local issues, and local bargaining power. Democracy-promotion projects are often criticized for being implemented within the vacuum of their own targets. Thus, attention is paid to the interaction between the projects and target levels, namely whether the promoter attempts to incorporate all its target levels to avoid resistance (from the state and political society levels) or reluctance (of the civil society and individual citizens) towards its projects.

Sectoral democratic transformation: the argument

Democracy promotion is not a straightforward process and cannot rely on the normative attractiveness or the benignity of democracy alone. However, democracy can still be achieved from outside, but the obstacles are more significant than anticipated by promoters. The main focus here is democratic transformation. Yet, it is also important to account for the entire process of the development and implementation of a democracy-promotion policy, since the institutional and decision-making structures of a promoter may influence policy formation and implementation. Thus, it is demonstrated that the mechanisms of foreign policy decision-making are likely to influence the implementation of democracy promotion. Incoherent foreign policy decision-making, burdened by institutional competition, is likely to hinder smooth implementation of democracy promotion and substantially curtails promoters' options.

Democracy promotion yielding advancement in local levels of democracy is a result of bargaining and persuasion, conditioned by a number of external and internal factors. In addition, it is a result of the strategic interaction of a promoter with regional powers that may be opposing the democratization of its neighbors. The chances of democratic behavior will increase provided the domestic costs of adaptation to democracy are moderate, promoters are actively involved in the resolution of pressing national issues, and there is no regional actor that blocks democracy and receives support from the target country. In addition to the analytical framework, the book further elaborates on the concept of a democracy blocker (Babayan 2012a, 2013a)—a powerful authoritarian regional actor. Even if not explicitly promoting autocracy, it is willing to and capable of blocking democratization in other countries. The mere adoption of a law does not guarantee rule-based behavior by domestic stakeholders. Consequently, a transformation of formal democratic rules and procedures into behavioral practices requires that democracy promoters achieve consistency in their efforts and follow-up on their activities. In addition, variation of democratic transformation within the three sectors indicates that democracy promotion needs to be simultaneously cross-sectoral, offering material incentives for democratic transformation. The analyses of these projects show:

1   the domestic requisites of successful democracy promotion may vary depending upon the target level;
2   the implementation strategy rarely varies depending upon the target level;
3   the outcome or the level of democratic transformation occasionally varies on different target levels given the implementation strategy is the same.

While factors influencing democratic transformation remain the same for any country targeted for democracy promotion, their values and importance may change from case to case. Nevertheless, despite legitimate and sometimes credible actions of democracy promoters, the incentives that they offer to authoritarian countries are too low. Thus, low incentives, which are not supported by cooperative actions of the promoters, are further weakened by their detachment from the domestic issues of the target country. It is apparent that the resonance of democratic rules and local identification with a democracy promoter do not positively contribute to local democratization either, and are merely intervening factors. The presence of Russia as a democracy blocker and the persistence of protracted conflicts are argued to be among the main, if not the main, obstacles to democratization in the South Caucasus. The absence of credible incentives, lack of cooperation between promoters, and the presence of a democracy blocker with local support make behavioral democratic transformation problematic in a country like Armenia. Yet, having faced similar domestic conditions but strongly opposed Russia's influence, and been supported in this opposition by democracy promoters, has likely resulted in tentative behavioral democratic transformation of Georgia. As the analysis shows, especially in the media sector of Armenia, the likelihood of a behavioral democratic transformation may increase should democracy promoters cooperate, actively offer credible incentives to different sectors of democracy promotion, and actively contribute to pressing national issues.

Effective democracy promotion entails not only intermediate success or completion of a democracy-promotion project, but also an overall improvement in the state of democracy in the target country. Depending upon the country-specific situation, overall improvement in democracy can involve a move to free and fair elections, reduction of political violence during campaigns, increased independence of the judiciary, or a reduction of political corruption. Thus, for example, elections-related projects should not only raise awareness by the voters about their rights or increase the understanding by political parties about the value of free and fair elections, but also ultimately contribute to the conduct of such elections and the peaceful transition of power. On the level of specific sectors targeted by democracy promoters, it can increase their own compliance with their primary functions based on democratic principles. While transition paradigms and democracy-promotion toolboxes focusing on one or the other sector have resulted in limited, if any, behavioral democratic transformations, simultaneous cross-sectoral democracy promotion may lead to enhanced effectiveness.

Case studies and the organization of the book

The findings of this book are based on in-depth comparative analysis of EU and US democracy promotion in three target countries of the South Caucasus region and three target sectors in each of the countries tracing democratic transformations. The analyzed period spans over the start of targeted democracy promotion throughout the latest general elections of 2013. By such tridimensional comparison, this book fills the gap of insufficient comparative research in democracy promotion. Although the volume by Magen *et al.* (2009) presents a comparative study of EU and US strategies of democracy promotion in different regions, it does not analyze their impact. Among potential democracy promoters, the EU and the US seem optimal choices for comparison, not only in terms of their strategies but also in terms of their possible impact on domestic politics due to their usual economic and political attractiveness for target countries and their leverage on the international arena. However, the comparison does not start with an assumption that these two actors are inherently different or similar. Instead, their strategies are confronted, looking for both similarities and differences, and possibilities for cooperation and complementation for enhanced results.

Despite two decades of dubious democratization, the South Caucasus has grown in importance for the EU and the US *inter alia* in terms of energy sources and routes, access to the Middle East, containment of militant fundamentalism, and proximity to Russia. In addition, the varying degrees of democratization of three South Caucasus countries allows for pinpointing the factors responsible for on-going progress or setbacks. Armenia, Azerbaijan, and Georgia have developed into competitive authoritarian regimes, even if with varying democracy scores. Georgia has so far come the closest to democracy, with Azerbaijan having consolidated its authoritarian regime, and Armenia staying in between. They rhetorically identify with democracy promoters but at the same time have been to varying degrees compelled to support Russia's democracy-blocking policies. The persistence of the protracted conflicts has hindered the economic development of Armenia and Georgia, and the behavioral democratic transformation of all three at macro level. Democratic transformations on the micro level of sectors within different election cycles are more nuanced. In addition, the South Caucasus still remains out of the spotlight of both academia and the media, even in comparison with other post-Soviet countries such as Ukraine. Though different in scale, the protests over joining the Eurasian Customs Union in Ukraine were widely covered by major English-speaking media outlets, while the ones in Armenia received more modest coverage (Nikolski 2013).

The book is divided into three major parts: theoretical considerations, local and international conditions of democracy promotion, and sectoral outcomes of democratic transformation. Addressing theory, Chapters 1 and 2 develop the analytical approach to democracy promotion and democratization, and apply it to democratic transformation. Based on literature, I classify types and sectors of democracy promotion, suggesting hypotheses for democratic transformation, i.e. the outcome of democracy promotion and domestic democratization. The following empirical chapters start with the analyses of the domestic socio-economic and political situation in Armenia, Azerbaijan, and Georgia after the independence from the Soviet Union. Chapter 3 introduces the conditions of domestic democratization and maps the environment where democracy promotion programs have been implemented. Chapter 4 proceeds with the analyses of EU and US democracy-promotion activities as part of their foreign policies, analyzing their strategies and approaches to democracy promotion. It also analyzes their relations with democracy-blocking Russia. The breakdown of Chapters 5–7 follows the approach of sectoral transformation adopted by the book. Starting with brief introductions into separate sectors, these chapters analyze democratic transformation and specific democracy promotion projects in each country within elections (Chapter 5), political parties (Chapter 6), and the media (Chapter 7). Part III concludes with a combined conclusion for Chapters 5–7, bringing together sectoral analyses and underlining different transformations.

Note

1 Partly to distance from the Bush agenda of democracy promotion, discourse has emerged to rename the promotion of democracy to "democracy assistance" (Burnell 2010, p. 17). However, the two phrases remain essentially the same without substantial differences in terms of strategies or targets.

Part I

Democracy promotion, democratization, transformation

1 The hybridism of democratic transformation[1]

Despite critical views, there is an extensive volume of literature that follows a normative understanding that democracy is the best type of government, with virtually no alternatives deserving consideration. The favoring view of democracy argues that democracy promotes "freedom as no feasible alternative can" (Dahl 1989, p. 89) and that it "provides by definition comparatively good protection for human rights" (Diamond 1999, p. 4). Proponents of democracy argue that it is desirable because it is "the best and therefore unbeatable means of political organization" and undeniably possible because "it is the one form of government which evolves constantly to ensure that it is possible" (Gilley 2009, pp. 124–125). However, others argue that democracy is not desirable because it causes repression and inequality (Riker 1982), promotes westernization, causes instability and inefficiency, and is impossible to achieve due to citizen stupidity and ignorance (Gilley 2009). Regardless of democracy's desirability and feasibility, it is currently the most celebrated form of governance which many governments try to promote and even more try, sometimes genuinely, to achieve. Even if refusing to fully adopt the championed liberal democracy, some have adopted a localized version of democracy, with adjectives and increasingly spreading single-party democracies (Tisdall 2010).

Notwithstanding the long history of democracy and its acceptance by virtually any country, at least rhetorically, to date it remains one of the most contested and debated concepts (Møller and Skaaning 2013). However, even if often treated as a "vague endorsement of a popular idea" (Dahl 1989, p. 2), democracy, as with other social science concepts, requires clear definition (Sartori 1970) to avoid vagueness when measuring it within different cases (Adcock and Collier 2001). The literature is filled with the multitude of "democracies with adjectives" (Collier and Levitsky 1997). However, while scholars debate the underlying components of democracy, the regime championed by democracy promoters—even if not always called as such—is liberal democracy, which consists of contestation and participation and is supported by the rule of law. These scholarly understandings of democracy, sometimes unwittingly, have translated into specific democracy-promotion sectors covering the political life of target countries. Given that these different sectors—elections, political parties, and civil society—may be on different levels of development in the target country, it would be logical to assume that democracy-promotion outcomes may be different depending on the sector and domestic conditions. These different outcomes in their turn are likely to produce democracies with adjectives, emphasizing that mere establishment of democratic institutions does not guarantee their democratic functioning. However, is there an analytical framework that would help in assessing the potential outcome and—even more importantly—anticipating it?

By closely analyzing comparative politics and international relations literature, I show in this chapter that decades of democracy promotion and its research have yet to produce a meta-theory that would wield some level of predictability. In addition, the scholarly literature has been characterized by an obsolete and artificial line between international and domestic factors of democratization. In other words, democracy promotion has often been viewed in the vacuum of promoters' strategies without paying attention to the facilitating or impeding factors provided by local milieu. While arguing that democracy promotion and local democratization should be analyzed as an interconnected process, the chapter turns *inter alia* to international socialization (Schimmelfennig *et al.* 2006) in its endeavor to develop an analytical framework for democracy promotion. This particular understanding of international socialization provides an opportunity to equally consider developments within the international and domestic realms, differentiating different types of strategies and democratic transformations. Such close consideration of international and domestic conditions and strategies of democracy promotion allows expectation of specific outcomes of democracy promotion depending upon varied values of international and domestic conditions. However, before proceeding to the analytical framework, the chapter provides in-depth analysis of the concepts of democracy, democratization, and democracy promotion to outline various democracy promotion projects and their objectives.

Democracy and democratization

Understanding of the outcome and impact of democracy promotion has often been limited due to scholarly disagreements over the conceptualizations of democracy. Thus, conceptualizing one of the most empirically and theoretically debated concepts can be a daunting task. The elusiveness of the definition of democracy mainly derives from its changing nature based on international and domestic processes, along with cultural and historical specificities of different societies. Thus, regardless of the currently prevailing definition of democracy, its conceptualization is closely interconnected with the context in which it is conceptualized and should be addressed by a "constructivist approach" (Whitehead 2002, p. 7). Definitions of democracy adopted for a study of democracy promotion—a highly practitioner-orientated concept—should be not only theoretically but also empirically grounded, carefully encompassing the existent literature but at the same time not being overly ambitious empirically. The scholarly definition adopted here is the classic one of liberal democracy, which is also the one type of government most praised and actually promoted by the practitioners, defined as:

> a meaningful and extensive competition among individuals and organised groups for all effective positions of government power; a highly inclusive level of political participation in selection of leaders and policies, at least through regular free and fair elections, and a level of civil and political liberties—freedom of expression, freedom of press, freedom to form and join organizations.
>
> (Diamond *et al.* 1989, p. xvi)

This classic definition, which is almost entirely adopted by the practitioners, as discussed later, may not be empirically applicable in all cases of democracy promotion, consequently hindering democratic transformation. Thus, one of the arguments here is that the definition of democracy in actual policies may need revision.

Whitehead (2002, p. 20) has observed that "democracy has some indispensable components without which the concept would be vacuous." However, these components are not stagnant and can be differently arranged. One such component is elections. Following Schumpeter (Schumpeter 1947), many scholars have regarded democracy as a system where the "most powerful collective decision makers are selected through fair, honest and periodic elections" (Huntington 1991, p. 7). The minimalist conception of democracy has helped to avoid conceptual overstretching by "moving up the ladder of generality" and might have been appropriate decades ago, encompassing a larger number of cases. However, this narrow approach equating democracy to elections is not compatible with the current situation on the democratic scene. Since the third wave of democratization, a record number of countries have adopted elections as government-choosing procedure. Nevertheless, in just a small portion of these countries are elections truly competitive, without massive fraud and voter intimidation, and they hardly correspond to the understanding of "good democracy" (Croissant and Merkel 2004). This is particularly true in the environment of a gradually decreasing number of democracies and an increasing number of democratic setbacks (Puddington 2013).

Gradually, the scholars of democracy have started including other requirements for a regime to be democratic, thus creating the "expanded procedural minimum" of democracy. Among the new features are the requirement for the elected officials to effectively govern without being overly constrained by non-elected entities, and the requirement for the civil powers to exercise control over the military. These features have been especially compatible with Latin American reality (Karl 1990; Huntington 1991; Schmitter and Karl 1991; Mainwaring *et al.* 1992). Other conceptions of democracy involve features corresponding to the established industrial democracy, which entails certain political, economic, and social features. The maximalist conceptions—hardly applicable to a handful of real cases—"include equality of social and economic relations and/or broad popular participation in decision-making at all levels of politics" (Collier and Levitsky 1996, p. 8). However, no regime should be considered democratic until the offices are contested (Cheibub *et al.* 1996).

With the spread of democracy around the globe and the subsequent develop-ment of democratization studies, simple distinction between democracies and non-democracies has become insufficient. Many formerly authoritarian countries took the road of democratization and, while some achieved democracy and even consol-idated it, others have stagnated in between. The research has shown that transfer from an authoritarian rule could be to a democracy but it also could result in a lib-eralized authoritarianism (dictablanda) or illiberal democracy (democradura) (O'Donnell *et al.* 1986), or hybrid regimes of competitive authoritarianism (Levit-sky and Way 2010). These developments have shown that "the trend toward demo-cracy has been accompanied by an even more dramatic trend toward pseudosemocracy" (Diamond 2002, p. 27). Transitology and consolidology assumed that new democracies can equally move either forward towards consoli-dation of democracy or backward towards authoritarianism (Carothers 2002). Thus, new classifications of regimes that initiated democratic reforms have emerged in the literature. Close examination of democratization literature has discovered more than 550 examples of "democracies with adjectives" (Collier and Levitsky 1997). These new definitions of democracies evolved because scholars on the one hand sought to increase conceptual differentiation in capturing new forms of democracy, and, on the other hand, sought to avoid conceptual stretching while working on cases of democracy which did not correspond to the previously discovered concep-tualizations (Collier and Levitsky 1997).

The need to better understand the mixed features of post-authoritarian regimes have often been voiced (Malloy and Seligson 1987; Karl 1995; Levitsky and Way 2010; Baracani and di Quirico 2013). The differentiated conception of democracy is also important as often it serves as a causal variable in research (Collier and Levitsky 1997). However, the boundaries between these differenti-ated conceptions are very often "blurred and controversial" (Diamond 2002, p. 27). The "diminished subtypes" (Collier and Levitsky 1997) of democracy have been generated based on the root concept of democracy, which was the pro-cedural minimum, expanded procedural minimum, or the established industrial democracy. The diminished subtypes of democracy are characterized as a par-ticular type of defective democracy through a specific missing or "weakened" component of the root concept of democracy (Collier and Levitsky 1997). Thus, while an authoritarian regime can become a democracy, different types of demo-cracies can also become more democratic (Diamond 2002, p. 34). Consequently, in research on democracy promotion, democracy should be regarded as a simul-taneous process within a country, and as the ultimate goal for promoters and the target country until the set objectives are achieved.

The presented divergent opinions on the notion of democracy and its value demonstrate that a comprehensive conceptualization of democracy that would satisfy both academics and practitioners is practically impossible. In addition, because conceptualization is an evolving activity that is closely correlated with the explanatory power of a theory (Kaplan 1964), the argument over the "correct definition" is redundant (Guttman 1994, p. 12). Thus, the suggestion is to "avoid the extremes of including too much or too little in a definition relative to their theoretical goals" (Munck and Verkuilen 2002, p. 9). While maximalist definitions of democracy are of little analytical use because they are too overburdened, the minimalist definitions bear the danger of including all actually divergent cases under one subtype (Munck and Verkuilen 2002). From a practitioner/democracy promoter point of view, adoption of a maximalist definition—which includes *inter alia* such attributes as freedom from war, provision of social rights, and transition to welfare state—might be unrealistic, especially when democracy promotion is implemented in a relatively poor country. On the other hand, there is hardly a rationale for the adoption of a minimalist electoral definition for a study on democracy promotion because it does not illustrate the democratic reality of the target country, as elections might be in place though still largely violated and even restrictive.

While the concept of liberal democracy or polyarchy (Dahl 1989) might be well-known and ideal-typical, democratization studies show that there are various types of "democracies with adjectives" (Collier and Levitsky 1997) in the real world. However, democracy promotion activities do not aim to develop hybrid regimes (Karl 1995), electoralist democracies (Vanhanen 1997), procedural minimums of democracy (O'Donnell *et al.* 1986; Mainwaring *et al.* 1992), and certainly not competitive authoritarianism (Levitsky and Way 2010). Though efforts of democracy promoters may be inconsistent and sometimes contradictory, they aim to promote liberal democracy, which includes effective participation, voting equality, inclusion of adults (Dahl 1989), and the provision of civil and political liberties. Thus, in Dahl's terms they should aim to ensure competition and contestation. While an electoralist regime can be the starting goal for a democratizing country, neither domestic nor international actors should be satisfied with short-term results. Excessive praise from a promoter for mere organization of elections, or absence of any social and especially material shaming for rigged elections, has the potential of endangering future democratic transformation as domestic actors may regard the current situation as the ultimate democratization goal of their donors.

Therefore, in order to not hinder the democratization process, democracy promoters should set feasible goals to achieve in a democratizing country, without falling into the minimalist trap. It is not assumed that promotion of liberal democracy necessarily results in its inevitable establishment. Instead, it may result in the establishment of a democracy with adjectives. Nevertheless, the definition of liberal democracy addresses the requirements of contestation and participation, and avoids the minimalist exclusion of attributes or maximalist overstretch of the concept. While contestation includes the right to form political parties and participate in elections avoiding intimidation mainly from the incumbents, participation ensures fairness of the voting process, access of candidates to public financing and media, freedom of expression, freedom of the media, and equal provision of these civil and political rights (see Table 1.1). The empirical

Table 1.1 Elements of liberal democracy

Potential goal of promotion	Element of liberal democracy				
	Contestation		*Participation*		
Components					
Subcomponents	Right to form political parties and civil organizations	Right to freely participate in elections	Right to vote	Fair voting process	Access to public financing and media	Freedom of the media and expression	Equal provision of civil and political rights

Source: partly based on Munck and Verkuilen 2002: p. 13.

definition of democracy within democracy promotion, which is the main reference point for the empirical research and is explored in relevance to the chosen promoters later in the text, may slightly differ.

As with democracy, democratization has been an issue of heated debate among scholars, who have not come to an agreement either on the nature of democratization, its preconditions, or the entire process of initiation and completion. If it is conceptually and practically appropriate to accept a contextually variable definition of democracy, then the definition of democratization cannot be rigidly fixed either, and may depend upon the contextual variations of certain processes. However, there are several methods of understanding the democratization process and, more importantly, when it is complete. The "two-turnover test" suggests that the process of democratization can be considered underway once the authoritarian regime has collapsed, and it is complete—and thus democracy is on the way to consolidation[2]—after there have been two successful and peaceful transfers of government between competing parties (Huntington 1991). Others argue that democratization is over when all actors consider the electoral process of democracy to be the "only game in town" (Di Palma 1990), and in this case actions of actors are not as important as their beliefs and perceptions. Apart from the debatable possibility of measuring beliefs and perceptions, this definition is rather dubious when thinking of the cases of Spain and Italy (Whitehead 2002). Thus, while taking these measurements into consideration, democratization should rather be viewed as an open-ended process, with the possibility of different outcomes, especially given recent backlashes (Ambrosio 2009).

The definition of democratization should be closely related to the adopted understanding of democracy. The understanding of the beginning and completion of democratization should closely correlate with the understanding of the promoted type of democracy. Thus, the practitioner's understanding of democracy and democracy promotion should play an even greater role than the scholarly one when evaluating the process of democratization from a policy point of view. The practitioner's understanding of democracy plays an important role because "democratization is best understood as a complex, long-term, dynamic and open-ended process [and] consists of a progress towards a more rule-based, more consensual and more participatory type of politics" (Whitehead 2002, p. 27), and can provide the necessary closure to the process. Thus, democratization is not determined by its outcome. It is rather determined by a process, which may lead to a specific outcome, clearly outlined in a democracy-promotion policy and the democratization initiatives of local actors. While the process of democratization may also vary, since actors may play important roles to varying degrees, democratization processes within democracy promotion can be predetermined by the adopted democracy-promotion policy. As for the theoretical understanding of democratization, it can be regarded as underway when certain actions are taken on the way to reach the outcome mentioned in the adopted definition of democracy. Thus, while there are certain approaches to democratization, these should be adapted to specific examples of democratization to provide a comprehensive understanding of the process.

Democracy promotion

The collapse of the Soviet Union became "an historic opportunity for a transition to a peaceful and stable international order" because the "international community has a vital interest in the success of this transition" (US Congress 1996), and donors have to provide necessary support and expertise. Democracy promotion has become one of the main foreign-policy objectives of many already-consolidated democracies and some of the "rising democracies" (Carothers and Youngs 2011; Petrova 2012). Reasons behind the rise of democracy promotion activities may range from materialistic pursuit of stretching economic and territorial power, and altruistic care for the well-being of other societies. In addition, promotion of democracy may sometimes conflict with other foreign-policy objectives (Wolff *et al.* 2013). One of the most influential theories of explaining rationales for democracy promotion is the democratic peace theory, arguing that democracies do not wage wars against other democracies (Kegley and Hermann 2002). Thus, in pursuit of a peaceful international system, democratic states opt for turning autocracies into democracies to avoid military conflicts and to achieve peaceful resolution of disputes. Democracy promotion is considered to be "the most effective long-term measure for strengthening international stability; reducing regional conflicts; countering terrorism and terror-supporting extremism; and extending peace and prosperity" (Bush 2006). Another rationale, though not in contradiction with the previous one, is the pursuit of a prosperous international system. Thus, democratic states promote democracy because of conviction that democracies are more effective and efficient in producing development and economic growth than are autocracies and dictatorships (Johnson 2002). However, the focus of this study is on democracy promotion itself rather than its rationales, which largely play a secondary role in the choice of implementation strategy and do not closely correlate with the chosen variables to be specified in the following chapters.

Scholars of democracy promotion have repeatedly expressed concerns over the lack of an adequate theoretical framework offering predictive value for democracy-promotion studies (Burnell 2007, 2008a). The literature mainly relates to the practitioner (Carothers 1999, 2004) and ex-post (Burnell 2008a) views of democracy promotion, which is overwhelmingly a narrative of the democracy-promotion efforts of the USA (Carothers 1999) and the EU (Gillespie and Youngs 2002; Youngs 2002), and the role of democracy promotion in their foreign policies. The lack of a theoretical framework for studying democracy promotion ex-ante as a process and indicating its potential effectiveness is obvious. So far, only some practitioner tools for ex-post evaluation of democracy promotion have been available. They have been developed by different foundations and development agencies—the United States Agency for International Development (USAID), the Swedish International Development Cooperation Agency (SIDA), the Deutsche Gesellschaft für Technische Zusammenarbeit (GTZ) etc.—and criticized by academics (Crawford 2003a, 2003b). Carothers even claims that "democracy promoters treat political change in a pseudoscientific manner" (2004, p. 102), thus their democracy promotion does not have a theoretical background. At the same time scholars criticize democracy promoters, arguing that they "rarely have much sense of history about what they do, either with regard to the countries in which they are working on or to the enterprise of using aid to promote democracy" (Carothers 1999, p. 19). Though this is potentially true, besides criticizing, academics should work on the development of an analytical framework that could help in the formulation of democracy-promotion policies. This section of the chapter presents analysis of different types and levels of democracy promotion, which are further used for developing an analytical framework.

Despite large volumes of academic work on democracy promotion there are less than a handful of works suggesting definitions which can be used when researching the phenomenon. Although there may be divergence between academic and practitioner understandings of democracy promotion, initial adoption of an academic concept is essential. Thus, democracy promotion consists of:

> overt and voluntary activities adopted, supported, and (directly or indirectly) implemented by (public or private) foreign actors explicitly designed to contribute to the political liberalization of autocratic regimes and the subsequent democratization of autocratic regimes in specific recipient countries.
>
> (Schmitter and Brouwer 1999, p. 12)

As mentioned in the definition, only activities officially labeled as democracy promotion are included in this study because other activities, regardless of their democratizing nature, may fall under covert intelligence efforts of international actors and not provide full understanding of variables under consideration. The given definition does not include the implicit actions of external actors, such as diplomatic and intelligence activities, health campaigns, and so on, and also omits international factors which do not require the presence of a promoter. Thus, it also excludes cases of contagion, while militarized democracy promotion is not taken into consideration by this study since the consent of a target is not required, reducing the chances for success from the beginning. This definition provides a general understanding of what democracy promotion is and leads to further classifications of democracy promotion.

While some distinguish four levels of democracy promotion targets—individual citizens, civil society, political society, and state institutions (Schmitter and Brouwer 1999)—others distinguish three sectors of democracy promotion: electoral process, state institutions, and civil society (Carothers 1999). Democracy promotion on the level of state institutions "supports institutions of public authorities not to improve their repressive capacity, but to reform those institutions" (Schmitter and Brouwer 1999, p. 21) by strengthening legislation, aiding the rule of law, and developing local government (Carothers 1999). Democracy promotion at the level of political society is understood as "assistance to the specialized organizations and movements of political society," usually involving competition for office (Schmitter and Brouwer 1999, p. 21), by political party building and electoral aid (Carothers 1999). At the civil society level, democracy promotion supposes assistance to "organizations that are at least partially voluntary and are relatively independent from the state" (Schmitter and Brouwer 1999, pp. 19–20) by NGO building, civic education, media strengthening, and union building (Carothers 1999). At the level of individual citizens, the objective of democracy-promotion programs is "to transfer knowledge about democratic institutions and practices, socializing individuals to democratic values, and changing their behavior" (Schmitter and Brouwer 1999, p. 19). Carothers includes individual citizens in the civil society sector. Though these categories were developed based on examining US democracy promotion, they can be applied to other promoters too and can be modified if necessary. These groups largely overlap, thus in Table 1.2 they are combined into one group which entails goals and types of promotion from both groups.

The template given in Table 1.2 makes clear the adherence of some democracy promoters to the idea that democracy should be promoted through bottom-up and top-down approaches. However, though these approaches should be used simultaneously, strategies usually differ from promoter to promoter. Encouragement of a multiparty system with increasing both supply (state institutions) and demand (civil society) are equally important for successful democracy promotion

Table 1.2 Sectors and levels of democracy promotion

Level/sector	Goal	Type of democracy promotion
State institutions	Democratic constitution[1]	Constitutional assistance
	Independent judiciary and other law-oriented institutions	Rule-of-law aid
	Representative legislature	Legislative strengthening
	Responsive local government	Local government development
	Pro-democratic military	Civil–military relations
	Free and fair elections	Electoral aid
Political society	Strong national political parties	Political party building
	Free and fair elections	Electoral aid
Civil society	Active advocacy NGOs	NGO building
	Strong independent media	Media strengthening
	Free and fair elections	Elections observation
Individual citizens	Politically educated citizenry	Voter education
		Professional and educational exchange

Source: based on Schmitter and Brouwer 1999, p. 44 and Carothers 1999, p. 88.

Note

1 Assisting in the establishment of a democratic constitution would mean that the promoters work from scratch and the transition to democracy has just began. However, in most of the cases of democracy promotion by consent, a democratic constitution has already been adopted based on the experience of other established democracies. Thus, in such cases the promoter moves to ensure that further democratic features enshrined in the constitution do not stay on paper only: free and fair elections, independent judiciary, representative legislature etc.

(Carothers 1999). Thus, state institutions should be established through a democratic process, be stable, and have the capacity to perform their functions without being pressured by the executive or the military. At the same time, vibrant and independent civil society should be able to represent the interests of the citizens and provide checks over the government. According to some promoters, the democratization process proceeds along a "relatively set path" (Carothers 1999, p. 87): a non-democratic regime faces popular demand for liberalization; opposition and civic actors consolidate their power; multiparty elections are held; an elected government achieves power; and democracy is further consolidated. Although this sequence may take place in many democratizing countries, the democratic quality of these events might be far from the imagined ideal. While civic actors may multiply and elections may be held, the quantity of civil society actors does not guarantee the fulfillment of their functions, and elections are not necessarily free and fair. Thus, though this sequence can be taken into consideration by promoters, instead of congratulating themselves and their domestic counterparts on groundbreaking performance, they also need to pay attention to whether these events carry a democratic character.

Schmitter and Brouwer (1999) also emphasize the importance of differentiation between democracy promotion and democracy protection. In contrast to democracy promotion, democracy protection is "overt and voluntary activities adopted, supported, and (directly or indirectly) implemented by (public or private) foreign actors explicitly designed to contribute to the *consolidation of democracy in specific recipient countries*" (Schmitter and Brouwer 1999, p. 14—emphasis added). Democracy protection does not intend to change the current political regime, especially if it is democratic, but acts to make it more effective and efficient. Likewise, organization of police training for enforcement of human rights and support for privatization of trade unions are activities directed at consolidation of democracy. While democracy-promotion activities are likely to be more effective on the state and political society sectors, democracy protection activities can be influential when targeting civil society and individuals. However, some of the target sectors in democracy promotion and democracy protection overlap, achieving more results in one case than in the other. In addition, the boundary between democracy promotion and protection is often blurred in the actual activities of promoters who do not strictly differentiate between the two.

The introduced analytical frameworks help with grasping the concept of democracy promotion and in differentiating between its types and sectors/levels. However, they do not elaborate on the mechanisms for implementing democracy-promotion policies. Moreover, they do not specify the conditions under which a democracy-promotion policy may have a certain outcome. This gap in the literature on democracy promotion is possible to bridge only by analyzing the interaction between the international and domestic variables. Further, an analytical framework is suggested that can be helpful in democracy-promotion studies. These projects are selected as operationalization of political-society projects (party development), civil-society projects (media development), and projects implemented on all levels (elections).

Democracy promotion varies not only in its possible implementation strategies but also in its targets and sectors. Classification of democracy promotion according to state, political society, civil society, and individual citizens helps to understand what the most important features of democracy are according to democracy promoters. It also helps in establishing a link between the academic and the practitioner approaches to democracy and democratization. Selection of elections, party development, and media-development projects not only reflects the academic definition of democracy as constituting contestation and participation, but also reflects the conventional democracy-promotion package of promoters. Although democracy promotion has been launched more than two decades ago and covered more than 100 countries, the academic world has not paid sufficient attention to its constituting elements and the practitioner world is still in a search for effective policies. In addition, not all sectors are equally targeted by all promoters. This overview shows that some of the projects overlap and a project targeting one component of democracy may also indirectly affect the other two. Another conclusion is that, despite at least two decades of democracy promotion, these projects still wander in twilight and need improvement and most importantly applicability to domestic contexts.

Democracy promotion through international socialization

Despite two decades of democracy promotion, "there is still a dearth of theoretically informed comparative studies" (Wolff *et al.* 2013, p. 3). In addition, there is a lack of analytical frameworks (Burnell 2007, 2008b) or "conceptual models" (Kumar 2012, p. 3) for democracy promotion with strong theoretical and empirical foundations. Schimmelfennig *et al.* (2006) have previously endeavored to fill this lacuna by developing a robust and empirically testable theoretical framework, based on the notion of international socialization, that can be applied to the implementation stage of democracy promotion and can also incorporate domestic democratization. However, this framework still needs development and application to other cases of democracy promoters and the targets of their activities in order to identify and provide full explanation of the concept of democracy promotion and identify the effective strategies. Here it is updated in terms of its structural and geographical scopes, as well as its independent and dependent variables. This section presents the original framework, providing definitions of important concepts, presenting the rationalist–constructivist debate, identifying the types of socialization and strategies, and specifying necessary international and domestic conditions for successful socialization. Since here the analytical framework of international socialization is applied to democracy promotion, any mention of international socialization components, approaches, and strategies should be equally regarded as those of democracy promotion.

International socialization is "a process in which states [or other targets] are induced to adopt the constitutive rules of an international community" (Schimmelfennig *et al.* 2006, p. 2). The state or another target for socialization is considered successfully socialized when it adopts rule-creating domestic mechanisms and powerful institutional and political processes that guarantee compliance and discourage opposition to this rule. From the point of view of democracy-promotion studies, this definition of international socialization is somewhat rigid and one-dimensional because it does not take into consideration possible varying degrees of democratic transformations. It is one-dimensional because it supposes the creation of institutions and processes to guarantee compliance to democratic principles, but does not elaborate on whether those principles are guaranteed to be complied with. Thus, this definition is used as a starting point for the development of a more comprehensive understanding that would encompass various possibilities of policy outcome. Analyzing international socialization from a forward-looking perspective, "as a process directed at or potentially leading to rule adoption by the target states" (Schimmelfennig *et al.* 2006, p. 2), addresses the concern that domestic political actors and processes have not received sufficient attention (Schmitter and Brouwer 1999; Schmitz 2004).

The literature on international socialization defines two general approaches through which international organizations promote their rules and norms. These methods are strategic actions of incentives and coercion on the one hand, and appropriate actions of persuasion and example on the other. The first one is the logic of appropriateness advocated by constructivists, and the second one is the logic of consequentiality advocated by rationalists (Olsen and March 2004), and these represent "opposing ideal-types" (Schimmelfennig *et al.* 2006, p. 16). From the rationalist perspective, states act in the technical environment of the international system, and international socialization is not a relevant concept per se. Socialization is only possible as a strategic action via incentives or coercion, and aims to change the behavior of the target but not its identity or interest (Ikenberry and Kupchan 1990; Schimmelfennig 2002; Jupille *et al.* 2003). From the constructivist perspective, international socialization argues that states act in a social environment and international socialization is based on the concept of appropriate action. Thus, an agency socializes target states by social persuasion and benign example, acting as a role model and changing the identity and interests of the socialized (Risse *et al.* 1999; Checkel 2001). However, none of the ideal-types alone can provide plausible and empirically grounded explanations for the success or failure of international socialization. Though international socializers or democracy promoters publicize the image of a socially constructed role model pursuing benign purposes, it is unlikely that these purposes do not derive from their material interests. Likewise, domestic actors, nurtured in their domestic yet non-socialized environments, are unlikely to regard foreign rules and norms as appropriate because of their mere internationality.

Schimmelfennig and his collaborators design an analytical framework that regards socialization as a "strategic action in a community environment" (Schimmelfennig 2003) and views it as "a bargaining process with normative constraints" (Schimmelfennig *et al.* 2006, p. 25). Thus, they adopt perspectives from both rational institutionalism and social constructivism, seeing domestic actors as rational and risk-averse, trying to maximize their utilities, while promoters are seen as "realist actor[s] in normative clothes" (Seeberg 2009, p. 95). While the framework adopts the constructivist vision of a cultural international environment and strong international organizations as socialization agents, it does not agree with the logic of appropriateness and disregards the possibility that domestic actors will change their self-defined interests based on interaction. Consequently, a theoretical framework of international socialization, analyzing the actions of international actors and relevant reactions of domestic actors, needs to consider that not always are actions based on rational calculations and not always are they driven by social and appropriate motives. To understand whether and how strategic action is formed under the influence of the international environment, Schimmelfennig and his collaborators proceed with theorizing based on a pure rationalist bargaining approach that can capture the concept of a strategic action in the international community.

From the rationalist perspective, the socializing agency and the target of socialization are motivated by their own self-interested political preferences, which, according to Schimmelfennig *et al.* (2006, p. 18), are "material and power-oriented." These can include security issues, welfare, or maintaining political power. Thus, a socialization agency and a target consider the socialization process as a pathway to achieve their own interests. Neither of them take the norms of the community for granted, but rather view them as undeniable facts that can either constrain or promote certain behavior. Following the same logic and echoing the critique of democracy promotion mentioned earlier, the socialization agency does not necessarily possess a genuine belief in democracy or other issues that they promote. They rather use the former to achieve other security or power-related goals. However, regardless of the motivation, the socializing agency has an interest in the socializing process, otherwise it would not venture into it. In addition, the spread of its own community rules would help create new alliances and prove the viability of its own system. Similarly, the targets when adopting the promoted norms or rules take into consideration potential benefits of adoption. However, the utility for the target in socialization, at least from its own perspective, is not taken for granted, otherwise the whole socialization process would be redundant because the norms would be adopted even without the socialization agency. Thus, in any case of socialization process there is a certain degree of domestic resistance (Schimmelfennig *et al.* 2006).

To overcome this resistance, a socialization agency has to be willing to employ certain strategies and tools that can also be costly to the international community. The extent to which a socializing agency is willing to pay to socialize a specific target depends upon the importance of the target to the interests and preferences of the agency. From this strategic perspective, the socialization agency reinforces its community rules or democracy, and the capability of reinforcement through punishments or rewards depends upon the bargaining power of the agency. The bargaining power of the agency at the same time is constrained by the credibility and the size of its rewards, and the credibility and severity of its punishment. Thus, to induce the target to internalize the socialized or promoted rules, the agency needs to be able to match its "offer" with domestic adaptation costs. If the adaptation costs of a target are higher than the promised rewards, then there is little chance for successful socialization. In a nutshell, the main proposition of the framework states that successful socialization depends upon the agency's bargaining power, credible constraints and incentives, well-developed monitoring systems, and the size of domestic adaptation costs. However, given the fact that socializers act within a social environment, the pure form of material bargaining is not possible and is constrained by structural features of the international community and the target.

Schimmelfennig *et al.* (2006) further distinguish between strategies of reinforcement and persuasion. Reinforcement entails specification depending upon the employment of incentives: reinforcement by reward, by support, or by punishment. The framework also categorizes incentives as tangible or intangible. A socializing agency can also opt for different channels of socialization: inter-governmental (targeting the governments directly) and transnational (targeting non-governmental actors such as social movements, interest groups, or business actors) (Schimmelfennig *et al.* 2006). The last categorization correlates with the categorization of levels in democracy promotion: state level with the intergovernmental channel, and civil society level with the transnational channel. The political society level of democracy promotion can be considered as intermediary because it also serves as the channel of expression for the public will to the government and the state. The targets of socialization face the reinforcement strategies that control incentives and disincentives, and persuasion strategies that imply arguing for the justification of the promoted norm. As research shows, socializing organizations employ both strategies, though not to equal extent (Schimmelfennig *et al.* 2006).

The reinforcement strategies in their own turn are categorized depending upon the tangibility of incentives they offer or withdraw. *Social reinforcement* employs "socio-psychological" (Schimmelfennig *et al.* 2006, p. 33) instruments of reward (international recognition or public praise), punishment (shaming or shunning), and support (additional meetings with the agency or arrival of expert groups). This strategy is generally used by the Council of Europe and the OSCE, which are socializing agencies without considerable economic or military leverage. The *material reinforcement* strategy is usually used by socializing agencies that have the capability to enforce the promoted norm by means of their material leverage, e.g. NATO and the EU. The most widely used strategy of material reinforcement is the reinforcement by reward, better known as political conditionality (Schimmelfennig and Sedelmeier 2005; Schimmelfennig *et al.* 2006). This strategy supposes tangible rewards when the target state complies with the conditions set by the socialization agency. While reinforcement by support supposes additional support in case of compliance, reinforcement by punishment supposes not only withdrawal of current support but also introduction of specific sanctions (as in the case of NATO's 1995 Operation Deliberate Force in Bosnia-Herzegovina). However, due to their costly nature, the last two strategies are used only if political conditionality fails and if due to high interdependence the socialization of a target state is more important than the actual costs of support or punishment (Schimmelfennig *et al.* 2006).

In choosing a socialization strategy, a rational socialization agency pursuing successful socialization should take into consideration not only its own preferences and capabilities but also the domestic conditions of the target state. As noted above, the usual strategy of socialization is reinforcement by reward, which leaves the decision of compliance strictly to the target state. Assuming that domestic political actors are rational and try to maximize their utilities, and taking into consideration "state-centric domestic structure and the electoral volatility [of post-communist states]" (Schimmelfennig *et al.* 2006, p. 53), it is unlikely that the target state complies with liberal norms threatening its current state of affairs if the domestic costs of adaptation are higher than the tangible rewards. Therefore, it is doubtful that social reinforcement alone would be a successful strategy of democracy promotion, especially in countries where adaptation costs are rather high.

Variables and arguments of international socialization framework

The dependent variable of Schimmelfennig and his collaborators' study is *compliance*, which analyzes how a state reacts to international conditions and under which conditions it complies or does not comply with promoted norms. Besides the set of already-presented variables, they also add a set of constructivist variables to reflect the choice of understanding international socialization as a strategic action in an international community. Being interested primarily in the "thresholds of effectiveness," Schimmelfennig *et al.* (2006, p. 57) prefer dichotomous categorization of their variables. The dependent variable is distinguished as compliance and non-compliance; whereas the independent variables are distinguished as having negative and positive values. The positive value implies the likelihood of compliance, while the negative value would most probably hinder compliance. The compliance is conceptualized as law passed or a treaty signed by a target state in accordance to the promoted rule or norm. However, Schimmelfennig and his collaborators do not proceed with a more in-depth analysis to see whether the target of the socialization actually adheres to the promoted rule after the initial compliance. Omission of the behavioral compliance as a dependent variable is explained by the difficulties in obtaining cross-national data and customary satisfaction by the socializing or promoting agent with the formal compliance of passing a law. However, in the case of democracy-promotion policies the behavioral compliance is the actual goal of promoters, and omitting it in research would lead to practically inapplicable results. This book intends to fill this lacuna and introduces its own dependent variable in the next chapter.

To test the hypotheses, the framework of international socialization uses a set of rationalist and constructivist variables that can also be distinguished on the basis of international–domestic divide (Schimmelfennig *et al.* 2006, pp. 57–60).

The rationalist independent variables are incentives (kind and size of tangible rewards), credibility (of promise to pay the reward), and costs (which are low in cases where rule conformity does not threaten the current distribution of power). The constructivist independent variables are legitimacy (measuring whether the socializing agency itself complies with the promoted norm and promotes it on a constant basis), identification (measuring the extent to which a target state identifies with the international community and promoted norms), and resonance (measuring the extent to which domestic institutional design matches with the promoted norms). Closer consideration of these variables is given in Chapter 3, which reveals the research design and main theoretical and methodological contributions of the book. The hypotheses containing the test and control variables are tested on nine European country-cases—Belarus, Yugoslavia (Serbia), Turkey, Slovakia, Romania, Estonia, Latvia, Northern Cyprus, and Montenegro—as targets of socialization by the European community organizations—EU, NATO, OSCE, and CoE—using the Qualitative Comparative Analysis (Ragin 1989).

Schimmelfennig *et al.* (2006, p. 55) argue that "credible membership perspective and low domestic political costs of rule adoption are both individually necessary and jointly sufficient conditions of successful socialization." Thus, their research findings support the rationalist perspective of understanding the mechanisms of international socialization. Schimmelfennig *et al.* also argue that, though social constructivist factors of identity, legitimacy, and resonance can to some extent constrain the decisions of socializers in choosing goals and targets, they do not account for the mechanisms of successful socialization. The rationalist variables tend to explain better the successful mechanisms because the main targets of the socialization process studies by Schimmelfennig and his collaborators are states that are not members of the community yet. Being outside of the community and not facing conditional incentives makes them exempt from social obligations to the community norms. This comparative-static analysis also demonstrates that "the gap between liberal countries with or without major minority rights problems first narrowed and then disappeared" (Schimmelfennig *et al.* 2006, p. 253), proving socialization to be a continuous rather than a short-term process.

The international socialization framework focuses on the promoters' strategies and domestic conditions of the target countries, thus enabling the researcher to identify effective democracy promotion strategies in the presence of specific domestic conditions. The Schimmelfennig *et al.* study (2006) was completed with cases of international socialization in Europe by Western international organizations. They conclude that successful socialization requires a specific set of domestic conditions supported by a membership incentive. Thus far, the framework has been applied exclusively to international organizations and has examined exclusively European cases, limiting the scope of its applicability. However, individual states ignored by the framework, such as the USA, also have an important role in democracy promotion, even though they cannot offer membership per se. In addition, the EU, the primary promoter in the research of Schimmelfennig *et al.* (2006), also promotes democracy without offering membership. Thus, the geographic and structural dimensions of the framework should be widened by applying it to other types of cases: those outside of Europe and those not offering membership. Only by doing so would it be possible to provide plausible arguments and reasonable recommendations on democracy promotion, avoiding the limitations of generalizing based on exclusively European and "membership-offer"-based research. This study has adopted the international socialization framework and adapted it to democracy promotion by widening its scope of applicability, changing its dependent variable to democratic transformation, and introducing new independent variables.

Notes

1 Minor parts of this chapter have appeared previously in Babayan 2009 and in Babayan and Huber 2012.
2 For more in-depth discussion of consolidation see Schneider 2009.

2 Conditions of democratic transformation, cases, and methods

This chapter brings together the theoretical and empirical parts of the book. It further specifies the research questions and hypotheses, and operationalizes variables used in this comparative research on the outcome of democracy promotion and democratization. Afterwards, it elaborates on case selection and describes how the cases are analyzed.

This book has derived from an observation which has led to empirical and theoretical puzzles. Since the collapse of the Soviet Union, numerous democracy-promotion activities have been launched with various targets and strategies. However, while some post-communist or authoritarian countries quickly democratized and even launched their own democracy-promotion programs (e.g. the Baltic states, Poland, and the Czech Republic), others are still democratic laggards despite almost two decades of democracy promotion activities (e.g. Armenia, Georgia, and other post-Soviet states). Though on a law-making level some countries have at least embraced democratic principles, others have not even bothered with democratic pretence, creating the paradox of long-lasting and widespread democracy-promotion activities and domestic championing of democracy, but scarce spread of liberal democracy on the global level. This discrepancy has triggered the main puzzle of this study: *why, despite numerous and extensive democracy promotion initiatives, has democracy not become "the only game in town" even in countries where these initiatives are welcome?*

Effective democracy promotion entails not only intermediate success or completion of a democracy-promotion project but also an overall improvement in the state of democracy in the target country. Depending upon the country-specific situation, overall improvement in democracy can involve a move to free and fair elections, reduction of political violence during campaigns, increased independence of the judiciary, or a reduction of political corruption. Thus, for example, elections-related projects should not only raise awareness by the voters about their rights or increase the understanding by political parties about the value of free and fair elections, but also ultimately contribute to the conduct of such elections and the peaceful transition of power. On the level of specific sectors targeted by democracy promoters, it can increase their own compliance with their primary functions based on democratic principles. In addition, domestic political actors should not only speak but also behave democratically (Linden 2002). There is a need to understand the combination of international and domestic conditions used in promoting democracy in countries without a membership incentive. Based on these considerations, and in an endeavor to develop an analytical framework while understanding the outcome of democracy promotion policies, this study posits the following question: under what conditions is democracy promotion more likely to result in democratic transformation?

There is a need to understand the combination of international and domestic conditions used in promoting democracy in countries without EU-membership incentive. To assess the effectiveness of a democracy-promotion policy, this research analyzes different outcomes the policy may have and whether outcomes of the same type of democracy promotion are different or the same depending upon the target sector of democracy promotion. Echoing the lament of the scholarly community that democracy promoters simply transfer their policies and success indicators from country to county, it is important to observe possible changes in policies in the target country in the course of democracy promotion and depending upon specific socio-political and economic developments in the target country.

Democratic transformation

The dependent variable of this study is *democratic transformation* as the combined outcome of democracy promotion and democratization. Taking "compliance" as their dependent variable, Schimmelfennig *et al.* (2006) are only interested in whether or not the country complies with the rule of the international organization, having as an indicator "legal rule adoption" (Schimmelfennig *et al.* 2006, p. 58). They do not investigate further to see whether the new rule or law is actually enforced because "the Western organizations were generally content with legal adoption and greeted the passing of norm-conforming laws as indications that their demands were fulfilled" (Schimmelfennig *et al.* 2006, p. 58). However, the examples of many post-Soviet countries show that mere legal adoption of a rule does not guarantee rule-based behavior within any of the sectors of democracy promotion or democratization. In addition, the assessments of democracy promotion projects acknowledge that, even if the rule has been legally adopted, "the challenge, however, lies in converting new formal rules into working rules" (ARD 2002, p. 24). Moreover, the formal adoption of the rule on civil-society level does not guarantee its prevalence also on political or state levels, often due to the weakness of the civil society in democratizing countries. Thus, while "compliance" is useful to understand short-term effects of rule promotion, democratic transformation within domestic political and societal systems as a dependent variable is more useful for understanding the potential overall outcome of democracy promotion, providing a better understanding of its impact.

Exclusively, democratic transformation as an outcome is taken as a dependent variable, and not "success" or "effectiveness," as the latter two concepts, though widely used in literature, are too subjective and normative. What may be a measurable and an achieved success for the promoter can be a failure from the standpoint of the improvement of democracy in the target country. In its own turn, democratic transformation cannot be always the same on all levels of promotion, and will often depend upon the implemented policy and domestic conditions. Meanwhile, long-term outcomes and unintended outcomes of democracy promotion are harder to detect since these often remain "unforeseen" and "unforeseeable" (Morell 2005) and are similar to impact (Kumar 2012). Within literature on evaluating democracy promotion, an outcome is operationalized as "behavioral changes that result from outputs" (Kumar 2012, p. 64), which in their own turn are the immediate results of democracy-promotion activities. Since democracy promotion does not happen in vacuum, the analyzed outcome is the result of a complex interaction between specific domestic and international factors. The outcome of democracy promotion cannot be measured looking only at democracy-promotion strategies but should also involve analysis of domestic factors. Thus, while still identifying a number of independent variables, my goal here is not to measure direct causal effects but rather to identify the complex interaction by case studies and comparative analysis (Ragin 1997; Wolff *et al.* 2013).

The variation in the outcome of democracy promotion—formal, behavioral, and unintended (Schimmelfennig 2002, p. 9)—is based on the discussion on conceptions of norms (Finnemore and Sikkink 1998) and is often used in the norm diffusion literature (Raymond 1997; Cortell and Davis Jr. 2000; Risse 2013). Though this research partially adopts the terms used in the literature, it operationalizes the outcome of democracy promotion differently in order to show the transition from legal rule adoption to rule-based behavior and to account for unintended consequences of democracy promotion.

While the international socialization framework uses a dichotomous categorization of its dependent variable (compliance versus non-compliance), to fully account for possible outcomes this research opts for a trichotomous categorization. At the same time, taking into consideration the implementation process of a policy and customary monitoring and evaluation strategies of promoters, the measurement of democratic transformation involves indicators from two dimensions: promoter and target. This is justified by the fact that often promoters measure the effectiveness of their projects not by domestic political dynamics but according to their checklists of completed activities. In addition, it is important because the outcome of democracy promotion occurs as a result of interaction between promoters and targets.

The formal democratic transformation of this study most resembles the compliance variable of Schimmelfennig *et al.* (2006). Formal democratic transformation from a promoter's perspective occurs upon project completion and the accomplishment of specific project goals, such as training of a specific number of officials or reporters, organization of a number of conferences etc. Within the domestic target realm, formal democratic transformation entails formal adoption of a law (in the case of the state level), of a code of conduct or a specialized law (in the case of political society) or a code of conduct/ethics and a law on the media (in the case of the civil society/media). It is less likely to occur on the individual target level of democracy promotion. Knowing that democracy promotion projects do not always proceed smoothly, this book also introduces the possibility of an unintended outcome. Unintended outcome/transformation is understood as an early project shutdown (regardless of reasons), democracy setback, neglect of democratic functions of the target level, or worsened evaluation in comparison with previous assessments. Essentially, an unintended outcome is a negative trend in democratization, which can also entail regress to autocratic tendencies.

Behavioral democratic transformation entails the overall improvement of democracy, which is *inter alia* understood as the conduct of free and fair elections and a free media, and is measured by various democracy indices such as Freedom House, Polity IV, and the Bertelsmann Transformation Index. This category of democratic transformation fully resembles the components of liberal democracy and happens when those are not only theoretically but also practically adhered to. Behavioral democratic transformation is also the most difficult one to achieve because it would mean that democracy has become "the only game in town." In addition, behavioral democratic transformation is measured within each analyzed sector of democracy promotion (elections, party politics, and media freedom) and entails fulfillment of specific functions ascribed by democratic rules. Thus, if elections are not free and fair, it is concluded that behavioral democratic transformation has not happened. Each sector under consideration is assessed based on its specific functions and indicators (see Table 2.1). Following Levitsky and Way (2010, p. 366), elections are considered as unfair in the evidence of *any one* of the indicators given below. Consequently, if *all* the indicators are absent, behavioral democratic transformation has happened.

1   At least one major candidate is barred for political reasons;
2   Centrally coordinated or tolerated electoral abuse is asserted by credible sources. Indicators include:

   - serious partisan manipulation of voter rolls;
   - large-scale voter intimidation or disruption of voting
   - ballot-box stuffing, multiple voting, or other forms of ballot tampering;
   - falsification of results;

3   Significant formal or informal impediments—coordinated or tolerated by the national government—prevent the opposition from campaigning nationally on reasonably equal footing. Indicators include:

   - violence against opposition party activists, candidates, or infrastructure;
   - use or abuse of law regulating public meetings limits the oppositions ability to campaign;

4 Uneven electoral playing field. Indicators include:

- electoral authorities systematically biased in favour of incumbent;
- highly uneven access to media;
- highly uneven access to resources.

(Levitsky and Way 2010: 366)

While parties are bestowed with numerous functions to fulfill (Diamond and Gunther 2001), the most important one within new democracies is "to make the elected government accountable" (Burnell 2006, p. 17). Nevertheless, to make the government accountable, undemocratic parties should become democratic themselves, and this will constitute their behavioral democratic transformation to match with the rhetorical liberal constellation of parliamentary convocations. Even if this kind of accountability is a matter "left for future discussion" (Burnell and Gerrits 2010, p. 1078), it is suggested that behavioral democratic transformation of parties in the parliament happens if *all* of the following holds true:

1 lack of broad access to state resources by a single party or group of parties (Bader 2010);
2 lack of domination by a narrow leadership (Bader 2010);
3 stable and clear political platforms;
4 being elected in free and fair elections, without using illegal methods before or during elections.

The main function of the media within a democratic framework is that of a watchdog, "keeping the elected accountable to the electorate, and ... to disseminate information, which will enable citizens to make informed choices and to participate in a meaningful way" (USAID 1999a, p. 22). Thus, behavioral

Table 2.1 Sectoral indicators for behavioral democratic transformation

Elections	Parties	Media
Major candidates are not barred for political reasons	Lack of broad access to state resources by a single party or group of parties	Reports on topics of its choosing
Credible sources assert there is no coordinated or tolerated electoral abuse	Lack of domination by a narrow leadership	Critically covers powerful political actors, including the incumbent
The opposition campaigns nationally on a reasonably equal footing	Stable and clear political platforms	Does not impose self-censorship
Electoral playing field is even	Elected in free and fair elections, without using illegal methods before or during elections	Provides equal and unbiased coverage to all election contestants
		Does not show bias towards the incumbent

Source: author's own compilation based on Waisbord 2000; Hughes 2006; Bader 2010; and Levitsky and Way 2010.

democratic transformation happens when the media performs its watchdog function, which is within the powers of the media to choose whether or not to perform. Partially based on definitions of watchdog media given by Waisbord (2000) and Hughes (2006), behavioral democratic transformation within the media sector is registered if media outlets do *all* of the following:

1   report on the topic of their choosing;
2   critically cover powerful political actors, including the incumbent;
3   do not impose self-censorship;
4   provide equal and unbiased coverage to all election contestants;
5   do not show bias towards the incumbent.

The choice of being a watchdog may depend upon other conditions, including economic or physical pressures, state regulations, or imposed censorship, which boil down to freedom of the media. Although freedom of the media does not indicate behavioral democratic transformation within the media sector, it indicates overall democratic improvement in the country, and its absence is a possible reason for not performing the watchdog function. Thus, freedom of the media is also observed and measured by indices of Freedom House, Reporters without Borders, IREX, and the Committee to Protect Journalists, chosen based on their "prominence and longevity" (Annenberg School of Communication 2007, p. 26) in evaluating media freedom.

Factors influencing democratic transformation

While the initial independent variables of the international socialization framework are investigated, additional international and domestic (independent) variables are added to account for the absence of a membership incentive and enhance the explanatory leverage of the framework. Yet again taking into consideration the importance of the promoter–target interaction, this book looks into the combination of international and domestic independent variables. Independent variables borrowed from the international socialization framework are incentives, credibility, and legitimacy on the international dimension, and costs, identification, and resonance on the domestic dimension. Initially assigned positive and negative values, these variables were also originally categorized as rational (incentives, credibility, and costs) and constructivist (legitimacy, identification, and resonance) (Schimmelfennig *et al.* 2006, p. 59). However, a dichotomous classification of the variables and their sometimes limited operationalization does not allow capturing of the full picture of promoter–target interaction and possible variations in international and domestic factors. Thus, substantial modifications are made, and each of the original and new variables is assigned a low (–), moderate (+), or positive value (++). In addition, more detail is given to the elaboration of variables and one of the variables is assigned a different term merely to fall under the logical reasoning of the methodological approach. The operationalization of the variables is empirically motivated, taking into consideration possible outcomes of democracy-promotion projects rather than the original constructivist–rationalist divide, which, though it seems a solid theoretical motivation, does not add to policy-driven research.

Relying only on the attractiveness of democracy's virtues would be short-sighted for promoters, inducing them to offer certain incentives for democratic transformation of their targets. *Incentives* are understood as the type and size of rewards offered to the target country for compliance. While a combination of political and economic incentives (++) are more likely to produce behavioral democratic transformation, economic incentives without the political ones would have only a moderate effect on behavioral change (+). The absence of any incentives would make the chances of a behavioral democratic transformation highly unlikely.

Credibility is understood as "the credibility of the threat of withholding the rewards or inflicting punishment in case of non-compliance, and the credibility of the promise to pay the reward or abstain from punishment in case of compliance" (Schimmelfennig *et al.* 2006, p. 59). The credibility of threats and promises can be of major importance for the outcome of democracy promotion not to create an image of Westerners who "will make a fuss [about violations of democracy] for a few days, and then they will calm down and life will go on as usual" (Shevarnadze in Karumidze *et al.* 2005, p. 24). Lack of credibility—not fulfilling the threat or promise (–)—is likely to damage the target's reliance on the promoter, making further similar actions useless. Such threats or promises are as a rule made with an expiration date, thus a fulfillment that passed the deadline set by the promoter or a partial fulfillment (+) will not be as negative as in the case of the lack thereof, but would signal the target that it may in future either receive a small reprimand instead of the promised sanction or get a marginal reward despite good performance. In contrast, timely fulfillment of a threat or a promise has the potential of underlining the commitment of the promoter and encouraging similar commitment from the target.

Legitimacy refers to the application and observation of promoted rules by the promoter, in order to avoid resistance from the target that may claim the "incompetence" of the promoter. Thus, "the minimal condition is that demands on the target governments must be based on organizational rules rather than ad hoc interests" (Schimmelfennig *et al.* 2006, p. 59). The legitimacy of the promoter would be low if it shows neither rhetorical nor behavioral commitment within its own territory or structure (–), in other words if it neither talks nor walks the walk of democracy. Merely rhetorical commitment without corresponding behavior would make the promoter moderately legitimate (+) for democracy promotion, while demonstrating both rhetorical and behavioral commitment would also have a positive (++) influence on achieving behavioral democratic transformation.

As mentioned, the variable of *costs* (Schimmelfennig *et al.* 2006, p. 59) is changed to the variable of *utility of adaptation* to harmonize its operationalization with the ones of other variables and reflect the utility for the domestic stakeholders to adapt to democratic rules. This variable is defined as any material or physical costs or the imminence of losing status quo by the target that can occur in case of compliance with promoted democracy rules. An imminent threat to the status quo or its loss makes the utility of adaptation to democracy low, as it may *inter alia* result in a loss of the occupied position (–) if elections are free and fair, in exclusion from governing coalition by the non-complying counter-parts, or loss of professional occupation or even physical damages to civil-society members. An uncertain possibility of losing the status quo would make the utility of adaptation moderate (+), while preservation of the status quo would have a positive (++) influence on behavioral democratic transformation.

Identification implies the willingness of domestic targets to be associated with the promoter. Identification expressed through rhetoric would be low if domestic stakeholders show commitment to non-democratic principles (–). Uncertainty between non-democratic and democratic principles and the promoter would make the identification moderate (+), while firm commitment to democratic prin-ciples and the approval of the promoter would have a positive influence on behavioral democratic transformation (++). However, there is no pretence made by this research of measuring genuine attitudes of local stakeholders towards democracy and democracy promoters. Rather than claiming the vague possibility of measuring ideas and beliefs, this research analyzes rhetorical identification of local stakeholders through their discourse. Thus, this research allows for the pos-sibility that, in the case of strong identification but no behavioral democratic transformation, local stakeholders may simply pay lip-service to democracy. Nevertheless, even such lip-service identification provides better opportunities for democratic transformation than a pronounced opposition to democracy.

The final variable of Schimmelfennig *et al.* (2006) is *resonance*, which sup-poses cultural or institutional reflection of the promoted rule with domestic laws, rules, and customs. To avoid arbitrariness, this variable is measured by docu-mented rules and declarations and not by individual attitudes. Presence of oppos-ing concepts makes the resonance of the promoted rule low (–), lack of corresponding concepts and rules makes resonance moderate (+), while presence of such rules and concepts makes resonance positive (++).

All these variables are investigated in this book. However, I argue that they are not enough to account for possible changes in the domestic situation of a target and for possible variations of democratic transformation. Thus, this research introduces an additional six variables, which, as with the previous ones, can be distinguished on international–domestic dimensions. However, there is no goal of choosing variables according to the rationalist–constructivist divide. Rather than taking solely theoretical assumptions as the basis for the choice of variables, this research bases its choice of variables, as well as on empirical evidence and actual practice in the field. The newly proposed variables of the international dimension are cooperation, consistency, and involvement. The vari-ables of the domestic dimension are party constellation, a democracy blocker, and ownership. It should be clarified that international variables do not reflect the current international situation but are attributed to the democracy promoter itself, thus are under the full control of the latter. Similarly, domestic variables are associated with the target of democracy promotion. Following the setting of the international socialization framework, these variables are also assigned values—low, moderate, and positive. However, because the dependent variable is not categorized dichotomously, there is no absolute threshold value for the independent variables. Nevertheless, the highest positive value is assigned to the operationalization of the variable that has the strongest potential to result in a behavioral democratic transformation, as this is the ultimate goal of democracy-promotion policies and domestic democratization.

Cooperation primarily refers to the joint programs between promoters in a target country and the involvement of at least two sectors of democracy promotion within the framework of one project, e.g. involving the state while the primary target of the project is civil society. As the same area of democracy promotion is often a simultaneous target for democracy promoters, democracy promotion starts being a competition for promoters. This makes the promoters hastily design democracy-promotion programs without close consideration of domestic conditions, thus leading to one-size-fits-all approach. This not only negatively affects the quality of a democracy promotion project itself but also decreases its potential influence on the overall level of democracy in a given country. Cooperation as described above is believed to alleviate the pressure from the state and to tackle reluctance from civil society and individuals, at the same time combining the resources of different promoters for augmented results. Cooperation is low (–) when it is either absent or is present only in the form of annual promoter meetings or dinners, where the yearly activities are presented. Cooperation is moderate (+) in the case of any programmatic joint activities, though targeting only one sector because in this case the promoters assure that their strategies do not conflict (which is sometimes the case in the field). Finally, cooperation is positive (++) and more conducive to behavioral democratic transformation in the case of joint activities targeting more than one sector.

Democracy promotion and the practice of individual promoters is characterized by "variance and inconsistency" (Wolff *et al.* 2013, p. 8). Democracy promoters tend to work on the short-term, without much-needed follow-up to their projects (Zeeuw and Kumar 2006) which is necessary to avoid the usual lip-service of domestic actors. To avoid the stagnation of democratic progress on a lip-service level, democracy promoters need *consistency,* which entails a follow-up to the completed project with further deepening of the initiative, targeting a particular level and issue. Consistency in democracy promotion is important because "the danger is that donors and financing agencies will declare victory when the formal rules have been modified … and will not follow through to ensure that they are enforced" (ARD 2002, p. 24). In the case of low consistency (–), the promoter is satisfied with the legal adoption of the rule (formal democratic transformation), especially if that is the final objective of a specific project, and shuts down the project without overseeing whether the rule is actually adhered to (the behavioral democratic transformation). In the case of a moderate consistency (+), the promoter launches a similar project, sometimes changing the implementer of the project and not following-up on the previous activities. In contrast, a promoter with positive consistency (++) follows-up with the issue and initiates projects or activities that are directed at the actual enforcement of the newly adopted rule, building on previously completed projects.

Involvement measures the level of presence of the promoter in the issues of national or regional importance, since positive and effective participation in the other issues of a target country (or region) may enhance domestic identification and the promoter's credibility. In addition, such involvement may eliminate outstanding issues that hinder or stagnate democratization. The involvement of the democracy promoter in areas other than democracy promotion is especially important in countries with outstanding conflicts, a low level of economic or human development, or other issues that are internally considered as national priorities. The degree of importance of a specific issue to the domestic politics can be determined through available surveys and political discourse. Involvement is considered low (–) in the case where the promoter limits itself to democracy promotion and related issues, moderate (+) in the case of mostly rhetorical involvement in other issues, and positive (++) in the case where the promoter tries to regularly and substantively engage in other local issues. However, such encompassing involvement may be possible only for large democracy promoters whose agenda can also accommodate additional issues. Smaller promoters can, however, seek cooperation with larger promoters to boost their local presence and give more weight to their democracy-promotion activities.

The first domestic variable of *party constellation* is borrowed from further analysis of Schimmelfennig *et al.* (2006, p. 245), who argue that "effective international socialization [democratization] will depend upon the party constellations in the target countries and their respective domestic power costs of compliance," as the course of reforms would depend upon the coalitional government formed by these parties. Party constellation can be distinguished as liberal/positive (++), mixed/moderate (+), and anti-liberal/low (–). Liberal party constellation is understood as liberal-, West- and democracy-oriented programs and declarations of parties with parliamentary seats. By contrast, in an anti-liberal party constellation the party programs and declarations are based on nationalistic, authoritarian, communist, and/or populist grounds. In the case of a mixed constellation, parties do not enjoy consensus on liberal reforms and, despite liberal coalitions, some of them are still in the process of reshaping their authoritarian or communist pasts. Thus, a liberal party constellation is the most conducive for behavioral democratic transformation, especially in cases of party-development projects. Although this variable is argued (Schimmelfennig *et al.* 2006) to have substantial influence on smooth norm transfer, here it is assumed to play a decreased role in countries with semi-presidential or presidential regimes, where the executive dominates over the parliament. Thus, it is expected that party constellation is rather an intervening variable, which encourages or further discourages democratization depending upon the values of other variables.

Democracy promoters are often blamed for unilateral programmatic decisions and for not involving local stakeholders in the development or implementation of democracy-promotion projects. This issue was first addressed in 1999 when World Bank introduced its Comprehensive Development Framework, emphasizing the importance of country ownership in developmental programs. Thus, another domestic variable to be considered is *ownership*. It is acknowledged that local ownership of a democracy-promotion program by an authoritarian government may block the advancement of the project. However, exclusion of local stakeholders is unlikely to have positive results either, because reforms would be blocked in any case. On the other hand, the exclusion of civil-society actors from projects developed for them is likely to result in indifference and in accusations of local inapplicability. Often local stakeholders are given limited ownership in project development but not in the implementation and moreover not in the monitoring and evaluation. Accordingly, the absence of any local involvement in the project is considered as a low (–) level of ownership. Limited involvement only in the developmental stage is considered as moderate ownership (+), and involvement or ownership in the course of the development and implementation of a project as positive (++).

Following the argument by Whitehead (2005) that successful democratization is possible if there is no major power in the region opposing democracy, another domestic variable of *democracy blocker* is introduced.[1] Democracy blocker is understood as a kind of a regional bully that is a powerful authoritarian regional actor and has the potential and is willing to influence—though not always directly—the domestic policy choices of a democracy-promotion target. The potential to influence stems from military, economic, and to some extent cultural interconnectedness with the target country. A mere proximity of a non-democratic neighbor is not considered as an indicator of a democracy blocker. Russia's influence over the post-communist territories may be considered as a sign of democracy blocker, while for example Iran's shared border with Armenia does not influence its political choices. It is important to note that the democracy blocker is regarded as a domestic variable even if it may seem as external to the target country, because it is not in the powers of the promoter to control its presence. Nonetheless, it is in the powers of a promoter to contain a democracy blocker's negative influence on democratization by alleviating the reasons of its influence. However, in the case of a democracy blocker the opposition to democracy is not necessarily outspoken and can be covert, aiming at distancing the target country from the democracy promoter. The absence of such an actor is a positive (++) condition for behavioral democratic transformation, whereas the presence of it with local resistance may moderately (+) hinder democracy promotion. The presence of democracy blocker with local support is likely to lower (–) the chances of the behavioral democratic transformation. In addition, understanding the reasons for support is important to give recommendations on the democracy promoter's *involvement* in specific areas and possible minimization of the democracy blocker's influence.

The dependent variable of democratic transformation is measured separately for each of the target sectors and is expected to have different results. Among

Table 2.2 Factors influencing democratic transformation

	Low (−)	Moderate (+)	Positive (++)
Incentives (international)	Social incentives	Economic but no/almost no political incentives	Economic and political incentives
Credibility (international)	No fulfillment of the threat or promise	Past-deadline or partial fulfillment of the threat or promise	Timely fulfillment of the threat or promise
Legitimacy (international)	No rhetorical and no behavioral commitment to democracy	Only rhetorical commitment to democracy	Rhetorical and behavioral commitment to democracy
Utility of adaptation (domestic)	Imminent loss of status quo/threat to status quo's survival	High possibility of losing status quo	Status quo preservation
Identification (domestic)	With non-democratic principles/against democracy promoter	With democratic principles/democracy promoter and partly with non-democratic countries	Only with democratic principles/democracy promoter
Resonance (domestic)	Opposing concepts	Lack of/confusion over specific concepts	Corresponding concepts
Cooperation (international)	Absent or annual meetings, dinners etc.	Joint promoter activities targeting only one level	Joint promoter activities targeting more than one level within the same activity
Consistency (international)	Closure of the project without follow-up	Similar project with a different implementer	Follow-up to the completed project
Involvement (international)	Only democracy promotion	Rhetorical involvement in other issues of national importance	Other issues of national importance
Party constellation (domestic)	Anti-liberal	Mixed	Liberal
Ownership (domestic)	Absent	Local involvement either in the development or implementation of the specific project	Local involvement both in development and implementation
Democracy blocker (domestic)	Present with local support	Present with local resistance	Absent

Source: author's own compilation.

the independent variables, the ones that need to be measured separately are the international variables of incentives, credibility, cooperation, and consistency, and the domestic variables of utility of adaptation, identification, resonance, and ownership. Thus, only the variables of involvement, democracy blocker, and party constellation do not need to be measured vis-à-vis each sector of democracy promotion. Consequently, when measuring, for example, incentives provided by a democracy promoter, a differentiation should be made between elections, parties, and the media, as the incentives (and other factors/variables) may not be the same for all three sectors. These are the test variables which are part of the main hypothesis that behavioral democratic transformation is likely to be achieved if credible material incentives provided by the democracy promoter are matched by at least moderate utility of adaptation, and the absence of or low support for a democracy blocker.

While it is argued that democratic transformations happen as a result of the interaction of all the presented variables, it is nevertheless assumed that, depending upon the target country, some of the independent variables will have greater importance. For example in the case of the post-Soviet countries, the variable of democracy blocker is likely to be more distinct due to Russia's constant strategic interests in the region. If so, then the efforts of democracy promoters should be supported by cooperative actions and positive involvement in resolution of national issues.. Based on the theoretical frameworks and the variables, the following hypotheses are suggested:

Democracy-promotion policies are distinguished into specific democracy-promotion projects, relevant statements, actions, and strategies. To incorporate both components of liberal democracy—contestation and participation —elections, party development, and media-development projects are studied. The analysis is presented in blocks of information that represent the status of the variables before, during, and after election cycles. Democracy-promotion projects represent the general democracy-promotion policies and allow full observation of the interaction of the selected variables. Democracy-promotion projects are analyzed within the course of their development, implementation, and—depending upon the availability—the evaluation. This includes all the trainings, conferences, statements, visits, financial transfers, and other related activities conducted in the course of the project implementation. However, projects alone cannot account for the changes in the domestic milieu, because individual projects are always accompanied by other democracy-promotion actions, statements, or discussions. Given that the dependent variable of this study is democratic transformation, the book also studies the state of democratic functionality of each analyzed sector and country. The research looks at the state of democratic functionality in line with the analyzed projects before, during, and at the end of project implementation.

This book draws on elements from both inductive and deductive approaches by starting from an empirical observation, then identifying theory (deductive), applying theory to later chosen cases, and investigating for additional variables (inductive). This research employs qualitative research methods of case studies by choosing a target country where two chosen promoters engage in the same type of democracy promotion within different target-sectors. Case studies "provide the intensive empirical analysis that can find previously unnoticed causal factors" (Achen and Snidal 1989, pp. 167–168). The study analyzes democracy-promotion projects according to sectors and types, from the year of launching democracy promotion (in the early 1990s) until shortly after the latest general elections. Democracy-promotion policies (further categorized as projects) are analyzed by tracking their initial development and further evolution. The selected countries represent states that have legally embraced the fundamental democratic principles and have been in interaction with selected promoters since the initial transition to democracy. The domestic conditions of the target country (from the first "democratic" general elections until shortly after the latest general elections) are also classified within the analytical framework to observe the interaction with the international conditions and to provide a full account of possible effects. Domestic and international changes after the latest general elections will be discussed, albeit without covering their outcome which, according to the adopted framework, is to be revealed after the next elections. To avoid static results and account for the dynamics of democracy promotion, the country-case is viewed beyond the limits of a single observation (Kubicek 2003; Flockhart 2005). Thus, because the observations of this research are based on the interaction of various international and domestic conditions, any change in those leads to a new observation.

Following the example of Schimmelfennig *et al.* (2006), this research uses the methods of within-case analysis—the congruence method, before–after comparison, and process tracing. Cross-case comparison is used in regard to different projects of the promoters (mostly ones targeting the same sector) to account for similarities of their strategies given the same domestic conditions or to pinpoint their differences. Comparisons between promoters and targets of democracy promotion help to explain possible differences between the strategies and effects in various domestic milieus and identify the variables that account for the specific outcome of a certain policy. These methods also provide detailed examinations of cases, which is necessary in identifying missing variables (George and Bennett 2005). Thus, comparison will be made between promoters' policies and strategies, possible outcomes of democracy promotion on different levels of promotion within the country-case by looking at the state of democracy before promotion programs and after (before–after comparison), and possible outcomes on the levels of democracy promotion (cross-case comparison).

According to George and Bennett, when using the congruence method:

> the analyst first ascertains the value of the independent variable in the case at hand and then asks what prediction or expectation about the outcome of the dependent variable should follow from the theory. If the outcome of the

case is consistent with the theory's prediction, the analyst can entertain the possibility that a causal relationship may exist.

(George and Bennett 2005, p. 181)

Thus, the values of a theoretically defined variable are checked against the expected outcomes within the period of observation. The ultimate goal of this method is to find one set of conditions that result in one type of outcome, even if the establishment of a causal link between democracy promotion and "observed changes in democracy" (Kumar 2012, p. 4) are difficult to establish.

One of the methods for verifying the results of the congruence method is the before–after comparison. Because the country-case is not treated as a single observation, it is possible to perform the before–after comparison each time one of the conditions (variables) or the value of the variable changes. This method allows controlling for the possible changes in the outcome and comparing different sets of conditions (independent variables). To further refine the findings and limit the possibility that simultaneous—though not causal—change has occurred in both dependent and independent variables, process-tracing analysis is used.

Even if not presented here in its entirety due to space constraints, process-tracing helps to identify the links between the independent and dependent variables and contributes to further development of an analytical framework. It also helps in identifying the hypothesized conditions. Since the outcome of democracy promotion is the result of interaction between different variables, process-tracing will help to identify "interacting causal variables" (George and Bennett 2005, p. 212) and understand the link between the international and domestic conditions of democracy promotion and its effect. In addition, it will help to "overcome the dilemmas of small-n research by providing more observation to the implications of a theory" (King *et al.* 1994, p. 227). The first step is the identification of the current state of the dependent variable in the case studies. With the help of process-tracing, as discussed by George and Bennett (2005), the next step is tracking the design and implementation strategies of democracy-promotion projects and their influence on domestic change by observing the reaction of domestic actors to the conditions of promoters. Process-tracing also helps to understand whether "similarity or variance of the independent variable [democracy-promotion strategy and domestic conditions] leads to different outcomes [in the dependent variable]" (George and Bennett 2005, p. 219).

Democracy promoters

While a vast amount of literature is available on individual democracy-promotion efforts of specific countries or organizations, limited comparative knowledge is available. Among the reasons for the lack of comparative research has been the alleged incomparability of democracy promoters, given their structural differences as an individual state or an international governmental or non-governmental organization, and the absence of an adequate and generally applicable theoretical framework. The choice of democracy promoters is primarily based on their comparative influence as international actors, as considerable leverage is needed to persuade domestic actors to change their behavior. In addition, the general assumption characterizes them as pursuing different strategies which, however, given the low level of democratic progress, result in similar outcomes.

Despite an array of international actors, the EU and the USA are the most prominent democracy promoters (Burnell 2008b). Initially these actors seem to represent two absolutely different and incomparable structures. However, closer consideration shows that "they are two different species of the same political genus" of compound democracy (Fabbrini 2007, p. 3), which is "based on territorial or state cleavages and necessarily function without a government" (Fabbrini 2007, p. 203), and where "decision-making capacity is constrained and limited through the sharing of its resources by distinct institutions" (Fabbrini 2005, p. 190). Similarities and differences between EU and US democracy promotion-policies in comparative perspective are not yet established using a clear analytical framework. The usual perception of the EU is as "one of the most important, if not the most important, normative powers in the world" (Barroso 2007), while the US is seen as a power that for the sake of democracy promotion can "send [its] soldiers, when [they] are needed" (Bush 2002). However, here the actions of the EU and the US are not viewed in isolation or in confrontation, but as complementing each other and in their own way influencing the potential outcome of democracy promotion and democratization processes.

The EU promotes democracy to its candidate countries by its powerful instrument of membership incentive. However, it also promotes democracy to countries that do not have membership incentives. The US is one of the largest and most visible democracy promoters that cannot offer membership incentive per se. The case of the US broadens the geographic and structural applicability of the analytical framework, giving an opportunity for its further development. This book analyzes the democracy promotion of USAID—the largest democracy-promotion instrument of the US. Though the US also uses military means in democracy promotion, this project does not take this into consideration as it does not require the consent of domestic actors, thus increasing the probability of non-compliance with promoted principles and rules of democracy. According to the mainstream literature on democracy promotion and foreign policy, these two promoters represent different images of normative (EU) and hard (US) powers; they are supposed to have different policies of democracy promotion though still not always resulting in democratic change in the behavior of domestic actors. However, this study shows that that, despite seeming differences, the strategies of these two actors have started to gradually converge.

Targets of democracy promotion

The case selection reflects the independent variables of this study and activities by both selected democracy promoters. Thus the selected cases need to have all variables present, with special focus on important variables that can be assigned negative values without in-depth research. Researching a case where the important variables have negative values would make findings generalizable, as democracy promotion is likely to be more effective and efficient in cases where these variables have positive values. Based on the argument of Schimmelfennig *et al.* (2006) that rationalist variables of costs (here utility of adaptation) and incentives account for the success of norm transfer, they are taken into account when selecting the target case. On the other hand, it was hypothesized above that the democracy blocker variable would account for the variations in democratic transformations, and if powered by domestic support would have negative effect on democracy promotion and democratization. The chosen country-cases do not account for their own democratization only, but rather serve as a democracy-promotion environment, where specific variables deemed crucial are particularly pronounced.

To find cases that would allow for testing of all the selected variables in the vast number of democracy-promotion targets and where both promoters are active, the initial selection is narrowed to European Neighbourhood Policy (ENP) participants. Selection of the cases also needs to be based on the possibility to test all the variables and yet again the feasibility of the research. In regard to the feasibility of testing all the variables, the variable of a democracy blocker is mostly relevant to the countries of the South Caucasus. Russia is an important actor for all post-Soviet countries in the ENP. However, the domestic stance towards Russia is not the same everywhere, with Moldovan and Ukrainian official positions towards Russia changing after each election. The South Caucasus countries, however, demonstrate different attitudes towards Russia, allowing different observations. While the Georgian government and population demonstrate outspoken resistance to Russia's policies, Azerbaijan follows a more neutral and pragmatic approach, and Armenia has been dubbed as the stronghold of Russian influence in the region due to the former's energy and security dependence on Russia.

The focus on Russia and the South Caucasus allows disentanglement of diverging relations between democratizing countries, democracy promoters, and the democracy blocker. It also allows demonstration that the success of democratization and democracy promotion would depend not only on the willingness and actions of the promoter and the target but also on the willingness of powerful regional actors to allow the democratization of others. In addition, the book looks for the capacity and willingness of the South Caucasus countries to resist Russia's efforts and continue with democratization. While among other regional actors Iran may be mistaken for a democracy blocker, it has neither the leverage of Russia nor has it expressed any superpower ambitions, limiting its interests to trade and occasional scolding of Azerbaijan for "non-Muslim" behavior. Even regional stakeholders believe that the influence of Iran or Turkey in the region "will go only as far as Russia is willing to permit," considering Iran only as a tool for Russia's Middle East policy (US Embassy cable 2009a). Thus, Russia's role as a democracy blocker in the South Caucasus is taken as a constant, while the main attention is paid to capture the variation in support of the democracy blocker and to some extent the reasons for this support, outlining the areas for greater involvement of democracy promoters. The presence of Russia with outspoken domestic support is likely to worsen conditions of democracy promotion.

The empirical research draws on a variety of sources, mostly primary. Initial analysis starts with the overview of literature on the issue that allows observing the democracy-promotion policies of the promoters. To assess the domestic conditions (independent variables), the limited amount of literature available on the South Caucasus is also used. This is supported by the analysis of local and international daily news services (in Armenian, Russian, and English) to keep track on the domestic developments and democracy indices. Among the primary sources are the official documentation of democracy promotion of the EU and the USA, such as Country and Progress Reports, Strategy Papers, communiqués, project proposal descriptions, evaluations, and project highlights by the promoters available online or upon request. To assess domestic conditions of the target countries, this study analyzes official statements by the domestic political and societal actors, and official documentation of the target country. Chapters on elections, political parties, and the media cover all three countries, with slightly more detailed attention to Armenia due to the stronger presence of Russian influence coupled with local support.

To a lesser degree, semi-structured interviews were conducted in some of the target countries with democracy promoters and in the US. The results of the interviews are embedded into the following empirical chapters. Some democracy promoters were interviewed to double-check findings on the strategies. Local targets of democracy promotion were not interviewed, since the interviews may only partially reveal their attitudes towards democracy promotion. In addition, this book focuses on the behavioral dimension of democracy promotion rather than attitudinal or ideational ones, which, though often attempted, are rarely validly measured.

Note

1 The concept was first introduced in the doctoral dissertation preceding this book and further elaborated on in Babayan 2013a.

Part II

Local ingredients of the global democratic recipe

3 The South Caucasus

The road to democracy or a blind alley?

Before the independence proclaimed in the early 1990s, Armenia, Azerbaijan, and Georgia had a brief independent period between the Bolshevik Revolution and annexation to the Soviet Union. Some argue that these years marked the first democratic period in the history of the South Caucasus region; however, these cannot be considered democratic in the modern sense of the concept. The *perestroika* period of Mikhail Gorbachev and the popular movements in Eastern Europe triggered looming intentions of Armenians to annex the enclave of 75-percent-Armenian-populated Nagorno-Karabakh (Derluguian 2005). At the same time, Azerbaijanis and Georgians joined to the chorus of communist countries intending to break away from the Soviet Union. The first decade of transition in all three South Caucasus countries was turbulent. Russian-style shock therapy and rapid privatization of the economy benefited a few and resulted in widespread oligarchic corruption (Stefes 2008). Armenia witnessed a war, years of economic blockade, the resignation of its first president, and the assassinations of the popular prime minister and the speaker of the parliament. Azerbaijan was involved in the war with Armenia over the Nagorno-Karabakh region and had seen an influx of refugees but also further development of its oil industry. Since the early days of its independence, Georgia has been involved in intrastate conflicts with some of its regions intending to break away, with these intentions exacerbated due to the initial nationalist politics of Georgian authorities. Despite diverging economic and political developments in the South Caucasus, Armenia, Azerbaijan, and Georgia have not ceased proclaiming their rhetorical adherence to democratic values. Nevertheless, not everywhere has their rhetorical democratic commitment transformed into a behavioral one.

Although several independent variables such as identification, resonance, and utility of adaptation are examined in this chapter, the main focus is on the democracy blocker variable. Russia's role as a democracy blocker is scrutinized and is considered as a domestic variable, since it is not in the power of promoters to control its existence. In addition, as the chapter further demonstrates, Russia's influence is inseparable from the position of some political elites and the developments within South Caucasus' protracted conflicts. In addition, this chapter sets the context for the discussion of the involvement of democracy promoters in the main pressing issues in Armenia, Azerbaijan, and

Georgia. This chapter demonstrates the importance of protracted conflicts on the internal and external politics of the South Caucasus countries, and outlines the differences between them and the negative influence that an unresolved conflict may have on democratization attempts. On the other hand, it is argued that, despite popular conviction, such actors as the Armenian diaspora are not as influential in political matters, and economic development is not necessarily accompanied by democratic progress. However, Russia's ubiquitous and controversial activities in the region, coupled with its dubious and often provocative promotion of conflict resolution, has kept Armenia from democratization despite the latter's identification with democracy promoters, while seemingly having an opposite effect on Georgia.

The haunting nightmares of protracted conflicts and international involvement

Nagorno-Karabakh

The regional conflicts in the South Caucasus are unavoidable when analyzing political and economic aspects of the three countries. Nevertheless, this book does not venture to assess the validity of claims over any of the breakaway regions, neither does it propose a potential resolution to the conflicts. It rather aims to demonstrate the nature of the conflicts as an intervening negative factor for democratization and democracy promotion, as a possible influence on local politics, and as an area which needs active involvement by a democracy promoter. The inter-state conflict between Armenia and Azerbaijan over Nagorno-Karabakh (NK), and up until 2008 the intra-state conflict of Georgia with its regions of Abkhazia and South Ossetia (SO), have been initially regarded as of marginal threat to international and European security. However, frequent sniper fire and casualties on the Line of Contact (LoC) between Armenian and Azerbaijani forces, and the 2008 full-scale armed conflict between Georgia and Russia, have reminded that, even if nominally frozen, these conflicts have a dangerous potential to heat up.

The conflict between Armenia and Azerbaijan over the former's defense of the right to self-determination of the Nagorno-Karabakh population and the latter's claims over its territorial integrity had been active from 1988–1994. The conflict had resulted in thousands of deaths on both sides, had caused hundreds of thousands of Armenians and Azerbaijanis to become refugees, and fuelled several espionage cases (RFE/RL 2014a, 2014b). While the Armenian population of Azerbaijan had been forced to flee to Armenia, the Azerbaijani population of Nagorno-Karabakh had been forced to flee to Azerbaijan. Despite the international involvement, the Nagorno-Karabakh conflict has achieved "frozen" status with occasional skirmishes, with 2008's Mardakert skirmishes being one of the most publicized, with further escalation in early 2014. As some analysts argue, "Armenia's pro-democracy movement … merged completely with the Karabakh issue" (Goldenberg 1994, p. 165).

The OSCE Minsk Group was created in 1992 and has since been holding peace talks over a resolution of the Nagorno-Karabakh conflict. Under the co-chairmanship of France, Russia, and the USA, the OSCE Minsk Group is comprised of the representatives of another six EU members (Germany, Italy, Portugal, the Netherlands, Sweden, and Finland), Belarus, and Turkey, as well as Armenia and Azerbaijan. However, the OSCE Minsk Group has so far failed to produce tangible results, subsequently undermining its potential with both Armenians and Azerbaijanis (Corwin 2006; Medzhid 2011; Babayan 2012b). The primarily Russia-negotiated ceasefire was signed in 1994, with Nagorno-Karabakh proclaiming its de facto independence.

Despite the ceasefire, the Nagorno-Karabakh conflict has dominated Armenian and Azerbaijani domestic and foreign politics and has caused almost 3000 lives from both sides since 1994 (International Crisis Group 2011). As of 2014 the independence of Nagorno-Karabakh has not been recognized by any state, including Armenia. Nevertheless, a large presence of Karabakh natives in Armenian politics demonstrates the extent of the interconnectedness and importance of the Nagorno-Karabakh issue to Armenia.[1] The former president Levon Ter-Petrosyan was more open to the option of Nagorno-Karabakh remaining on the territory of Azerbaijan. Among other points, the Minsk Group co-chairs proposed in 1997 that Armenia cedes all Azerbaijani territory outside of Karabakh and the Shusha province within Karabakh, with OSCE peacekeepers responsible for the security of returning Azeri refugees and the Karabakh population (Migdalovitz 2001; Zourabian 2006). Azerbaijan was proposed to allow Karabakh Armenians to maintain armed forces which, at the end of the Baku-Stepanakert talks, would have been reduced to a militarized police (Migdalovitz 2001). Arguing that neither Azerbaijan nor the international community would accept the independence of Nagorno-Karabakh, former president Ter-Petrosyan called the plan realistic. However, Ter-Petrosyan's position went in sharp contrast with the positions of his government members, especially then Prime Minister Robert Kocharyan and defense minister Serzh Sargsyan, and diaspora and local Armenians (Migdalovitz 2001, p. 9). Eventually he was forced to resign.

After 14 meetings within 1998–2001, the two sides expressed their dissatisfaction with the OSCE mediation and even voiced the possibility of a regionally grown solution (Peuch 2001). The meetings, however, continued, though with disruptions due to the inability of the presidents to prepare their publics for a settlement (Migdalovitz 2001). The 2001 Paris and Key West negotiations did not result in a settlement, prompting arguments that "all hopes for a possible agreement were demolished" (Ziyadov 2010, p. 119) after Heydar Aliyev died, passing the presidency of Azerbaijan to his son Ilham. The Prague process was a round of negotiations with "no agenda, no commitment, no negotiation, but a free discussion" (OSCE 2004a, p. 1). It proposed the concept of an interim status, which would have ensured Azerbaijan's legal recognition of Nagorno-Karabakh. However, both Armenian and Azerbaijani sides understood the concept differently, since Armenia has demanded an international status for

Nagorno-Karabakh in line with the one of Kosovo, while Azerbaijan would agree to a temporary status only (Ziyadov 2010). They agreed to the preamble of the Madrid principles presented by the mediators in 2007 and updated in 2009, however, while still negotiating on the other parts and generating further disagreements (Musayelian and Harutyunyan 2013). While Armenia and Nagorno-Karabakh support a referendum on independence among the current population of Nagorno-Karabakh, Azerbaijan does "not like the Madrid document" (US Embassy cable 2009b), insisting on a referendum after the return of Azeri internally displaced persons (IDPs). The inability to agree on the "basic principles" resulted in a freezing of negotiations for two years (Fuller and Giragosian 2011) with eventual resumption in late 2013 (RFE/RL 2013a), which was widely hailed by the US (Psaki 2013; RFE/RL 2013b) and the EU (RFE/RL 2013c). This round of negotiations not only did not result in a signed agreement, but was followed by accelerated condemnations of ceasefire violations and exchanges of fire (RFE/RL 2013d, 2013e; News.az 2014) and casualties on both sides (News. am 2014a; RFE/RL 2014c).

Sniper fire exchange and the regional "weapons spending spree" (Kucera 2010a) have made the Nagorno-Karabakh conflict "one of the most worrying" (European Parliament 2012, p. 1; Mohammed 2012) and complex "because it involves a number of regional actors" (Vasconcelos 2012: 101). The presence of Armenian and Azerbaijani snipers on the 220-km LoC cost 25 lives in 2007 (Orudzhev 2008), 30 in 2008 (OSCE 2009), and 19 in 2009 (Caucasian Knot 2010a). Armenia increased its military spending from US$93 million in 1999 to US$217 million in 2008, and Azerbaijan from US$133 million in 1999 to US$697 million in 2008 (SIPRI) and to US$3.1 billion in 2011 (Caucasian Knot 2010b). Bellicose statements by the Azerbaijani government (Osborn 2009) that they "have to be ready to liberate [their] lands by military means, and [they] are ready" (RFE/RL 2008a; Interfax 2012) and promising to shoot down civilian planes if they fly to Stepanakert (Bulghadarian 2011) impede peaceful resolution. The presidential pardon and rank promotion for an Azerbaijani officer convicted of murdering with an axe his Armenian colleague at a NATO training exercise in Budapest has exacerbated an already tense atmosphere (OSCE 2012; RFE/RL 2012a). Being less combative, Armenia nevertheless opts for political pressure and expects military support from Russia. Armenia maintains close economic and political connections with Nagorno-Karabakh and sends recruits to the Nagorno-Karabakh army (Gradirovski and Esipova 2007). The urgency of need for a settlement cannot be undermined since "heightened rhetoric, distrust on both sides, and recurring violence along the LoC increase the risk of miscalculations that could escalate the situation with little warning" (Clapper 2012, p. 21). Mutual denunciation by Armenian and Azerbaijani leaders (United Nations News Service 2011) indicates little intention of cooperation between the conflicting parties, despite rhetorical commitment and occasional hopeful statements by the OSCE on the progress of negotiations (RFE/RL 2014d).

The importance of the Nagorno-Karabakh issue to Armenian politics is echoed by the population. According to a series of USAID-funded surveys conducted by the International Republican Institute (IRI) in Armenia and the Armenian Sociological Association in 2006–2008, the Nagorno-Karabakh conflict has been a major source of problems and fears for the Armenian population. Thus, it is not surprising that over 70 percent of the respondents considered solution of the Nagorno-Karabakh problem a priority for the Armenian government. The positions on the ultimate solution to the conflict, however, may vary among the population, government officials, and international actors as demonstrated by the ousting of the former president Ter-Petrosyan in 1998. However, taking into consideration that the conflict hinders economic development, endorses an atmosphere of insecurity, and places democracy issues at the bottom of the priorities list[2], this makes conflict resolution and regional cooperation an area to be given priority attention by democracy promoters. The conflict also reiterates the dominating position of Russia in Armenia and in the South Caucasus.

After the Cold War, the US launched developmental, democracy promotion, and reconstruction projects in the South Caucasus despite the lack of consensus between observers on whether the US should be involved in the region (Nichol 2010). The proponents of US engagement in the South Caucasus argue that conflict-resolution efforts help in restraining warfare, smuggling, and Islamic extremism, and may contain Russian and Iranian influences over the region. Azerbaijan as a supplier, with Armenia and Georgia as transit countries, are important actors for US counterterrorism actions and for the energy-supply diversification plans of US "European allies" (Gordon 2009). New transit routes depend on the resolution of frozen conflicts and opening the borders between Armenia and Azerbaijan. Otherwise, more time and financial resources would be spent, as in the case of the US-supported Baku–Tbilisi–Ceyhan crude oil pipeline, which connected Azerbaijan to Turkey through Georgia instead of directly through Armenia. Through Azerbaijan, the South Caucasus also provides the US with access to the Central Asia and Afghanistan, making the presence of conflicts undesirable for US security interests (Cornell 2005).

Given a substantial Armenian lobby in Congress and its own security interests in Azerbaijan, the US cannot openly support any of the sides. However, the status quo is not within its interests either, nor is conflict escalation. US officials have repeatedly stated that the conflict has to achieve an exclusively peaceful resolution and any skirmishes were met with condemnation. While Russia was pre-occupied with its own domestic issues in the 1990s, the US also pushed NK conflict mediation down its priorities list in the 2000s after engaging in the War on Terror. Before passing the mediating torch to Russia, the US organized five meetings between Armenian and Azerbaijani presidents over 2008. US–Russia relations worsened after the NATO attacks on Serbia in 1999, however, with slight improvement after the 11 September terrorist attacks and further worsening following Putin's strengthening authoritarianism and the Russo–Georgian armed conflict of 2008. The "reset" in US–Russia relations agreed on by the presidents Medvedev and Barack Obama in 2009 underlined the change of US foreign policy and symbolically entrusted the resolution of the NK conflict to Russia, while claiming that the US "works inconspicuously" (Kerry in News.am 2014b).

The protracted Nagorno-Karabakh conflict damages the democratization prospects of Armenia by giving its authorities a reason to justify undemocratic measures during elections or censoring the media. In addition, it negatively affects the utility of adaptation of the incumbents to democracy promoted from outside if proffered rewards are conditioned by concessions in conflict resolution or friendly relations with neighbors, as it may endanger their position with hardliners. On the other hand, the persistence of the conflict damages trade and energy plans of the promoters in the region, especially of the EU. Strained relations between Armenia and Azerbaijan force them to refrain from multilateral cooperation projects, making promotion of not only democracy but also regional cooperation an ordeal (Babayan 2012b). Constrained by their strategic interests in the region, the international actors will not openly take sides. However, ignoring the Nagorno-Karabakh problem and merely resorting to moral support of the peace process will not produce a peace settlement and may result in an unwanted war. As further elaborated, active involvement in conflict resolution is a necessary condition for successful democracy promotion in the South Caucasus, especially in light of Russia's self-appointed and meticulously guarded mediation plans. Moreover, positive involvement in the conflict may help the EU and the US to advance their other strategic interests, such as energy diversification for the EU and the fight against terrorism for the USA.

Abkhazia and South Ossetia

South Ossetia opposed Georgia's independence from the Soviet Union and decided on its own unification with North Ossetia in the Russian Soviet Federative Socialist Republic. This was followed by the South Ossetian autonomous region appealing to Moscow to recognize its independence within the Soviet Union. A number of mutually unrecognized elections in Georgia and South Ossetia led to an armed escalation in 1991 between ethnic Georgian forces and South Ossetia. A Russia-brokered ceasefire agreement of 1992 divided South Ossetia into areas controlled by the Georgian government and unrecognized South Ossetian government. However, the ceasefire did not result in a definitive settlement of the conflict, with major clashes and attacks occurring in 2004, 2006, and 2008.

As Nagorno-Karabakh has tried to leave Azerbaijan, Abkhazia has repeatedly attempted to leave Georgia. The collapse of the Soviet Union triggered stronger calls for expanded autonomy in Abkhazia, turning into a fully fledged war in August 1992. The war has been characterized by a lack of military control on both sides and a vast number of atrocities against civilians, which was arguably instigated by Russia providing arms to rebel groups (Human Rights Watch 1994). A Russia-brokered ceasefire in 1993 ended the armed conflict until 1998, with Abkhazians later demanding US$13 billion in compensation from Tbilisi (RIA News 2007). The anti-Georgian policy of Abkhazia continued, officially demanding the departure of all ethnic Georgians from Abkhazia and declaring independence in 1994. A shorter armed conflict broke out in 1998, followed by other two confrontations in Kodori Valley, involving Abkhaz and Georgian troops and Chechen insurgents. The secessionist conflicts have also negatively influenced Georgia's relations with Russia due to the latter's on-going covert involvement and mass-issuing of Russian passports to Abkhazians and South Ossetians, arguably for humanitarian purposes (International Crisis Group 2006).

As warned (Lavrov 2008), the independence of Kosovo set a precedent for Abkhazia and South Ossetia. Accusing Georgia of military build-up, the break-away regions appealed to the international community to recognize their independence. The ceasefire brokered by then French president Sarkozy ended the armed conflict of 2008, which had also involved Russia. With no settlement achieved, Russia recognized Abkhazia and South Ossetia's independence. The complexity of the Georgian conflicts is emphasized by the mixed roles of the involved parties. While after 2008 Georgia regards Russia as a conflicting party resorting to sabotage (US Embassy cable 2008) that armed rebels shortly prior to the conflict (Guardian 2010c), Russia sees itself as merely a mediator (Economist 2011a). Despite the insistence of the breakaway regions on independence, president Mikheil Saakashvili emphasized their political belonging to Georgia and the readiness of Georgian missions abroad to serve them (Interfax 2009), also issuing "neutral passports" to allow travel outside of Georgia (Bigg 2012).

The 2008 conflict has been mediated within the format of Geneva talks co-chaired by the EU, the OSCE, and the UN. The commencement of the Geneva talks was "rocky" (Fuller 2008). Abkhazia and South Ossetia demanded participation in the talks on an equal basis with Georgia; however, the latter refused (Civil.Ge 2008a). To avoid a dead-end in negotiations, mediators would meet separately with the representatives of Georgia and the breakaway regions, adding to the confusion over the format of the talks (Civil.Ge 2008b). The Abkhaz delegation went as far as to request a change of the format (Civil.Ge 2012a). The Geneva talks provided a forum for negotiations and mediation, but the added value of this forum in changing the status quo is marginal. The participating parties either claim they are not involved—Russia—or they do not want to recognize others' involvement. Russia's dubious involvement was underlined by its accession deal to the World Trade Organization (WTO). The deal provided for an independent company to conduct customs checks on trade between Russia, South Ossetia, and Abkhazia (Civil.Ge 2011a) Though the two break-away regions have perceived the deal as "stab in the back," that is apparently "the price for its [Russia's] continued financial support and military protection" (RFE/RL 2011a).

European and American (Robbins 2011) insistence on humanitarian issues have continued throughout the 22 rounds of negotiations. The 20th round was held against the background of the suspended Incident Prevention and Response Mechanism, which according to Georgia's chief negotiator in case of collapse may leave the participants without an information exchange mechanism (Civil. Ge 2012b). Even if Russia and Georgia seem to deduce different meanings out of the same discussions, the UN representative noted positive developments at least within free movement of the local population. However, drafting of the document—'Agreed Undertakings'—on rehabilitation of housing and damaged facilities, supply of water; the legal situation of refugees and IDPs, and facilitation of their voluntary and safe return has generated open opposition from Abkhazia and South Ossetia. They preferred to walk out from the discussions (Civil. Ge 2010a), while Abkhazia renounced its participation from the second working group (Abkhaz Government 2010).

Even if Russia and Georgia "can get along when they want to" (Economist 2011b), authorities of both countries instigate an atmosphere of mutual blame and personal insults (Telegraph 2008; Tsotniashvili 2011). While Georgia has detained and prosecuted over a dozen alleged spies (Civil.Ge 2010b; ICC 2011), Russia has considerably increased its military presence in Abkhazia and South Ossetia (Felgenhauer 2010; Socor 2010). The distrust was exacerbated in October 2010 when Georgia lifted visa requirements for residents of Russia's North Caucasus republics "to deepen the relationship between the peoples" (BBC 2010a). Russia called the move a "political travesty" (Nikolski 2010) and "provocation" (Pesov 2010). In July 2011, Georgia alleviated the tensions by allowing all Russian citizens to be issued visas at the Zemo Larsi–Kazbegi border crossing point (Civil.Ge 2011a). The parliamentary victory of Bidzina Ivanishvili's party in October 2012 and his appointment as prime minister may improve relations with Russia, despite him being portrayed as incompetent (Walker 2012). Putin, however, sees Ivanishvili sending "positive signals" (BBC 2012a; RIA 2012a), even if these will not change Russia's decisions in regards to Abkhazia and South Ossetia (RIA 2012b).

The democracy blocker: Russia in the South Caucasus[3]

Russia's first decade after the break-up of the Soviet Union was highlighted by the armed conflicts in the Northern Caucasus, economic "shock therapy," the financial crisis of 1998 with a further decline in GDP, the constant search for a prime minister, and its declining weight in international politics. Nevertheless, Russia maintained a democratizing image, emphasizing friendly relations with Western leaders with the "Bill and Boris" friendship (Rutland and Dubinsky 2008; Pushkov 2010) being the most notable. Nostalgia for the imperialistic past and undeniable political influence became even stronger after NATO's bombing of Yugoslavia in 1999 despite strong Russian opposition, and the eventual disillusionment with the US "spinach treatment" (Talbott 2003). Russia's second president, Vladimir Putin, opted for a "harder" approach towards foreign affairs and economic development. Admitting slim chances for Russia to liberalize to the extent of the US or the UK, Putin (1999), nevertheless stated that Russia had been and was a superpower. Putin's further statements and actions spread concern among Western observers due to the "breaking away from the core democratic values of the Euro-Atlantic community" and "the return of rhetoric of militarism and empire" (Ahlin *et al.* 2004).

Underlining Russia's awakening from hiatus, in 2000 president Putin approved a less-cautiously worded foreign-policy strategy. The strategy overtly called the US a threat to a multipolar world and Russia's interests as a great power. It pointed to the dominance of the US, international terrorism, promotion of regional groupings, and globalization of the world economy as Russia's main challenges. However, understanding that the forced allegiance of Eastern Europe was long lost to the EU, Russia gave the post-Soviet countries priority in its foreign policy. President Putin's annual address to the Federal Assembly of 2002 underlined the importance of post-Soviet countries (Babayan and Braghiroli 2011). Asserting its great power status and regaining its traditional sphere of influence have become the primary task of Putin's Russia (Secrieru 2006). Through military cooperation and economic investments, Russia has taken direct action to stabilize authoritarian regimes in the post-Soviet space (Grävingholt *et al.* 2011). Its own energy resources, the initial Western neglect, and the economic indebtedness of the former Soviet republics have together provided a rather fertile ground for Russia's authoritarian maneuvering.

Russia aims to shape the domestic environments of neighboring countries according to its interests, at the same time resisting to the presence of other international actors (Babayan and Braghiroli 2011). Given Russia's frequent usage of its energy resources as a powerful political tool and its frequent mediating efforts, it is argued that, in the South Caucasus, Russia mainly pursues two intertwined *modi operandi* or frameworks for influencing neighboring countries: business-energy and politics-security (Babayan 2013a). Due to its own authoritarian regime, Russia would be unlikely to target civil society, which is usually a partner for democracy promotion, no matter how weak. The frameworks are intertwined due to the merger of Russia's own economic and political realms, where prominent businesspeople have close government ties and sometimes even occupy state positions.[4] However, the suggested frameworks should not be considered as governance models in the same manner as the EU's efforts at exporting its "good governance" or US's in exporting liberal democracy. These are rather *modi operandi* through which a democracy blocker, in the case of this chapter Russia, attempts to halt democratization and make its own policies or cooperation with them attractive for neighboring countries. Nevertheless, the attractiveness of such cooperation would largely be influenced by these countries' internal developments and the degree of their bargaining powers, with higher bargaining power to be likely to lead to lower attractiveness of cooperation.

Within a business-energy *modus operandi*, Russia aims to dominate the local energy market by providing the consumed energy and by monopolizing delivery or export routes. Investing in other financial sectors without conditionality, which often accompanies democracy-promotion funding, or simply buying out the industry of the target country, gives the democracy blocker leverage that is often unattainable for democracy promoters. In addition, in the South Caucasus, where frozen and occasionally active armed conflicts have dominated the scene, Russia's involvement within political and security issues can potentially streamline the developments to Russia's benefit. To show how Russia may apply these frameworks, the chapter proceeds with outlining Russia's interests in the South Caucasus and its willingness to project authoritarianism and the role of a democracy blocker, even if not always overtly. Discussion of Russia's foreign-policy objectives and strategies is an important part of the analysis, since it allows for shaping the suggested frameworks and explains how cooperation with Russia may become more attractive than association with democracy promoters or further democratic progress. The analysis then proceeds with the discussion of the economic and political dynamics within the region and Russia's involvement, especially since the first presidency of Vladimir Putin, when Russia's authoritarianism started to consolidate.

Georgia's Rose Revolution of 2003 and Ukraine's Orange Revolution of 2004 were initially regarded as a challenge to Russia's dominance in the neighborhood. However, they rather provided Russia with a justification for more pro-active and aggressive policies, putting its democracy-blocker potential and willingness to act as one beyond doubt. Subsequently, concerns have been raised about the increasing authoritarianism of Russia's regime and its authoritarian influence projected over the countries of the former Soviet Union (Abushov 2009; Ambrosio 2009; Tolstrup 2009; Grävingholt *et al.* 2011). Russia's growing authoritarianism has been masked by neologisms and euphemisms, such as *suverennaya demokratia* (sovereign democracy) and *vertikal vlasti* (hierarchy of power),[5] increasing its attractiveness to the countries struggling with the consequences of their dubious transitions. In addition, following a "Machiavellian approach" of supporting whatever regime it deems profitable for its own purposes (Shapovalova and Zarembo 2010), Russia has also used democracy-promotion rhetoric. Stating that Russia "has a sphere of privileged interests" (Averre 2011, p. 13), president Medvedev (Medvedev 2008) claims Russia's commitment to "the development in all possible ways of rights and freedoms, the struggle with corruption." However, the swap of positions in 2012 between Putin and Medvedev and Putin's plans for building a Eurasian Union (BBC 2011; Blockmans *et al.* 2012) seem to further consolidate authoritarianism in Russia.

Given Russia's authoritarian tendencies and its growing regional ambitions, democracy promotion by other international actors, such as the EU's enlargement and various neighborhood policies, have been viewed by Russia as the "apple of discord" (Arbatova 2006). One of the major concerns of Russia has been the launching of the Eastern Partnership (EaP). Despite the reassurances from the former EU foreign policy chief Solana that the EaP had not been designed against Russia, Russia's foreign minister Lavrov interpreted the choice given to EaP partners as "either you are with Russia, or with the European Union" (EUobserver 2009). The first and second wars in Chechnya (Haukkala 2011), the conflict in Georgia in 2008 and the subsequent monitoring of the Russia–Georgia border (Grevi 2007), and a number of gas crises, added to the oft-voiced disapproval of Putin's policies. Although the "reset" in relations between the EaP advocate Poland and Russia has helped to overcome some divisions, Russia has been indirectly trying to hinder smooth implementation of the EaP, *inter alia* promising Azerbaijan "serious consequences" (US Embassy cable 2009c) for its participation in the EaP and the Nabucco pipeline project. In addition, the EU's indecisive role in frozen conflicts has added to Russia's dominant role in its neighborhood. The tiptoeing politics of the EU over conflicts in the South Caucasus and its outright refusal to engage in Nagorno-Karabakh conflict mediation (Jozwiak 2012) have emphasized Russia's economic and military dominance.

Thus, Russian foreign policy after the USSR has been guided by the endeavor of regaining Russia's status of superpower, which *inter alia* included keeping its *blizhnee zarubezhy'e* (near abroad) under its direct influence. Thus, Russia initiated the creation of the Commonwealth of Independent States (CIS) in 1991, which has become one of its main tools for projecting influence. However, the appeal of the CIS in comparison with other regional organizations has been weak due to a lack of any financial aid (Rywkin 2003). Nevertheless, due to certain economic and security policies and despite certain local resistance, Russia's role in the South Caucasus has been more assertive in the 2000s than in the 1990s. Thus, through energy dependence, economic pressure, occasional military aid, and despite its allegedly weakening grip over the region, Russia tries to fuel "Putin's fantasy" (Nixey 2012, p. 7) of a Eurasian Union.

Energy, security, and the Eurasian Customs Union

While the US and European countries have provided unconditional aid, Russia has usually engaged in specific business development based on its own strategic interests. This strategy of "if not by tanks, then by banks" (Tsygankov 2006) underlined the recent employment of non-military instruments in reinforcing Russia's policies and obtaining dominant status in the economies of the South Caucasus. Russia forgave Armenia's post-Soviet debt of US$98 million in exchange for five Armenian state-owned military-industrial enterprises (Migdalovitz 2004). Some arguments go as far as claiming that former president Kocharyan "effectively sold off Armenia … to Russian commercial and political interests" (Nixey 2012, p. 5). Further economic integration has happened as Russia purchased large shares in Armenian telecommunications (RFE/RL 2012b), energy, electricity networks, and banking industries. The Russian Vneshtorgbank purchased a controlling 70 percent stake in the 1923-established Armenian Savings Bank in 2004 and, after renaming it to VTB Armenia in 2006, in 2007 purchased the remaining 30 percent from Mika Armenia Trading to become its sole shareholder. Then head of the Armenian side in the Armenia–Russia Economic Cooperation Commission and later president Serzh Sargsyan welcomed Russia's investments and did not see "any risk at all in the growth of Russian capital in our country" (Socor 2006), which has eventually resulted in 500 out of the 800 largest firms being Russian-owned (Elliott 2010). This positive opinion, however, has not been always shared by others in the South Caucasus (Tsereteli 2005; Saakashvili 2006).

Despite the disagreements between former presidents Yeltsin and Shevar-nadze on placing Chechen refugees in the Pankisi Gorge in Georgia (Baran 2001), in the 1990s Russia–Georgia relations were rather pragmatic and without major disputes. The first economic entry of Russia happened in 2003 with the acquisition of an electricity-distribution company, Telasi, and the only working block of the Gardabani power station (Tsereteli 2005). In addition, Gazprom acquired the right to manage and upgrade gas pipelines running through Georgia; a move supposed to provide Russia with influence over Georgia's economy, rather than Gazprom with profit (Baran 2003). Energy acquisitions were fol-lowed by purchases in the banking and commodities sectors.

The pragmatism was reversed by the new course of foreign policy adopted by succeeding president Saakashvili. He not only insisted on in-revolt Abkhazia and South Ossetia reconsidering their independence claims, but also called for closer integration with the EU and NATO at the expense of its bilateral relations with Russia. Using Georgia's negative trading balance and dependence on Russian gas, Russia has employed its economic force to compensate for this Georgian "rebellion". In March 2006 Russia imposed an embargo on Georgian wine (Corso 2006), justified by an unusually high number of pesticides in tested bottles (Regnum 2006). In May 2007 Russia banned imports of Georgian mineral water Borjomi, citing violations of water-purity standards (BBC 2006a), prompting accusations by Georgian authorities of a politically motivated eco-nomic embargo (BBC 2006b). Since 50 percent of annual Borjomi production was sold to Russia, and with another decade to wait until Georgian products become competitive in the EU (Patsuria 2010), Russian embargoes have sub-stantially curtailed Georgian economy. The moderate bargaining power of Georgia had been its veto power in the WTO, blocking Russia's entry since 2004. However, a Swiss-brokered bilateral deal on unblocking Russia's bid was signed in November 2011 (RFE/RL 2011b), paving its entry into the WTO in August 2012. The deal provides for an independent company to conduct customs checks on trade between Russia, South Ossetia, and Abkhazia (Civil.Ge 2011a). The two breakaway regions have perceived the deal as a "stab in the back" that is apparently "the price for its [Russia's] continued financial support and military protection" (RFE/RL 2011a).

Unlike Armenia and Georgia, Azerbaijan, rich with natural resources, has had better opportunities for economic maneuvering, thus increasing its bargaining power. Trade restrictions imposed by Russia at the beginning of the second Chechen War (Hunter *et al.* 2004) did not have a severely negative influence on Azerbaijan's economic development. Nevertheless, to curtail Azerbaijan's eco-nomic leverage, Russia sought to prevent Azerbaijan's participation in the US-supported Baku–Tbilisi–Ceyhan pipeline project. However, the pipeline started operation in May 2006, giving Azerbaijan entry into the international energy market by bypassing Russia. One of Azerbaijan's levers of influence over Rus-sia's decisions, even if not a significant one, might have been Gabala radar station—one of the nine radar stations built in the USSR to detect possible missile attacks—with a positive contribution to Azerbaijan's budget due to an annual US$7 million lease to Russia (President of Russia 2002), which Azerbaijan has announced to raise starting from 2012. Despite Russia's initial claims that a station in Armavir, Russia, has the same capacity as Gabala and that the lease would be pointless (Ghazinyan 2011), Russia was ready to sign the extension until 2025 (RIA 2011). However, the deal lost any attractiveness to Russia after Azerbaijan increased the rent from US$7 million to US$300 million per year. Russia even entertained the option of building another radar station in Armenia and closed down its operation in Gabala in December 2012 (Abbasov 2012; Fomitschev 2012; Shakaryants 2012).

Despite Azerbaijan's comparative leverage, the energy relations between Russia and the South Caucasus countries have been characterized as "highly asymmetric" (Perovic 2005, p. 1) and potentially endangering the ability of small states to make independent decisions (Inbar and Sheffer 1997). Privatization of state-owned facilities, under the pressure of Russian energy companies but allegedly to increase the effectiveness of governance, have made Western companies reluctant to invest in the South Caucasus energy sector (Tsereteli 2005). However, Russian companies closely associated with Russian authorities use energy revenues to invest in other sectors of the economy (Tsereteli 2005), making their "partners" even more dependent.

Gas is procured to Armenia by the ArmRosGazprom (ARG) CJSC. ARG was founded jointly by Armenia and Russia in 1997, with Russian gas monopolist Gazprom and the Armenian Energy Ministry each owning 45 percent and the ITERA company 10 percent of stocks. However, Gazprom's share has risen to 80 percent with the Armenian government holding 20 percent of shares. The dependence upon Russian gas was supposed to be ameliorated by the 2007 inauguration of the Armenia–Iran natural gas pipeline, meant to supply 400 million cubic meters towards the annual Armenian consumption of 1.5 billion cubic meters (Socor 2007). Russia did not meet the initiative of another pipeline with enthusiasm, and the latter's construction and launch had been repeatedly postponed (Markarian 2005). However, the Iran–Armenia pipeline was put under the control of Russian-dominated ARG after Gazprom had threatened to substantially increase gas prices for the South Caucasus from January 2006 (Markarian 2005). Armenian officials replied with a rare criticism of Russia, calling the move politically motivated (Danielyan 2005a) and suggesting charging Russia for stationing its troops in Armenia (Bedevian 2005). Gazprom replied that Armenia would be charged a higher price unless it transferred the control over the Armenia-Iran pipeline to Russia (Kalantarian 2006). Consequently, regular Armenian concessions and Russian bullying secured gas prices to stay the same in 2011 (Harutyunyan 2011a), thus keeping it at US$180 for 1000 cubic meters. Moreover, though subsidized by the Armenian government (Harutyunyan 2011a), the gas price for economically vulnerable Armenian households was lowered for at least one heating season (Avetisian 2011a). However, in July 2013 the price of gas was increased, prompting talks that it may be subsidized within the Customs Union (Stepanyan 2013a). Yet, as it was later revealed, the Armenian government had "secretly subsidized" gas prices prior to presidential elections of 2013, as a result increasing its total debt to Russia even more which was then paid by ceding the remaining 20 percent of ARG to Gazprom (Stepanian 2013a). This was followed by further announcements that due to new agreements with Russia gas prices may not increase for the next five years (RIA News 2013).

Georgia's "disobedience" and the arrest of four Russian nationals suspected of espionage were classified by president Putin as "an act of state terrorism with hostage-taking" (BBC 2006c). Consequently, adding to the embargoes on wine and mineral water, Russia doubled gas prices for Georgia (BBC 2006d). The increase in gas prices could have been avoided by Russia's customers, including Georgia, by handing over to Russia the domestic pipeline systems (Sindelar 2006). Amid talks over gas prices, two explosions occurred in January 2006 on the Mozdok–Tbililsi pipeline in North Ossetia, which cut gas supplies to Georgia and to Armenia. While Russia blamed pro-Chechen insurgents, president Saakashvili claimed that "it was an attempt by Russia to force Georgia to surrender ownership of its domestic gas pipeline" (Sindelar 2006). Calling Saakashvili's statements "hysteria" (Sindelar 2006), in November 2006 Russia announced construction of a direct pipeline to the Georgian breakaway region of South Ossetia, and raised gas prices for Georgia in January 2007. Relations were further strained by the August 2008 armed conflict between Russia and Georgia, which forced Azerbaijani state energy company SOCAR to halt its oil exports to Georgia (Yevgrashina 2008). Despite views that the 2008 armed conflict might have been due to Russian energy interests (Martin 2008; Tsereteli 2009), Russia and Georgia have continued pragmatic business relations, with president Saakashvili encouraging more investment despite certain domestic fears that Russian companies are state controlled (Rozhnov 2010; Trend 2012). In an attempt to further boost economic ties with Russia and dubbed by Saakashvili as "a sign of strength" (Civil.Ge 2012c), even if still pursuing its territorial integrity by returning the breakaway regions, Georgia also lifted the visa requirement for Russian citizens (Civil.Ge 2012d). However, this action has not been reciprocated by Russia, which demanded restoration of diplomatic ties and a change of Georgian law on the breakaway regions (Civil.Ge 2012e).

In the case of the oil-rich Azerbaijan, which fully realizes its economic potential (Regnum 2010), energy-manipulation does not work similarly due to the initial unwillingness of Russia to invest in the Azerbaijani energy sector and further competition with European companies (Musabeyov 2010). Nevertheless, Gazprom has managed to pave its way into the Azerbaijani market. In 2000–2006, due to "severe weather conditions and shortages of electricity in Baku" (Kelkitli 2008), Russia sold natural gas to Azerbaijan. In 2006, when the BTC pipeline was inaugurated, Gazprom announced an increase in gas prices from US$110 to US$230 and a cut in gas supplies from 4.5 billion to 1.5 billion cubic meters (Ismayilov 2006). Calling Russia an "unreliable partner" who "did not act as a gentleman" (Blagov 2007), in 2007 Azerbaijan halted oil exports to Russia "to fuel Azerbaijani power stations that formerly ran on Russian natural gas" (RFE/RL 2007a). Despite the Azerbaijani "revolt," Russia has not imposed an embargo or introduced a visa regime as in the case of Georgia, but preferred to offer a deal through Gazprom by buying Azerbaijani gas at market prices, and maintaining "positive dynamics in the trade turnover" (Popov 2010). The first deal signed by Russian Gazprom and Azerbaijani SOCAR in 2009 allowed for 500 million cubic meters of gas to be sold to Gazprom. In September 2010 Gazprom and SOCAR signed an addendum to the contract, increasing the sales volume to 2 billion cubic meters per year in 2011 and to above 2 billion cubic meters from 2012. The Russian strategy of buying large amounts of Azerbaijani gas is viewed as targeting the construction of the EU-backed Nabucco pipeline project to leave it empty, without the gas from one of its main suppliers (Zaynalov 2009). Selling large amounts of gas to Russia may endanger Azerbaijan's export diversification plans and decrease its bargaining power against Russia (Niftiyev 2010).

Russia's presence in political security matters is as vivid as in business and energy, especially in regard to Armenia. The Russian-promoted Collective Security Treaty Organization (CSTO) was signed by Armenia in 1992, with Azerbaijan and Georgia joining in 1993. Though involving all South Caucasus states, the organization has not contributed to the resolution of the regional conflicts (Saat 2005). In addition to the CSTO, Armenia and Russia signed a Treaty of Friendship and Cooperation in 1997, which was characterized as an "element of alliance" by former president Ter-Petrosyan (Migdalovitz 2004, p. 4). The treaty allowed Russian guards to patrol the borders of Armenia with Turkey and Iran. Accordingly, the Russian 102nd Military base is stationed in Gyumri, Armenia. After the withdrawal of two Russian military bases from Georgia in 2005–2007, a significant part of the military hardware was moved from Batumi and Akhalkalaki, Georgia, to Gyumri (Martirosyan and Mir Ismail 2005). According to Azerbaijan's president Aliyev the move induced an arms race in the region and forced Azerbaijan to increase its military spending (Martirosyan and Mir Ismail 2005). Thus, while reducing its military presence in Georgia due to the latter's NATO aspirations, Russia has not reduced its military presence in the South Caucasus but simply moved its troops from Georgia to Armenia. Moreover, the number of contract soldiers within the base in Gyumri will double by the end of 2012 (Harutyunyan 2012).

The confidence that the military pact with Russia protects it "against some of the vocal and demonstrated threats by ... [the] neighbour to the West" (Oskanian 2002) increased, especially after the dissolution of the Soviet Union. In addition to strained Armenia–Turkey relations, Russia has used the Nagorno-Karabakh conflict to preserve Armenia as its closest ally and pressure both Armenia and Azerbaijan whenever needed (Nichol 2011). Closed borders with Azerbaijan and Turkey, and Turkey's financial and military assistance to Azerbaijan, have made Armenia turn to Russia for protection. As then minister of defense Sargsyan put it in 2002, such security cooperation makes Armenia feel protected in its "difficult region" (PanArmenian.Net 2002). Due to Georgia's efforts to lessen Russian influence and Azerbaijan's increasing leverage due to its natural resources, Armenia seems a natural partner for Russia in maintaining its influence over the

South Caucasus. With dozens of similar agreements, security protocols signed between Armenia and Russia cemented the latter's presence in the South Caucasus by extending the deployment of Russian troops in the region until 2044, underlining that Russia "is crafting its policy around Turkey–Armenia normalization and Nagorno-Karabakh" (Elliott 2010).

While the extension of the security agreement was viewed in Armenia as an assurance against possible aggression from Azerbaijan, the latter voiced concerns over Russia's increased and impartial presence in the region (Smbatian 2010). Russia's military presence in the region showed to be even more controversial and less loyal to its partnerships after reports in the Russian media (Kucera 2010b) that defense systems had been sold by Russia to Azerbaijan. Though considered a "bluff" by some (Aysor 2008), the possible purchase was considered as a "betrayal" (News.am 2010) and negative meddling in the region's affairs by others. Even if Russia's continued military support to Armenia seems to some extent to upset Azerbaijan (US Embassy cable 2009d), relations with the latter are rather balanced, as when dealing with the Nagorno-Karabakh issue it both supports the principles of territorial integrity (Azerbaijan) and self-determination (Nagorno-Karabakh/Armenia). Previously sympathetic to the Chechen cause, Azerbaijan not only cut its support to Chechen fighters in the 2000s but also has been less eloquent in its NATO ambitions than Georgia (Kelkitli 2008). Closure by Azerbaijan of a Chechen school and centers on its territory improved its political relations with Russia (Schriek 2002). Although for Azerbaijan's transport and energy plans a pro-Western government in Georgia would be more beneficial, in the aftermath of the 2008 conflict Azerbaijan "chose a strategy of soft support for Georgia while refraining from making harsh statements against Russia" (Valiyev 2009a).

While Russia's relations with Armenia are the friendliest and with Azerbaijan the most neutral, with Georgia they are the most strained. Officially concerned by Georgia's relaxed treatment of Chechen militants fleeing to its territory, in 2000 Russia imposed a visa regime on Georgia. The issue of the Pankisi Gorge being a safe haven for Chechen fighters has been a long-time dispute between Russia and Georgia. Accusing Georgia of giving shelter to terrorists and plotting against it, Russia bombed the valley in 2001 and in 2002 (Giorgadze 2002; Myers 2002). Following Russia's ultimatum to attack Georgia if it did not secure the Russia–Georgia border, Georgia arrested a number of Chechen fighters (Yalowitz and Cornell 2002). Despite Russia's successful diffusion of Adjara's uprising and removal of previously supported Aslan Abashidze in 2004 (Tsygankov and Tarver-Wahlquist 2009), relations were still tense after the 2003 Rose Revolution and Saakashvili's statements on Georgia's EU and NATO aspirations. The espionage scandal and the arrest of four Russian military officers in Georgia followed by a temporary recall of the Russian ambassador in 2006 strained political relations even more. Even though Georgia soon handed the alleged spies over to the OSCE, Russia suspended air, rail, road, sea, and postal links to Georgia, stopped issuing visas to Georgian citizens, raided Georgian businesses in Russia, and deported more than 100 Georgian citizens.

The apogees of Russia–Georgia strained relations became the five-day armed conflict in 2008 and Russia's further recognition of the independence of the two Georgian breakaway regions of Abkhazia and South Ossetia, which allegedly was done to prevent NATO enlargement due to the border dispute (US Embassy cable 2009a). Despite ceasefire agreements signed by Russia and Georgia and even if "they can get along when they want to" (Economist 2011b), authorities of both countries instigate an atmosphere of mutual blame and personal insults (Telegraph 2008; Tsotniashvili 2011). While Georgia has detained and prosecuted over a dozen alleged spies (Civil.Ge 2010b; ICC 2011) Russia has considerably increased its military presence in Abkhazia and South Ossetia (Felgenhauer 2010; Socor 2010), while proclaiming its role not as a party to the conflict but as a mediator (Economist 2011a). The distrust was exacerbated by Georgia's move in October 2010 to lift visa requirements for residents of Russia's North Caucasus republics, as detailed earlier in this book.

Local perceptions of Russia

The Armenian population has shown mixed sentiments towards relations with Russia. Despite the threats of increasing the prices of commodities, the approval ranking of bilateral relations has increased over the course of three years. This may be explained by the increasing levels of fear towards the Nagorno-Karabakh conflict and the presence of the Russian military base in Armenia that provides the feeling of security. Thus, 65 percent of Armenian respondents were in favor of the Russian military base, 11 percent (in 2006) and 18 percent (in 2007) were indifferent, with only 2 percent (in 2006) and 1 percent (in 2007) against. Relations with Russia have continuously been considered as positive by more than 90 percent of respondents, while more than 80 percent of respondents qualified Russia as a trustworthy ally.[6] Given the low approval ranking of the authorities, the high level of popular support cannot be credited to the pro-Russian rhetoric of the government. It is rather a result of general apathy with the government and lackadaisical approach of the international actors. The combination of these factors in Armenia results in local support for Russia's actions, which potentially endorses Russia's anti-democracy actions, with a number of political party representatives considering Armenian politics to be "completely dominated by Moscow" (US Embassy cable 2009e).

The attitudes of the Georgian population towards Russia drastically diverge from the Armenian ones. Even before the 2008 conflict, 90 percent of respondents assessed relations with Russia as bad and 74 percent saw Russia as a threat as opposed to 32 percent seeing Russia as a partner. After the 2008 conflict, the picture became even gloomier for Russia's image as 97 percent of the respondents assessed the relations with Russia as bad and 90 percent saw Russia as a threat to Georgia. Local attitudes towards Russia have not changed since 2008, however, but the preference for providing a peacekeeping mission went from the EU to the USA and NATO in 2011 as compared to 2009 and 2010.[7] All political parties participating in the 2012 parliamentary elections, including the New

Rights Party sympathetic to the creation of a constitutional monarchy in Georgia, have advocated further democratization (de Waal 2012). While president Saakashvili's party has widely named the US as its main strategic partner, Ivanishvili's victorious Georgian Dream party's main difference seems to be a lack of open hostility towards Russia (Kucera 2012). However, despite Ivanishvili's efforts and a partial embargo lift on Georgian wine and mineral water, relations between Georgia and Russia have remained strained: while Russia extended its 2014 Winter Olympics security zone into the breakaway regions, Georgia contemplated boycotting the Games.

Azerbaijani analysts have argued that perceptions of Russia in Azerbaijan can be divided into three stages: Yeltsin's presidency, Putin's presidency, and the aftermath of the 2008 conflict with Georgia (Valiyev 2009a). Putin's presidency managed to dissolve Russia's biased and unpredictable image among the Azerbaijani public, instead making the image of a more reliable partner (Valiyev 2009b). However, the 2008 conflict re-instated the public fear of Russia and "had an effect on Aliyev's thinking" (US Embassy cable 2009e). Despite general support for Georgia, Azerbaijan's public preferred not to voice its NATO aspirations too loudly (Valiyev 2009b). The scarce opinion polls on Azerbaijan give mixed results, to some extent supporting the pragmatic vision on Russia of both Azerbaijani government and public. While Caucasus Barometer finds that the Azerbaijani public's support for friendship, doing business, or marriage with Russians has decreased, the BBC poll shows that the support for Russia's influence stood at 51 percent in 2010, with 41 percent of young respondents thinking that Azerbaijan would develop more if cooperating with Russia (ADAM 2010). Representatives of political parties in Azerbaijan agree on the importance of democracy but disagree on the level of Azerbaijan's democratization, stating that the country is now seen by Russia as an element of its zero-sum game in the region (US Embassy cable 2009f).

Conclusions

The constitutional break-up of the South Caucasus countries from the Soviet Union, the high levels of literacy and education of their populations, the subsequent rapid economic growth, and a readiness to integrate into democratic structures seemed to be the required prerequisites for successful democratization. However, two decades after their independence, the outcomes of the democratization process are far from established democracy. While more in-depth research of elections, party politics, and media development will reveal the nuances of the regimes, it is clear that, since the break-up of the Soviet Union, Armenia has transformed into a competitive authoritarian regime, Azerbaijan has strengthened its authoritarianism, while Georgia has managed to turn the negative tide a few years after the Rose Revolution. Formally existing democratic institutions are "viewed as primary means of gaining power," especially in Armenia and Azerbaijan; however, "incumbents' abuse of the state" makes competition "real but unfair" (Levitsky and Way 2010, p. 5).

Even with varying degrees of intensity, the South Caucasus countries have highly identified with democracy promoters on the rhetorical level. Nevertheless, it seems the population has not always been aware of the principles or rights that accompany democracy, making governmental manipulation less complicated. Strong support and confidence in EU institutions has had the potential to overcome the confusion over the concept of democracy and the apathy towards democratic institutions. The receptiveness of the population to democratic ideas should have been further supported by democracy promoters, but without abandoning the efforts of democracy promotion through state and political society. Given the geopolitical situation of the South Caucasus countries, democracy promoters must primarily address the needs of the target levels and country overall.

However, low effectiveness of international mediation in the Nagorno-Karabakh conflict (Babayan 2012b) has provided the authorities both in Armenia and in Azerbaijan with a basis to justify their undemocratic behavior by invoking security concerns. In addition, the Nagorno-Karabakh conflict is one of the main sources of other maladies in Armenian politics, such as halted rapprochement with Turkey and economic and energy issues due to closed borders. The situation may be slightly different in the case of conflicts in Georgia. However, what all these conflicts have in common is the involvement of Russia in different capacities. Russia's role as a democracy blocker in the South Caucasus is beyond doubt and is largely fuelled by the protracted regional conflicts.

Russia's regime and foreign policy thrive on its natural resources, thus making adoption of its model of governance along with its foreign policy "not attractive" (US Embassy cable 2009a) and often not feasible. However, its natural resources make cooperation with Russia attractive and strategically important for neighboring countries, whose regimes are likely to have fallen into democratic stagnation as a result of Russia's more aggressive policies, not as a result of specific regime promotion. Russia has tried to keep the South Caucasus countries divided by using distinct *modi operandi*: business-energy and politics-security (Babayan 2013a). The military support to Armenia, the allegedly disguised selling of weaponry to Azerbaijan, and the recognition of independence of Georgia's breakaway regions, while flirting with the status of Nagorno-Karabakh, show that Russia's interest in regional cooperation or conflict resolution is merely oratorical. Such penetrating involvement does not contain Russian influence only to security matters, but also spreads it over political and economic issues. Georgia's resistance to Russia's political and military involvement does not spread to Russia's economic involvement in the country. However, the close ties of the main Russian investors to the state, successful relocation of Russian troops from Georgia to Armenia, and the predominantly hands-off approach to the region of the EU and the US, render Georgian efforts at keeping Russia at bay futile. Azerbaijan, the only country in the South Caucasus having considerable leverage over Russia due to its natural resources, neither resists nor supports Russian involvement but follows a pragmatic and rational approach of maximizing its own utilities.

Armenia's long-adopted complementary foreign policy of having good relations with every important actor possible stands for its government and public's understanding of its low bargaining power, due to its land-locked position and a scarcity of high-valued natural resources. The bargaining power of Georgia is limited to its being a transit route for Azerbaijani oil, and is to decrease even more with Russia's entry into the WTO. However, the chances of using its position as a transit route as a bargaining chip are low because of the dependence on Azerbaijan's own actions. Azerbaijan's energy resources provide it with high bargaining power not only in relations with Russia but also with the EU. Both the EU and Russia value Azerbaijani oil, and while Russia tries to build partner relations with Azerbaijan, the EU condones violations of democracy. While Azerbaijan has the greatest potential to shake off Russia's authoritarian grip, its authorities' utility of adaptation to democracy is low. Despite emerging arguments of its waning influence (Nixey 2012), operating within business-energy and politics-security *modi operandi* and staying involved in the region's affairs serve Russia's goals. In the case of the South Caucasus, Russia may achieve desired results in its authoritarian projection, not due to the appeal of its regime over democracy but mainly due to the geopolitical situation in the region.

Notes

1 Both former president of Armenia Robert Kocharyan and the current president Serzh Sargsyan are from Nagorno-Karabakh. Kocharyan has also served as the president of Nagorno-Karabakh.
2 In 2008 democracy was ranked 12th in the list of issues that Armenians are concerned about. The importance of democracy in 2008 had decreased by seven percent in comparison with 2006.
3 Parts of this section have earlier appeared in Babayan 2013a.
4 Prime Minister Dmitry Medvedev served as the chairman of the Gazprom board of directors in 2000–2001 and 2002–2008, while Viktor Zubkov has simultaneously served as first deputy prime minister and chairman of the Gazprom board of directors.
5 For more details (in Russian), see www.kommersant.ru/Doc/718419, www.russ. ru/Mirovaya-povestka/Suverennaya-demokratiya-ili-demokraticheskij-suverenitet and www.inop.ru/publication/page78/; http://politike.ru/dictionary/472/word/%C2%C5%D 0%D2%C8%CA%C0%CB%DC+%C2%CB%C0%D1%D2%C8
6 Based on the Armenian National Voter Study by IRI, the Gallup Organization, and American Sociological Association, with funding from USAID, 2006, 2007, 2008.
7 For more information on the surveys, see www.iri.org/news-events-press-center/news-iri/show_for_country/1690

4   The EU and the US

Confusion, ambitions, and the reality

While the previous chapter focused on the domestic context of democratization in the South Caucasus, this chapter analyzes the international context. It assesses the legitimacy and credibility of the EU and the US in promoting democracy, and their actual and potential involvement in the resolution of pressing national issues in Armenia, Azerbaijan, and Georgia. An overall assessment of credibility within democracy-promotion policies and instruments is developed in this chapter, while the credibility of each promoter within target-sectors is evaluated in more detail in the next chapters. One of the international conditions—legitimacy—is inherently connected with democracy promoters and, though playing an important role in the interaction with the target, it mainly derives from the internal political situation of a promoter. To evaluate the legitimacy of each promoter in their democracy-promotion activities, the commitment to democracy and related internal developments are assessed. The chapter argues that both the EU and the US have been legitimate in their democracy-promotion policies, targeting areas that enjoy a high democratic stance in their domestic milieu. However, their legitimacy has been repeatedly undermined by their often laissez-faire approach to their own credibility, with US legitimacy in promoting democracy likely to be undermined due to global surveillance by the NSA.

Initially preferring to channel their democracy-promotion activities through different targets, both the EU and the US have nevertheless chosen similar strategies, which suffer from similar shortcomings. Lenient and inconsistent interest in national and regional issues and often tiptoeing policies towards a democracy blocker are likely to leave democracy-promotion policies without success. While showing a varying degree of involvement in issues other than democracy promotion, neither EU nor US strategies result in long-awaited resolutions. In addition, to assess their capacity and willingness of formulating policies vis-à-vis another important regional actor and the general feasibility of exporting democracy, the factor of a democracy blocker is brought back in by the analysis of EU and US relations with Russia, with sufficient attention paid to transatlantic relations in the NSA aftermath.

The European Union: slowly but surely?

The abundance of terms describing the EU points to disagreement not only in academic circles but also to the often-voiced inability of the EU to "speak with one voice." Despite the adoption of a common foreign policy, individual member states did not act unanimously on a number of foreign-policy issues, with the Iraq war, the Palestinian UN bid, and the Eurozone crisis being among the examples. The descriptions of the EU vary from the sympathetic "normative power" (Manners 2002) and a "quiet superpower" (Moravcsik 2007) to the fashionable "metrosexual power"[1] (Khanna 2004) and the rather negative "irrelevant" and a "neo-colonialist" entity (Kagan 2003; Crook 2007). The negative descriptions usually reach their peak when dealing with EU foreign policy because European governments seem to be "entirely preoccupied with their internal, intra-European machinations" (Crook 2007) and are reluctant to cooperate, leaving the EU's foreign policy inconsistent even in times of important international developments, such as the Georgia–Russia crisis of 2008 and earlier crises in Albania, Kosovo, Rwanda, and most recently the events in MENA. Thus, many mention the non-cooperation of member-states as the biggest obstacle towards an effective and coherent EU foreign policy (Hoffmann 2000; Smith 2008). The EU's foreign policy consists of the least arguable options for action, ones to which even the most reluctant member state could, theoretically, agree (Smith 2008). This disagreement over interests and preferences, and the constant search for consensus, blocks the creation of a supranational mechanism of foreign policymaking, as does the member states' unwillingness to pool their sovereignty or alter their preferences due to a desire to stay in full control of their foreign policies (Gordon 1997).

Disagreements between member states and the notoriously low actorness of the EU in pursuing its policies have prompted some analysts to claim that the EU and its member states could become an obstacle to the development of the multilateral order (Emerson *et al.* 2011). The multitude of voices within its decision-making process results in its indecisive role in the international arena and the image of the EU as an important donor but not as an important international player. However, despite internal disagreements and inconsistency, the EU has been an attractive club of states and an important and major donor for developing countries. The number of countries striving for EU membership has increased. However, even if these discrepancies may not negatively affect the magnetism of the EU, it may substantially affect its credibility and its ability to be taken seriously by its partners and other international players such as the US and Russia. This section demonstrates that, even if the legitimacy of the EU in promoting democracy is beyond doubt, its credibility is often undermined by its own actions and the inability or even reluctance to be involved in "turf wars" with other rival actors. To support the latter point, the section focuses on the case of Armenia and its preference to join the Eurasian Customs Union over signing an EU Deep and Comprehensive Free Trade Agreement (DCFTA).

Commitment and legitimacy: good intentions versus confused actions

Despite the EU's rhetorical commitment to democracy, a "widespread feeling" has been expressed on the EU's actual commitment to promote democracy and human rights:

> Within the EU, there is an apparent absence of political will fundamentally to revise approaches to democracy support, even if the shortcomings of these policies have been apparent for some time.
>
> (Youngs 2008a, p. 7)

In addition, profound criticism has been raised over the quality of democracy within the EU itself. Rejection by France and the Netherlands of the European Constitutional Treaty (Bogdanor 2007), low turnout during elections, and widespread unawareness and indifference towards the EU's policies have prompted critics to speak of a democratic deficit in the EU (Marquand 1979; Chryssochoou 2006). The term democratic deficit coined by Marquand (1979) has even entered EU terminology, referring to the domination of the EU's institutional set-up by an institution which combines legislative and government powers (the Council of the European Union) and an institution which lacks democratic legitimacy (the European Commission). However, others have either maintained the view that there has been no need to bother fully democratizing the EU (Schmitter 2000) or have outright rejected the existence of such a deficit (Moravcsik 2002). In addition, others have taken into consideration the arguments of both camps regarding the issues of democracy and accountability as "absolutely fundamental to the success of the European Union" (Bogdanor 2007, p. 5). Since the central decision-making bodies of the EU—the Council of Ministers and the European Parliament—result from democratic elections, the EU "is fully legitimate" (Bogdanor 2007, p. 5). Nevertheless, due to the complex system of decision-making and representation, the issue of accountability still triggers questions from Eurosceptics. However, these issues that bother EU scholars are not directly related to the legitimacy of the EU in promoting democracy. The states and populations of target countries rarely question democracy within the EU because of its low level of accountability to its own citizens. They are rather interested in the democratic nature of the issues that the EU supports, namely free and fair elections, a multiparty system, and a free media.

"Democratization is by no means a new departure for the EU" (Ferrero-Waldner 2006, p. 2) because "the best protection for our security is a world of well governed democratic states" (Council of the European Union 2003, p. 10). Many even claim that the most important function of the EU is to serve as a democratic model (Petersen 1995, p. 62 quoted in Olsen 2002, p. 137). The EU recognizes the importance of democracy promotion by stating in the Maastricht Treaty that "Community policy in this [development cooperation] area shall contribute to the general objective of developing and consolidating democracy and the rule of law and that of respecting human rights and fundamental freedoms" (Article 130U, Section 2).

This commitment to democracy is reiterated in the Agenda 2000 of the European Commission (EC), which states that "the Union must ... promote values such as peace and security, democracy and human rights" (European Commission 1997, p. 27). In addition, Article 8A of the Lisbon Treaty states that "the functioning of the Union shall be founded on representative democracy." Due to lack of military power and internal political structure, when exporting its democratic model the EU supposedly acts as a normative power, trying to have an ideational impact on its partner and target countries (Manners 2002). At the same time, the EU has the highest membership criteria, which were set during the European Council meeting in Copenhagen in 1993. These criteria include requirements for candidate countries, or the countries ever endeavoring to have closer cooperation with the EU, to embody institutions that guarantee democracy, the rule of law, and respect and protection of minority rights.

Though a part of the Copenhagen criteria is labeled as democratic, the EU has preferred to distance itself from such concepts as "democracy" and even more "liberty" (Magen *et al.* 2009), preferring the term "good governance." Wherever democracy was mentioned, it was always followed by a group of other concepts such as human rights, stability, and rule of law that can actually be included in the overall concept of democracy (e.g. ENP documents). Similarly, EU democracy promotion included a whole variety of policies that aim to address social modernization, human equality, and peaceful resolution of conflicts (Cremona 2004; Leonard 2005) in addition to emphasizing "the importance ... of the principles of parliamentary democracy and the rule of law" (European Community 1987). The Paris Charter provided one of the clearest understandings of democracy by the EU and its members:

> Democratic government is based on the will of the people, expressed regularly through free and fair elections. Democracy has as its foundation respect for the human person and the rule of law. Democracy is the best safeguard of freedom of expression, tolerance of all groups of society, and equality of opportunity for each person. ... Democracy with its representative and pluralist character, entails accountability to the electorate, the obligation of public authorities to comply with the law and justice administered impartially.
>
> (OSCE 1990)

These conceptualizations and commitments have put the EU understanding of democracy—which includes contestation, participation, and representation with further advancement to conflict resolution and social modernization—in between the minimalist and maximalist academic conceptualizations. In its democracy promotion, the EU has aimed to handle a range of issues which, however, were more likely to address democratic consolidation rather than foster democratic transition or promote democracy in its early stages. Clearly dividing one process from the other and preparing the target level for further advancements should be one of the important objectives for the EU in these initiatives.

After two decades of democracy promotion, the EU acknowledged that there was no "ready-made recipe for political reform. While reforms take place differently from one country to another, several elements are common to building deep and sustainable democracy" (European Commission 2011). The establishment of deep and sustainable democracy, a new buzzterm in the EU's vocabulary, requires a strong and continuous commitment on the part of governments and includes:

- free and fair elections;
- freedom of association, expression and assembly and a free press and media;
- the rule of law administered by an independent judiciary and right to a fair trial;
- fighting against corruption;
- security and law enforcement sector reform (including the police) and the establishment of democratic control over armed and security forces.

(European Commission 2011)

The ambiguous novelty or usefulness of the concept of deep democracy has left many unimpressed (Emerson 2011; Kurki 2012; Wetzel and Orbie 2012). However, what the review of the ENP did was to advance the "more funds for more reform" European Union approach, as if underlining that the previous ENP mechanisms had not taken conditionality seriously. Scholars even go so far as to argue that, even during successful cases, such as the Eastern enlargement, the EU did not have a well-defined view of democracy promotion (De Ridder and Kochenov 2011). This "'fudging' of the meaning of democracy" (Kurki 2012, p. 3) has prompted calls for "tightened categorization" (Youngs 2008b, p. 14), also because the EU's partners have preferred dealing with "clear-cut 'liberal' democracy supporters such as the US" (Kurki 2012, p. 1). It has been argued that the ambiguity of the EU's definitions of democracy has negatively influenced its performance (Wetzel and Orbie 2012), which has required discursive adjustments introduced after such external pushes as the Arab Spring (Babayan and Viviani 2013).

EU strategies: a pile of policies

In the regions where a membership perspective is not applicable but domestic conditions are less conducive, the EU pursues a strategy of persuasion and example, e.g. South Caucasus, Africa, and the Middle East. The EU's policies of democracy promotion to non-candidate countries follow the usual practice of the EU on norm promotion: slight political conditionality with some economic and boosted political incentives, putting a strong emphasis on the "shared values" notion. The EU has developed numerous policies and instruments for promotion of democracy and human rights, targeting countries in different regions of the world: PHARE, TACIS, MEDA, the Barcelona process, the

European Instrument (formerly Initiative) for Democracy and Human Rights (EIDHR),[2] and others. Practically every region of the world has been given its own policy to underline the context-tailored projects. However, all the policies have followed the same line of development and implementation, and have often met the same criticisms.

The main instruments of EU democracy promotion in the CEE were the Copenhagen criteria and thousands of pages of the *acquis communitaire*. Through democracy promotion, the EU aimed to strengthen the international order by "spreading good governance, supporting social and political reform, dealing with corruption and abuse of power, establishing the rule of law, and protecting human rights" (Council of the European Union 2003, p. 10). Though, these democracy-promotion priorities can be addressed on all the target levels mentioned previously, EU democracy promotion through the enlargement policy was marked by an evident top-down approach, which preferred to tackle the state rather than society. Instead of focusing on civil-society groups, elections, or political parties, the EU opted for strengthening the state capacity through constant monitoring of the enlargement policy implementation. Thus, the whole EU accession process was characterized by the "preference of order over freedom" (Kopstein 2006). The enlargement policy has become the great success of EU foreign policy in general and democracy promotion in particular. The alluring membership incentive, closely tied to conditionality of any material or social benefits, played the most important role in the success of EU democracy promotion in the CEE. The EU follows the same approach with current candidate countries. However, lack of membership incentive and a credible conditionality in relations with other target countries is likely to negatively affect the performance of its initiatives (Kelley 2006; Schimmelfennig *et al.* 2006; Babayan 2009).

TACIS was initiated in 1991 with an allocation of ECU 54 million as a technical assistance to the CIS to improve nuclear safety. TACIS funding for 1991–1999 was mainly "demand-driven" as CIS ministries would send requests based "on scarcely existing information," and assistance was mainly provided as "single small-scale projects" (Frenz 2007, p. 6). However, in 1998 the European Commission revised TACIS to include *inter alia* closer collaboration on democratization, the rule of law, trade, border management, and trafficking. In addition, for 2000–2006 it moved to a "dialogue-driven" strategy (Frenz 2007, p. 6). However, the EU grouped its budget headings and activities on human rights and democratization under the EIDHR. The EIDHR was based on macro- and micro-projects promoting justice and the rule of law, fostering the culture of human rights, promoting the democratic process, and advancing equality, tolerance, and peace. Through the EIDHR, the EU contracted NGOs and international organizations and could operate even without the consent of host governments. This feature may seem advantageous in preventing unwanted interference of authorities in the allocation of funds or project implementation. However, it runs the risk of retaliation from authorities in the case of exclusion and diminished ownership, through stricter control over civil society. The EIDHR (European Commission 2010) was launched in Armenia in 2003 to support NGOs through

11 selected projects, while in Azerbaijan for 2007–2008 and 2012 it supported nine and 16 projects respectively (EU Delegation in Azerbaijan 2012).

Encouraged by enlargement success, the EU created the ENP, which, however, does not offer membership to target countries. The ENP differs from other geographically limited EU policies because it includes countries from Africa, Eastern Europe, and the Middle East. The ENP, a response to enlargement (European Commission 2004) and first outlined in the Commission Communication on Wider Europe, calls for bridging the dividing lines between EU member states and their neighbors by promotion of democracy, stability, and security. In its Strategy Paper on the ENP published in May 2004, the EU outlines the strategies of cooperation with its target countries (European Commission 2004). Further, in December 2006 and December 2007 the EU proposed strategies for strengthening the ENP (European Commission 2006, 2007).

A policy without a "uniform acquis" (Kelley 2006, p. 36), the ENP has offered its partners a "privileged partnership" and "sharing everything with the Union but institutions" (Prodi 2002), based on "mutual commitment to common values principally within the fields of the rule of law, good governance, the respect for human rights, including minority rights, the promotion of good neighbourly relations, and the principles of market economy and sustainable development" (European Commission 2004, p. 3). The neighboring countries can reach the "privileged partnership" depending upon the "extent to which these values [respect for human dignity, liberty, democracy, equality, the rule of law, and respect for human rights] are effectively shared" (European Commission 2004, p. 3). Taking into consideration the "joint ownership" (European Commission 2004, p. 8) of the action plans, it can be assumed that on the initial level the determination of the extent of adherence to shared values will be carried out based on the country's declarations and country reports.

The EU strategies of democracy promotion usually follow the path of reinforcement by reward with a positive political conditionality (Schimmelfennig *et al.* 2006; Schimmelfennig and Scholtz 2008). The political conditionality is also present in the ENP on the stage of acceptance into the policy. In its ENP Strategy Paper in regard to the countries not yet ready to be included in the initial stages of the ENP—the South Caucasus countries—the Commission has stated:

> the EU should consider the possibility of developing Action Plans ... in the future on the basis of their individual merits. With this in view, the Commission will report to the Council on progress made by each country with respect to the strengthening of democracy, the rule of law and respect for human rights.
>
> (European Commission 2004, p. 10)

However, the EU has not always followed its own rules, since it included the South Caucasus countries in the ENP largely due to Georgia's Rose Revolution (Kurowska 2009; Bardakçı 2010) and despite lack of democratic progress in the other two states of Armenia and Azerbaijan (Babayan and Shapovalova 2011).

On January 1, 2007 the EU reformed its external funding structure and replaced MEDA, TACIS, and other programs with the European Neighbourhood and Partnership Instrument (ENPI), which financially assists the implementation of the ENP in target countries. For the budgetary period of 2007–2013 EUR 12 billion is available to support the reforms in the countries according to the priorities mentioned in their Action Plans. For this assistance the EU introduces conditionality, stating:

> where a partner country fails to observe the principles referred to in Article 1 [once again confirming the shared values principle], the Council, acting by a qualified majority on a proposal from the Commission, may take appropriate steps in respect of any Community assistance granted to the partner country under this Regulation.
> (European Parliament and the Council 2006, Article 28:1)

However, the conditionality and the threat of exclusion have been only partial since the Parliament and the Council further clarify that "Community assistance shall primarily be used to support non-state actors for measures aimed at promoting human rights and fundamental freedoms and supporting the democratization process in partner countries" (European Parliament and the Council 2006, Article 28:2). Youngs (2009) also finds that, at least in the Mediterranean and East Asia, the EU has started implementing a bottom-up approach, increasing the budget for civil society support, mainly through human rights NGOs. However, even in the case of non-compliance the EU does not completely withdraw the financial assistance, simply changing the channel from the state to the civil society. The effectiveness of such a strategy is doubtful because most of the ENP countries are autocracies with weak civil societies and the transnational channel of international socialization has "proved ineffective" (Schimmelfennig *et al.* 2006, p. 9). In addition, a question arises of how consistent and impartial the EU conditionality will be given that it does not always adhere to its own criteria.

To make the conditionality work, the ENP has to offer certain incentives to encourage countries' compliance with the promoted rules and norms, which otherwise either do not officially exist or are violated. Even if the benefits of the ENP "may be substantial," there have been doubts "whether governments agree to submit to a system of rules in which they have little decision-making power" (Kelley 2006, p. 37). To increase the attractiveness of the ENP, the Commission elaborates the following incentives:

- a perspective of moving beyond co-operation to a significant degree of integration, including a stake in the EU's internal market and the opportunity to participate progressively in key aspects of EU policies and programs;
- an upgrade in scope and intensity of political co-operation;
- opening of economies, reduction of trade barriers;

- increased financial support;
- participation in Community programs promoting cultural, educational, environmental, technical and scientific links;
- support for legislative approximation to meet EU norms and standards;
- deepening trade and economic relations.

(Kelley 2006, p. 37)

At the same time as trying to encourage compliance, the EU has developed the Governance Facility, which allocates EUR 50 million annually for countries making progress. (Ukraine and Morocco were the first to receive this support for reinforcement.) Though these might seem as considerable incentives for compliance, the membership incentive has still been absent.

However, some of the EU member states deemed the ENP insufficient, especially in light of the existing Northern Dimension covering the Baltic States and Russia, and the Union for the Mediterranean (UfM) covering 16 Mediterranean partner countries from MENA and the Balkans.[3] In addition to these policies, Poland and Sweden put forward an initiative to strengthen the EU's policy towards its Eastern neighbors, which seemed to be a timely undertaking given the outbreak of conflict between Georgia and Russia (Shapovalova 2009). The initiative met a positive response from other member states, including France, which was looking for support for its own UfM initiative. The main argument of the Eastern Partnership (EaP) supporters was the inclusion of partner countries' interests, unlike in the cases of previous policies (Runner 2008). The EaP has covered ENP partners Armenia, Azerbaijan, Belarus, Georgia, Moldova, and Ukraine. With a budget of EUR 600 million through the ENPI, the EaP offers political association and economic integration through Association Agreements (AA), Deep and Comprehensive Free Trade Agreements (DCFTA), and visa liberalization. However, just as with the ENP, the EaP has been considered another weak instrument of the EU because it does not offer a membership perspective (Boonstra and Shapovalova 2010) and yet again fails to reward the frontrunners and punishes the laggards (Babayan 2011).

Introduced and perceived by some as an upgrade to the ENP (Danielyan 2010) and conditioned on the performance of partner countries, the EaP, however, included all South Caucasus countries, despite their poor democratic performance. Some local observers have noted that the EaP will have a positive effect "on democratic changes in Armenia only in one case: if the European structures put forward very serious demands before our authorities" (Danielyan 2010). Association Agreements are supposed to be signed only with functioning democracies demonstrating "good progress" (Avetisian 2011b). However, as shown later, some EaP partners have turned away from the EU, undermining years of negotiations. To ensure the readiness of these countries to sign AAs, DCFTA, and visa liberalization agreements, the EU has provided additional funding (Shoghikian 2009). With visa liberalization talks, the EU has seemed to bid on the strategy of additional support prior to compliance to incentivize democratic performance in upcoming elections. However, the EU's inconsistency regarding political conditions decreases its credibility and future bargaining power. Thus, the added value of the EaP as a policy that can address the needs of partner countries and promote the goals of the EU is dubious. The attractive terms of notions of "free trade" and "visa liberalization" have lacked both substance (Boonstra and Shapovalova 2010) and specific terms and conditions that provide an effective framework for implementation.

Despite its rhetoric and emphasis on the importance of civil society for democracy, the EU has implemented its democracy promotion through intergovernmental channels. While pursuing an exclusive approach with EU candidates, with other countries it has pursued an intermediary approach. Despite conditioning inclusion into a new policy by democratic progress, the EU has included non-complying countries shortly afterwards. It is unlikely that the current conditionality or incentives approach towards non-candidates will change. Considering assistance to opposition parties and NGOs as "an interference into a country's internal affairs" (Risse 2009, p. 251), the EU follows a statist and top-down approach to democracy promotion, with uncertain intentions and inefficient learning techniques. In its democracy-promotion activities within the EaP framework, the EU has channeled its funding through civil society only in Belarus, where the authorities refuse to cooperate.

In an attempt "to retool our [the EU's] armoury" (Sikorski in US Embassy cable 2009g), Poland proposed the establishment of the European Endowment for Democracy (EED), which was established as a private foundation operating under a Board of Governors. The EED is independent from the EU, co-functions with already-existing EU instruments, and draws its budget from voluntary contributions from member states. However, this arrangement seems far from successful despite its current "decent budget" (Pomianowski in Dempsey 2013a) and the financial contributions pledged by Belgium, Denmark, Sweden, the Netherlands, all the new member states, and Switzerland. Nevertheless, the EU considers the establishment of the EED to be a "concerted effort" by its institutions and member states (Füle 2013a) which is especially important for improving the performance of the recently established European External Action Service. Its budget will be used to "support the unsupported" who, according to the European Commission, are "journalists, bloggers, non-registered NGOs, political movements (including those in exile or from the diaspora), in particular when all of these actors operate in a very uncertain political context" (European Commission 2012).

The establishment of the arguably redundant EED (Dempsey 2013a) and the appointment of the Special Representative for Human Rights come despite calls at such critical junctures as the Arab Spring for the EU to avoid "becoming more concerned with creating new structures than working concretely to support new democracies" (De Keyser 2011, p. 2). It seems that piling policies up instead of adjusting them to better respond to international developments has been the main strategy of the EU. However, given the intergovernmental nature of its foreign-policy decision-making, this approach should not come as a big surprise. With the consensus of all 27 member states required, each nurturing its own strategic interests, an accumulation of policies seems a less complicated solution. However, the establishment of the EED seems to be intended not only to advance human rights and democracy, but also to "[send] a clear message of solidarity to the peoples of the Neighbourhood" (Füle in European Commission 2013) and to react to complaints made about the ENP, which was said to reward the laggards and punish the frontrunners.

The EU in the South Caucasus: Eastern partnership versus the Eurasian Customs Union

Even if not immediately under the spotlight of the EU's attention, the import- ance of the South Caucasus is underlined by shared borders with Russia, Iran, and NATO-member and EU-candidate Turkey, and by large reserves of oil on the territory of Azerbaijan. Hence, the EU "has a strong interest in the stability and development of the South Caucasus" (European Commission 2004). Since the finalization of the 2004 enlargement, the EU has paid more attention to the region through regular financial injections for various reforms (Markarian and Stamboltsian 2004). The ENP Strategy Paper has identified the South Caucasus as a region that should receive "stronger and more active interest" than it does (European Commission 2004, p. 10). However, at the same time, due to political and economic factors within the country, Armenia has had to be patient despite distinctive hopes for a future in the EU (Lobjakas 2004a). The EU's interest also stems from three protracted conflicts in Nagorno-Karabakh, Abkhazia, and South Ossetia.

The interconnectedness of South Caucasus politics performed by politically and economically rather-different countries has led the EU to treat the region with "simplistic uniformity" (Babayan 2011, p. 4). The EU's habit of treating countries in regional blocks (Smith 2008) despite outstanding regional disputes has led to a simultaneous initiation of relations with the South Caucasus coun- tries, with Partnership and Cooperation Agreements (PCA) being signed and enforced in the same year with all three countries. The block treatment in some cases resulted in negative outcomes, as in the case of delays of the ENP Action Plan talks due to the dispute between Azerbaijan and Cyprus (Saghabalian 2005a), and positive, like the inclusion of all three countries in the ENP based on Georgia's promising democratic turn of 2003, and the inclusion into the EaP based on Azerbaijan's important role in energy diversification plans (Babayan and Shapovalova 2011). This approach, however, is not a characteristic of the EU only, but is also largely adopted by other organizations calling for similar reforms or advancement of democracy not in particular countries but the whole region (Zakarian 2003). However, the motives and consequences of this issue are not analyzed in depth here, but rather its importance is underlined when referring to EU policy formation.

Analysts argue that EU–South Caucasus relations have been shaped through three phases: the collapse of the Soviet Union, Armenia's accession to various international organizations, and its inclusion into the ENP (Minasyan 2005). The inclusion into the EaP can be added as the fourth phase. In 2001 the EU expressed its willingness for closer cooperation with the South Caucasus, one of the objectives of such cooperation being resolution and prevention of conflicts. The South Caucasus governments were ready to welcome this initiative and in 2003 the European Council appointed Heikki Talvitie as the first EU Special Representative (EUSR) for the South Caucasus. Taking into consideration the strongly expressed EU aspirations of all three states, the EU possesses the required legitimacy in acting as an external mediating actor. The region became closer to the EU economically because since 2004 the EU has been its primary trade partner (though for the EU the trade with the South Caucasus is only 0.5 percent of its overall figure), and geopolitically because of the Eastern enlargements of 2004 and 2007. The EU prefers to include previously weak and unstable South Caucasus states in its "ring of friends" (European Commission 2003) because now they are able to help their partners in fights against terrorism and trafficking (Council of the European Union 2003).

The appointment of a EUSR for South Caucasus (EU Presidency 2003) was taken as another token of the EU's increasing interest in the region (Grevi 2007). The first EUSR, Heikke Talvitie, was financed by Finland during his first year and was based in Helsinki during his whole mandate. The SR's mandate was to:

> contribute to the implementation of the EU's policy objectives, which include assisting the countries of the South Caucasus in carrying out political and economic reforms, preventing and assisting in the resolution of conflicts, promoting the return of refugees and internally displaced persons, engaging constructively with key national actors neighbouring the region, supporting intra-regional co-operation and ensuring co-ordination, consistency and effectiveness of the EU's action in the South Caucasus.
>
> (European Union 2003)

In fulfillment of these tasks the EUSR has regularly met government and parliament officials, opposition forces, and civil society. Before the changes introduced by the Lisbon Treaty, the EUSR reported to the Political and Security Committee, Committee on Civilian Crisis Management, and to the Council geographic working group on Eastern Europe. Despite regular statements and visits to the region, the role of the EUSR rather followed than shaped the developments in democracy-related areas in the South Caucasus (Tocci 2006). In addition to the low productivity of the EUSR and despite the calls from the European Parliament for a "firm approach," the importance of the region for the EU was put under question by the decision to scrap the post of EUSR to the South Caucasus. But, after months of doubts over the position, a former French Ambassador to Georgia, Philippe Lefort, was appointed EUSR for the South Caucasus and the crisis in Georgia in late August 2011.

One of the main tasks of the EUSR has been prevention of conflicts, assistance in the resolution of present conflicts, and preparation of peace (International Crisis Group 2006). However, despite initial hopes referring to the EU as an "honest broker" void of US–Russia rivalries (International Crisis Group 2006), the EU has not substantially contributed to conflict resolution in the South Caucasus (Grevi 2007). This was not surprising, due to "very limited human and financial resources with no political advisor based in the region" (Grevi 2007, p. 57). In 2006, Peter Semneby was appointed EUSR with his mandate using more specific language to "contribute to the settlement of conflicts and to facilitate the implementation of such settlement" (Council of the European Union 2006). While most of the EUSR's attention in conflict resolution was focused on Georgia's conflicts, more direct attention started being paid to Nagorno-Karabakh after the EUSR had asked for two political advisors to be based in Baku and Yerevan.

The importance of the resolution of the Nagorno-Karabakh conflict and putting an end to ongoing clashes has been yet again underlined by former EUSR Semneby (RFE/RL 2010a). Concerns over the possible escalation of the conflict *inter alia* stem from its potential to block the prospect of energy diversification, to result in another humanitarian crisis, and to deteriorate the EU's relations with Eastern Europe, Iran, and Turkey (Ghazaryan 2010). In addition, the peace is shaky "because it is … a self-regulated ceasefire with the two parties facing each other without any separation force in between" (RFE/RL 2010a). The EU has rhetorically committed itself to a resolution of the Nagorno-Karabakh conflict due to concerns that the "peace process has stopped since 10 years" and there is an "urgency" within the EU for solution (Prodi in Lobjakas 2004b). However, the urgency has not yet translated into an effective policy that would tackle the issue. Regular encouragements to end the stalemate and progress on the conflict resolution (Danielyan 2006a) were accompanied by seldom-concrete actions through the European Parliament, like first blocking calls (Melkumian *et al.* 2004) and then calling for Armenian withdrawal from Azeri lands (RFE/RL 2010a). However the efficacy of such actions is doubtful as they either demonstrate behavioral indifference or may be interpreted as predisposition to a solution favored by only one of the conflicting parties. Despite a survey of 100 members of the European Parliament claiming that there has been a general consensus for having a permanent non-military EU mission at the highly volatile Armenia–Azerbaijan LoC (ComRes 2010; Ghazaryan 2010), no such action has been taken.

Despite the rhetorical commitment of the ENP to facilitate cooperation in military-security matters, country-related ENP documents show more concrete actions and less vague language in economic matters (Babayan 2012b). Regardless of the nature of the cooperation issue, the ENP provides a long-term cooperation framework but does not clearly specify what partner countries can expect after the ENP implementation is over. The ENP entails regular rewards if applicable; however, the rewards do not vary depending upon the priority area and domestic utility of adaptation. Through regular progress and country reports, the ENP provides reliable information about both its own and, if possible, the partner states' actions. However, the feedback on changes in actions of the partner states might sometimes be absent or not actually relevant because, in the case of non-cooperation or non-compliance, instead of addressing the issue of divergence the EU simply opts for amending the Action Plan. In addition, while the rhetorical commitments of the EU, Armenia, and Azerbaijan to peaceful resolution of the Nagorno-Karabakh conflict are high, the ENP framework is vague and often sacrifices specific actions for consensus (Babayan 2012b). In their turn, Armenia and Azerbaijan strive for different outcomes of the conflict: Armenia advocates the independence of Nagorno-Karabakh, while Azerbaijan insists that the breakaway region is to be within its territory and shows readiness to advance its perspective through military means (Babayan 2012b).

Although the number of actors in the South Caucasus regional cooperation is not large and they are coordinated by the EU, the situation is complicated by the EU's inconsistent policy of conditionality. Unlike other international organizations present in the region, the EU due to its economic and political status has the leverage to sanction the regional actors in case they defect from cooperation. However, in ENP documents sanctioning is mentioned only as a change of target within the country, through which the assistance is channeled. Nevertheless, despite the participating countries either rhetorically or even sometimes by action defecting from the accepted framework of cooperation, the EU has not introduced any sanctions. The EU's reaction to the continuing arms race led by Azerbaijan, and joined by Armenia, has taken the form of lament on "less progress than we had hoped for in their peace talks which ... are attracting growing interest from the EU" (Avetisian 2011c) and hopes that "the Azerbaijani leadership is aware of the enormous risks and potential costs that would be associated with an attempt to resolve the conflict by military means" (RFE/RL 2010a).

Even if conflict resolution may not be the EU's main priority in the South Caucasus, conflicts that largely dominate the economy and politics of the region cannot be ignored. In addition, the ongoing conflicts may also be used by the partner countries as justification for their non-compliance. The mere rhetorical support given to the OSCE Minsk Group undermines the visibility of the EU in the region. However, delegating its own single representative to the Group, instead of having seven member states represented, would increase the involvement and stabilize the position of the EU in the region. Such an action seems timely given the creation of the EEAS and support by a number of MEPs of replacing the OSCE framework by the one of the EU (ComRes 2010). Increased involvement may also garner more "EU enthusiasts" and result in increased EU-ization of regional policies. However, the current approach of the EU, besides having marginal if any effect on conflict resolution in the South Caucasus, risks decreasing the leverage of the EU in the region, inducing the local actors to turn for more concrete action to Russia or the US.

The democracy promotion of the EU is conditioned by its relations with other regional players. Despite alleged "transatlantic divides" (Kopstein 2006), relations with the US have been amiable, while relations with Russia have been more strained due to Russia's poor democratic record and regular bullying thanks to its energy resources. The initial enthusiasm over Russia's democratization has been followed by disillusionment with Russian politics. Despite long-lasting democracy promotion in Russia, there has been no progress in democracy and surprisingly the regular EU–Russia consultations on human rights have coincided with a deterioration of the political situation in Russia (Youngs and Shapovalova 2011). In addition, the EU's role in democracy and human rights promotion is downgraded by Russian civil society actors as compared to the US (Shapovalova and Youngs 2012). The EU's policy towards Russia has been largely reactive; however, it is argued that it has become more coherent and realistic (Barysch 2011). The more-realistic approach to Russia is based on general acceptance by member states that the EU has limited influence over Russia (Barysch 2011) leading to democratization reluctance in areas that are unwilling to cooperate even rhetorically.

An initially accepted process of EU enlargement has started to be viewed by many in Russia as the "apple of discord" between the EU and Russia, causing their rivalry (Arbatova 2006). One of the major concerns of Russia has been the launch of the EaP. Despite assurances from the former EU foreign policy chief Solana that the EaP had not been designed against Russia, Russia's foreign minister Sergey Lavrov interpreted the choice given to EaP partners as "either you are with Russia, or with the European Union" (Brunnstrom and Harrison 2009). Though the "reset" in relations with EaP-advocate Poland and Russia has helped to overcome some divisions, Russia has been indirectly trying to hinder smooth implementation of the EaP. In 2010 the European Commission started negotiations on DCFTA with Ukraine, announcing that similar negotiations with Moldova would start in 2011. Russia reacted by urging both countries to join its Customs Union, which is incompatible with DCFTA. However, the battle for allegiance did not result in major tensions (ECFR 2010). The EU also managed to win over Moldova after being unusually proactive, dispatching Swedish and Polish foreign ministers to support the pro-EU coalition that later formed the Moldovan government. This hindered Russia's efforts to promote a centre-left coalition (ECFR 2010). However, Russian efforts at blocking the initiatives within the EaP peaked and became more successful in 2013, with Armenia's turn to the Eurasian Customs Union instead of its earlier intention to sign the DCFTA agreement.

The EU's representatives have repeatedly stated that signing any customs agreements with Russia would endanger signing of AAs, since the prerequisites of the Russian-aspired Eurasian Customs Union contradict the EU-offered DCFTA. Similarly, when addressing the determination of EaP countries in signing AAs, Russian Prime Minister Medvedev underlined the incompatibility of the two structures (Medvedev in Lazaryan 2013). The EU's repeatedly voiced view on the incompatibility between the Customs Union and DCFTA does not stem from ideological concerns but from legal ones, and the EU is not prone to pressure its partners (Füle 2013b). However, the Customs Union has been viewed not only as another alternative agreement but also as a possible leverage over the EU's neighbors, since Russia has been expected to apply pressure including:

- the possible misuse of energy pricing;
- artificial trade obstacles such as import bans of dubious WTO compatibility and cumbersome customs procedures;
- military cooperation and security guarantees; and
- the instrumentalisation of protracted conflicts.

(Füle 2013c)

In July 2013 the deputy foreign minister and chief negotiator for Association Agreements from Armenia, Tigran Mnatsakanian, "expressed confidence that the Association Agreements with some partner countries, including Armenia, will be initialed within the framework of the Vilnius summit" in November (RFE/RL 2013f). That did not happen. In addition, the head of EU Delegation in Armenia confirmed that the latter was on track for signing the Agreement (RFE/RL 2013f). At the same time, Armenian officials attempted to use a more pragmatic approach, calling Russia the "military security choice" and the DCFTA the "economic choice" since "this is not a contradiction … [and in] terms of security, Armenia is tied to Russia" (Kocharyan 2013). However, other Armenian officials opted for neglecting the remarks of the EU and Russia, stating that they "will not be going down the path of 'either or' " since "these two processes are mutually complementary" (Stepanian 2013b).

Russian media has publicized a number of preferential agreements and possible subsidies promised by Putin to Sargsyan in return for joining the Customs Union. Among those is US$18 million investment into modernization of the Armenian infrastructure by the Russian-owned South Caucasus RailRoads (ARKA 2013a). In addition, Russia has promised larger investments into prolonging the exploitation of the Armenian nuclear power plant (AtomInfo 2012; ARKA 2013b), which is deemed as obsolete by the EU. Moreover, the negotiations on the participation and investment by Rosneft in production of chloroprene rubber by the Armenian Nairit factory coincided with president Sargsyan's announcement on joining the Customs Union (Rosneft 2013; Simonyan 2013).

Despite the unexpected turn to Russia's Customs Union, Armenia has still been showing interest in a "watered-down" version of the Association Agreement, i.e. without the DCFTA (Stepanian 2013b). President Sargsyan even argued that since the political provisions of the agreement are strong enough to induce reforms, political and economic components of the agreement can be easily separated (Stepanian 2013b). Foreign minister Edward Nalbandyan has insisted that cooperation with the EU is still possible (Nalbandyan in Stepanyan 2013b).

However, EU officials are not as enthusiastic and accommodating, and the statement by the Swedish foreign minister, the country that pushed for the EaP, that "Association Agreement with Armenia is now off the table. We work with Ukraine, Moldova, Georgia" (Bildt 2013), sent a clear signal that the EU may actually keep to its conditionality. However, others expressed concerns on giving in "to sero-sum logic re our partners. Engagement remains important" (Linkevicius 2013). Saying that the EU, however, will not abandon Armenia and

Armenians (RFE/RL 2013g; Tamrazian 2013), Füle later confirmed that no agreement was planned to be signed with Armenia at the Vilnius summit (Stepanyan 2013c). Following the reaction of the EU, Armenian news agencies even reported that the EU had cancelled its twinning projects (News.am 2013); the EU, however, later refuted having done so (EU Delegation to Armenia 2013). While talks have emerged that the EU may suspend its programs, Armenian cozying up to Russia has been likely to lead to closer cooperation with China. Chinese Prime Minister Li Keqiang pledged additional US$16 million in aid, in addition to the sale to Armenia to multiple-launch rocket systems (RFE/RL 2013h). The agreement followed the statement by the Armenian prime minister of the country's plans of joining the Shanghai Organization Cooperation as an observer (RFE/RL 2013i).

Arguing that "Armenia has not taken a sensational step" since Russia is its "strategic partner," Sharmazanov downplayed the U-turn taken by Armenia and the potential of "breaking talks," along with the potential to add to EU–Russia tensions (BBC 2013). However, the surprise may as well be justified given previous statements by Armenian officials. Prime minister Tigran Sarkisian has repeatedly argued against Armenian entry into the Customs Union, saying that Armenia has no common borders with Russia, Belarus, or Kazakhstan (Banks. am 2013; Hayrumyan 2013a), with the deputy chairman of the ruling Republican party insisting on the upcoming initialing of the agreement hours before the president's announcement.

Sharmazanov, who is also a deputy parliament speaker, downplayed the significance of these statements, saying that Armenian foreign policy is formulated by president Sargsyan. The Chief of Presidential Staff also claimed that, given ongoing interest by the Armenian government to join the Customs Union, Russian–Armenian "expert groups" developed "solutions that allow us to overcome" the absence of common borders (Panorama 2013). Nevertheless, the decision sparked public discontent, with protesters gathering at the presidential residence and chanting "no return to Soviet Union" and objecting against decisions without proper public debate (Grigoryan 2013). The protesters' claims were cast away by the statements of the deputy chair of the ruling Republican party that, in such important issues, the president does not need to initiate a public debate and can make decisions on his own (Sahakyan in Grigoryan 2013).

The reaction of most of the political parties has been muted, with Prosperous Armenia waiting for a party discussion before announcing its position. The oppositional Heritage, which has only five seats in the 131-seat parliament, has argued that accession to the Eurasian Customs Union would jeopardize Armenia's independence and its sustainable development into a democratic state with a growing economy (Gevorgyan 2013). Armenian National Congress, chaired by former president Ter-Petrosyan, who organized after-election protests in 2008, called Sargsyan's decision "humiliating," but without rejecting the possibility of accessing the Customs Union (Hayrumyan 2013b). The Armenian Revolutionary Federation applauded the decision, citing the security of Armenia and Nagorno-Karabakh as the main issues to guide Armenia's foreign policy (Hayrumyan

2013b). The Prosperous Armenia party, known for its previous close ties with the president's Republican party, has not made an official statement at the time of writing.

Armenian officials have also claimed that the Customs Union brings greater benefits to Armenia, and most importantly different types of benefits. While acknowledging the EU's support in protection of human rights, training of the judiciary, and civil society building, National Security Council chairman Arthur Baghdasaryan argued that the agreements with the Customs Union is more beneficial to Armenia than DCFTA (PanArmenian.Net 2013). This certainty has been also echoed by Russia, confirming that Armenia can start the negotiations for accessing the Customs Union as early as October 2013, with full accession in May 2014 (Shuvalov in Lazaryan 2013). Thus, the process of accession to the Customs Union echoes the timetable of the planned initialing and signing of the Association Agreement.

After Armenia's turn to the Eurasian Customs Union, more questions are asked on the choices to be made by other countries neighboring Russia. While Moldova repeatedly stated that signing of the Association Agreement would not damage its economic relations with Russia and its export prospects (Interfax 2013), Russia has announced the possibility of banning the import of Moldovan wine (Moldova.org 2013) and proceeded to implement its threat (Heil 2013). The most vocal EU-supporter in the South Caucasus, Georgia, has reiterated its commitment to European integration and initialed the Association agreement in November 2013. However, while praising the EU as the finest creation of civilization, Georgian Prime Minister Bidzina Ivanishvili mentioned that accession to the Eurasian Customs Union was also possible. Meanwhile, president Saakashvili accused Ivanishvili of betraying Georgian foreign policy and equated the Customs Union to the Soviet Union (Stamboltsian 2013). The deciding factor, however, would be not much-praised European or other values but the strategic and economic interests of Georgia (RFE/RL 2013j). However, while other EaP countries may be at the crossroad of which agreement to choose, Belarus is not enthusiastic about Armenia joining the Customs Union, since the latter may compete for subsidies from Russia which so far went almost exclusively to Belarus (Lavnikevich 2013). This worry is aggravated by recent trade wars between Belarus and Russia: planning to sell its potash resources without its Russian cartel partner, Belarus simply arrested the CEO of the Russian potash-producing company in August 2013, which was followed by fury from the Kremlin and banning of pork imports from Belarus (Forbirg 2013; Heritage 2013), with a dairy products ban to follow (Razumovskaya 2013).

Though EU–Russia relations improved closer to 2011, there has been a number of tensions, including the first and second wars in Chechnya (Haukkala 2011), the conflict in Georgia in 2008 and the subsequent monitoring of the Russia–Georgia border (Grevi 2007), the gas crisis in 2009, and often-voiced disapproval of Putin's policies, especially when exercising pressure on EaP partner countries. Relations with Russia have also caused disagreements between the member states, with Italy's former premier Silvio Berlusconi over-enthusiastically supporting Russia, Germany's former Chancellor Schroeder more realistically assessing Russia's place in the EU and NATO, and UK leaders as a rule taking the toughest stance. Varying interests and preferences of the member states and energy issues have influenced the EU's generally soft approach to Russia, resulting in an ongoing confusion whether to firmly insist on democracy or not. In addition, the EU's indecisive role in protracted conflicts has added to Russia's dominant role in its neighborhood. Tiptoeing politics over conflicts in the South Caucasus emphasize Russia's economic and military dominance, leaving little chance for resolution.

The United States: business as usual

Unlike the EU, the US has rarely faced the challenge of proving or even defining its actorness in international politics. It has rather periodically debated the rationale for its involvement in the shaping of the international order. While the EU generated a line of neologisms derived from the term "superpower," the US has long been referred to as a hegemon, a "superpower" (Huntington 1999), or a "hyperpower" (Cohen 2004) after the collapse of its main rival, the Soviet Union, and even occasionally as a "besieged superpower" (Kolodziej and Kanet 2008). Though the degree of US influence on international affairs has varied over time, its influence per se has never been doubted. Unlike the case of the EU, the doubt over the US's role has come from within, questioning whether the US should be involved in international affairs (Deudney and Meiser 2008). US foreign policy has been marked by "searching for [a] purpose" (Dumbrell 2008, p. 88), and after the collapse of the Soviet Union the liberal internationalism or democracy promotion of Bill Clinton became the motto of US foreign policy. The election of George W. Bush reaffirmed the position of democracy promotion, but coupled it with a fight against terrorism produced by "the axis of evil," allowing military interventions under the banner of democracy promotion. Military interventions in Afghanistan and Iraq, dubbed by the neoconservative Bush administration as democracy promotion, provided a fertile ground for the opponents of democracy promotion, but arguably had little negative influence on peaceful targets of democracy promotion.

The US has been traditionally portrayed as an actor with a hard approach vis-à-vis the EU's soft and even pacifist (Speck 2011) approach to international affairs. The famous "Mars vs. Venus" (Kagan 2003) analogy underlined the transatlantic divide on democracy promotion. However, the divide was argued to be blown out of proportion as the differences between EU and US strategies were marginal (Magen *et al.* 2009) with subsequent strategies starting to converge (Babayan and Risse 2014). However, unlike the EU, the US has demonstrated little confusion on its actions. The unequivocal endorsement and alleged orchestration of color revolutions in Eastern Europe, at least rhetorically quick reaction to natural disasters around the globe, including the one in Haiti, and a comparatively cohesive reaction to the events in MENA demonstrate a more-efficient foreign-policy decision-making mechanism than the one of the EU.

However, despite advantages in decision-making efficiency, US foreign policy has often been marred by supporting "oily" and friendly autocrats. Nevertheless, the importance of the US in the international arena has not been put under doubt, maintaining its position as an acknowledged global actor whose stance has often shaped the positions of its partners.

Commitment and legitimacy: the way we are

"The advancement of human rights and democracy is not just the policy of the United States; it is the epitome of who we are as a nation" (Bureau of Democracy, Human Rights, and Labor 2010), underlying the US's "crusade for democracy" (Scott-Smith and Mos 2009, p. 237). From the early twentieth century, US external affairs have been marked by Woodrow Wilson's (1917) conviction that "the world must be made safe for democracy," but can be traced back to former president George Washington's assertion during his farewell address in 1796 of the US's mission "to give to mankind the magnanimous and too novel example." After Wilson's presidency, the US has continued "to foster the infrastructure of democracy" (Reagan 1982), to "enlarge the community of democracies" and "advance America's interests worldwide" (Clinton 1994) by means of foreign aid and sometimes military power. While the main mission of the US during the Cold War was not democracy promotion per se but rather the containment of the Soviet Union (Cox *et al.* 2000), democracy promotion neatly fit the "searching for purpose" task after the collapse of the grand rival (Dumbrell 2008, p. 90). Some (Robinson 1996) argue that there was a change in US foreign policy from supporting autocracies to promoting democracy. However, the policy goal has remained intact: "to gain influence over and try to shape their [national democratization movements'] outcomes in such a way as to pre-empt more radical political change, to preserve the social order and international relations of asymmetry" (Robinson 1996, pp. 318–319). However, notwithstanding the growth of democracy assistance, its examination by US policy analysts has been sporadic and its understanding has been limited to practitioner circles (Carothers 2000).

   Although democratic rhetoric has been present in US foreign policy since Wilson's presidency, prior to the 1980s most of the foreign aid was concentrated on economic and military assistance to friendly countries, in an effort to prevent their going communist (Carothers 2010). The limited efforts at democracy promotion were mostly funneled through modernization arguments, hoping that economic development would result in democracy. The emergence of an established US democracy promotion appeared with the first Reagan administration, which was concerned with the US's insufficient engagement in the "war of ideas" with the Soviet Union (Carothers 2000, p. 183). After some disagreements with Congress, the establishment of the National Endowment for Democracy (NED) became the major contribution to US democracy-promotion industry (Pishchikova 2010). Since the fall of the Soviet Union, the US has promoted democracy with an "explicit political purpose" (Carothers 2000, p. 184) to:

advance freedom for the benefit of the American people and the international community by helping to build and sustain a more democratic,
secure, and prosperous world composed of well-governed states that respond
to the needs of their people, reduce widespread poverty, and act responsibly
within the international system.

(US State Department 2010)

This expressed commitment to democracy promotion was, however, accompanied by "lack of a clear definition of democracy and a comprehensive understanding of its basic elements" (Epstein *et al.* 2007, p. 3). Lack of a clear
definition made it virtually impossible to determine the turning point when the
target does not require further assistance (Epstein *et al.* 2007). Having acknowledged the lack of a definition, Congress voiced its concern that "the State
Department and USAID do not share a common definition of a democracy
program" (Senate Appropriations Committee 2005). Thus, to "ensure a common
understanding of democracy programs among US Government agencies," it
defined democracy promotion as:

> programs that support good governance, human rights, independent media,
> and the rule of law, and otherwise strengthen the capacity of democratic
> political parties, NGOs, and citizens to support the development of demo-
> cratic states, institutions and practices that are responsible and accountable
> to citizens.

(Senate Appropriations Committee 2006)

With the commitment to the promotion of democracy remained unchanged,
the commitment to a specific mode of promotion has been changing from one
administration to the other, with adjustments to the policies triggered by
internal developments rather than external pushes, as has been the case with
the EU (Babayan 2013b). Democracy promotion under Bill Clinton was
dubbed as a "grand vision" of his administration (Yang in Carothers 2000).
The financial support to democracy promotion tangibly increased from the
Reagan years to the end of the Clinton administration (Carothers 2000). The
Clinton administration pursued the "enlargement of the world's free community of market democracies" (Lake 1993)—democracy promotion—in a
hope to replace the previous grand strategy of containment (Poppe 2010).
However, Clinton—a "pragmatic crusader" (Poppe 2010, p. 11)—did not
intend to place democracy promotion above other foreign policy or security
issues, but rather intended to complement one with the other. In addition, the
Clinton administration's democracy promotion followed a non-interventionist
character and preferred to promote democracy in countries that had already
showed signs of democratization. The policy towards states unwilling to
reform would be "to isolate them diplomatically, militarily, economically and
technologically" (Lake 1993). Meanwhile, if the process of democratization
stagnates, the US should act to renew it (Albright 2003). Thus, Clinton's

peaceful promotion of democracy to complement US strategic interests followed "pragmatic realism first, with idealism always a close second" (Brinkley 1997, p. 127).

The same cannot be said about the following George W. Bush administration and its "democracy promotion on steroids" (Carothers 2007, p. 11). President Bush codified democracy promotion even further through Institutionalizing the Freedom Agenda (State Department 2008) and by signing the ADVANCE Democracy Act in 2007 (House Committee 2007). Yet, even if Bush put democracy promotion on the map (Wolff *et al.* 2013), the first months of his presidency implied the possibility of axing democracy promotion (Carothers 2007) and focusing more on traditional interests by cutting foreign-policy commitments (Poppe 2010). However, after the 9/11 attacks Bush opted for a hard approach of military interventions and for reinforcement by punishment whenever the target country did not show any readiness for democratic change and posed any threat to US national security (Bush 2005). Promising to "finish the historic work of democracy in Afghanistan and Iraq" (Bush 2004), Bush acknowledged the policy of the US to "seek and support the growth of democratic movements and institutions in every nation and culture" (Bush 2005). In the early stages, those operations were presented as a long-awaited turn by the US towards democracy promotion, instead of pursuing "stability at the expense of democracy" in the Middle East (Rice 2005). Despite rhetorical elevation, the Bush doctrine put democracy promotion second to counter-terrorism, letting it climb the priorities ladder only when justifications were required for the operation in Iraq (Hassan and Hammond 2011). Always being a military and not only an economic power, the US unlike the EU has never constrained itself to a normative power image. Thus, democracy promotion under Bush was combined with the fight against terrorism.

Given the contemporary complexity of international affairs, the US has to "acknowledge its rivals and project a different message about democracy promotion" (Carothers 2012a). Obama was silent on democracy in his first inaugural speech (Obama 2009), prompting criticisms (Nau 2010) of the "abandonment of democracy" (Muravchik 2009). Some have claimed that "this American administration has put democracy and rights back in front" (US Embassy cable 2009h), with others hoping that peaceful instruments would not reinforce pragmatism over the commitment to promote democracy and human rights (US Embassy cable 2009g). Not only Republicans have voiced criticism of minimized democracy-promotion rhetoric, but Democrats have also occasionally felt as if the Obama administration prefers improving relations with authoritarian governments to democracy promotion (Hiatt 2010; Packer 2010). However, the initial cool-off in democracy promotion was followed by boosted rhetoric, as well as Obama's speeches in Cairo and Accra, and Secretary of State Hillary Clinton's speeches on human rights. In addition, when the engagement policy bore no fruit, as happened especially with Iran and China, Obama and Clinton stepped up their rhetoric on human rights (Carothers 2012b).

With his low-key democracy promotion, an "open door" approach, and without boisterous statements, Obama has brought the US's democracy-promotion approach closer to the one of the EU (Poppe 2010). In his 2013 inauguration speech Obama did not completely shy away from democracy and pledged to "support democracy from Asia to Africa; from the Americas to the Middle East" (Obama 2013). In addition, though "quantifying spending on democracy promotion is notoriously tricky" (Magen and McFaul 2009, p. 2), since Obama took office in 2009 budget requests to Congress for democracy promotion have steadily increased, meaning that cuts have been balanced by increases. Even if an uneven approach towards non-democratic countries continued, the Obama administrations have paid greater attention to the legitimization of US actions (Babayan 2013b). Yet, this legitimization may have evaporated because of NSA global surveillance and the toll it had not only on transatlantic relations but also on such a topical human right as the one to privacy. In addition, disregard of constitutional freedoms and democratic processes by the most celebrated promoter of democracy may have provided additional excuses for authoritarian regimes to shun democracy (Human Rights Watch 2014).

US strategies: wildly successful patience?

On the one hand, the US seemed unfazed by the declining number of democracies in the world. It considered its democracy promotion in Central and Eastern Europe and the former Soviet Union as "wildly successful" and saw EU membership as a token of democratic consolidation, even if it "cannot really prove cause-and-effect," opting for "strategic patience" (Rosenblum 2011). On the other hand, other senior officials, such as the USAID administrator, have voiced concern over a "disturbing pattern ... as new laws restrict civil society," insisting that in such circumstances "the vital connection [of democracy and human rights] to prosperity and growth" must be reiterated (Shah 2013). USAID's strategy for Democracy, Human Rights and Governance, released in June 2013, highlighted the centrality of participation and accountability and set the following objectives:

- Promote participatory, representative and inclusive political processes and government institutions.
- Foster greater accountability of institutions and leaders to citizens and to the law.
- Protect and promote universally recognized human rights.
- Improve development outcomes through the integration of DRG [democracy, human rights and governance] principles and practices across USAID's development portfolio.

(USAID 2013a)

Another US institution involved in democracy and human rights promotion, the Bureau of Democracy, Human Rights and Labor, emphasizes that promotion of democracy not only promotes its value per se, but also serves in promoting US national interest . It seeks to:

- Promote democracy as a means to achieve security, stability, and prosperity for the entire world;
- Assist newly formed democracies in implementing democratic principles;
- Assist democracy advocates around the world to establish vibrant democracies in their own countries; and
- Identify and denounce regimes that deny their citizens the right to choose their leaders in elections that are free, fair, and transparent.

(US State Department 2009)

The US has been inclined "to see a stable democracy as the product of a healthy and vibrant civil society" (Kopstein 2006, p. 89), with democracy being established as soon as the authoritarian leader is overthrown and elections are held. The overall institutional environment, however, does not seem to be so important (Kopstein 2006). But democracy is not only about elections, it is *inter alia* about independent media, political parties, checks on a democratic government that must face the check of electable opposition, and leaders that must hand over power peacefully (Epstein *et al.* 2007). Democracy-promoting organizations that are funded by US government concentrate heavily on elections, political parties, and civil-society organizations, in most of the cases preferring not to work with state-related organizations, focusing on the opposition, especially in the case of media development as part of civil society. The US has also largely invested in development of political and civil societies by supporting local NGOs and monitoring elections (Marinov 2004).

US democracy promotion is mainly channeled through USAID, the Department of State with its Bureau of Democracy, Human Rights, and Labor, and the non-profit NED. Apart from these, the Ministry of Defense, the Millennium Challenge Corporation (MCC), and the Department of Justice conduct limited activities of democracy promotion, albeit with much lesser budget and programmatic variance. USAID has spent approximately US$1.5 billion a year on democracy promotion, while the State Department has spent approximately US$500 million, and the NED US$100 million. Established by an executive order in 1961, USAID is the principal instrument of democracy promotion of the US government with its distinct Democracy and Governance (DG) portfolio, which focuses on rule of law, elections and political processes, civil society, accountable governance, and independent media. USAID receives overall policy guidance from the US State Department. In addition, it has to respond to several committees of Congress, which during the Republican domination of Congress in 1995–2006 saw considerable cuts in its budget (Thiel 2004). Some Republicans even proposed the elimination of USAID within a drastic reform of the State Department (Hook 2003). Nevertheless, USAID remains the main democracy-promotion instrument of the US, with its missions covering a large geographic and thematic variety. The strategic goal of the Department of State, titled Governing Justly and Democratically, has included the following four elements:

- Rule of Law and Human Rights supports constitutions, laws and legal systems, justice systems, judicial independence, and human rights.
- Good Governance supports legislative functions and processes, public sector executive functions, security sector governance, anti-corruption reforms, local governance, and decentralization.
- Political Competition and Consensus-building supports elections and political processes, political parties, and consensus-building projects.
- Civil Society supports media freedom, freedom of information, and civic participation.

(Epstein *et al.* 2007, p. 19)

USAID democracy promotion was launched after democratic transitions in Latin America and the former USSR in the mid-1980s (Epstein *et al.* 2007). Since then, USAID has initiated democracy promotion in more than 120 countries. US efforts at democracy promotion have been called a success due to transitions in Chile, the Philippines, Poland, and South Africa (Epstein *et al.* 2007). Despite the publication of regular success stories and reports, USAID's efforts are not as widely publicized as the ones of the State Department or the NED (Carothers 2000), even though they are more publicized than the ones of the EU. Although USAID develops a democracy-promotion program, in most of the cases its implementation is carried out by an international or local partnering NGO, which has won the bid for the program. USAID differentiates between implementing partners and contractors, as the former have more freedom in the development and sometimes the execution of the project.

The end of the Cold War resulted in the addition of new departments and tasks to USAID to account for the initiatives in post-communist satellites and later in post-Soviet countries. A New Independent States (NIS) Task Force was created in 1991, employing development professionals with little experience in the former Soviet Union (Pishchikova 2010). Later, in 1993, the NIS Task Force and the Eastern Europe Task Force were merged into the Bureau for Europe and NIS. Having little experience in the region, the Bureau employed based on Russian language skills and "nobody quite knew what they were doing there in that bureau but it was said to be different from everything else" (Hansen in Pishchikova 2010, p. 76). However, what the Bureau and USAID did know was that they needed to differentiate new activities of democracy promotion from the previous aid framework (Pishchikova 2010) in order not to hurt the feelings of countries that were claiming to be European and did not want to be associated with the derogatory "Third World." This differentiation, however, did not account for the differences between the NIS countries, treating them with the same simplistic uniformity as the EU.

The Freedom for Russia and the Emerging Eurasian Democracies and Open Markets (FREEDOM) Support Act (FSA) of 1992 spent a total of approximately US$30 billion on assistance to 12 countries of the former Soviet Union, excluding the Baltics.[4] USAID had to adapt to "new approaches, move quickly, and constantly adjust to changing circumstances" (Pressley 2000, p. ii) and some of the projects were "literally written on the back of the napkin" (Lyday in Pishchikova 2010, p. 79). Rushing to have funds approved by Congress, USAID seemed to have overlooked a similar urgency for developing a clear and tailored monitoring and evaluation system. After a decade of treating democracy-promotion targets in the former Soviet Union as a region, an attempt was made in 2001 to diversify the strategies based on country needs. However, the gradual change is still in the process (Melzig and Sprout 2007). The change in strategy mainly considers the proximity of the Central Asian and the South Caucasus countries to the strategically important region of the Middle East (Pishchikova 2010).

Being convinced that democracy should come from endogenous forces, USAID also partners local political forces aspiring for democratic reforms. However, the involvement of local actors is limited as USAID mainly works with its implementing partners and contractors. Based on its regulations, USAID very rarely channels funding directly to a local recipient, but rather announces a bid for US contractors. Upon winning the bid, a US contractor's headquarters regulates the implementation process through its branch in the recipient country. USAID works with implementers through contracts and cooperative agreements. In the case of the latter, the implementer has relatively more freedom in the creative implementation of a project, provided it stays within strictly regulated USAID requirements. Often the same implementer will apply and receive the contract/agreement for a similar project in many countries, making the project goals and evaluation indicators "travel from country to country without a change" (Zarycky 2010).

Despite limited local involvement in the development of the projects, and sometimes even in their implementation, USAID nevertheless claims that it has had a positive impact on democratization. Specifically, its own and other "donor assistance has helped fuel the explosive growth of NGO sectors in these countries" (USAID 1999b, p. xi). At the same time most of the efforts through the transnational channel are not backed-up by necessary governmental ones. As a former head of USAID's Armenia DG acknowledged, USAID had started planning a project that would involve both state and civil-society levels (Zarycky 2010), although the details of the project were still under elaboration. This move to include state actors into civil-society projects is a necessary and a long-awaited step, as "assistance to civil society strengthening can lead to human rights repercussions" (Epstein *et al.* 2007, p. 10), such as Russia's 2006 law limiting NGO activities and 2014 law allowing additional impromptu checks on NGOs.

Repercussions against USAID have recently become apparent, signaling for better coordination and cooperation not only among democracy promoters but also among different implementers of the same promoter. In 2012, USAID was expelled from Russia by president Putin's decision, under allegations of meddling in internal affairs and attempting to influence election results (McChesney *et al.* 2012), even though his own ruling party, United Russia, has allegedly benefited from USAID funding (RIA 2012c). USAID's decision to abide by Putin's demand was met by dismay from civil-society organizations, who have acknowledged long-term cooperation with USAID and comparative development of human-rights organizations in Russia (RIA 2012d). Elsewhere, following another accusation of attempting to undermine the national (leftist) government the USAID mission was expelled from Bolivia (AlJazeera 2013), only a month after the new USAID mission director was sworn-in in April 2013 (USAID 2013b). The decision of the Bolivian president Morales to demand the closure of USAID came after Secretary of State John Kerry had called Latin America the "backyard, neighbourhood" of the US (Reuters 2013). Exactly in such situations, potential cooperation with other democracy promoters may result in enhanced effectiveness and circumvention of the barriers erected by local governments. Even taking into consideration sovereignty claims of local governments, such incidents risk sending a disconcerting message to civil societies, which in some cases may feel "betrayed" (Freedom House 2012; Kramer in McChesney *et al.* 2012).

In its democracy-promotion efforts the US has rarely resorted to an official conditionality as the EU has, but often exercised conditionality and sanctions through statements and negotiations. The MCC, created by the Bush administration in 2002 and authorized in 2004 as a poverty-reduction tool, has become one of the rare conditionality examples. Due to its focus on democracy as a prerequisite for economic development, the MCC has been expected to be more successful than other instruments of democracy promotion (Beard 2009). Using 16 quantitative indicators based on the sources of Freedom House, the World Bank, the UN, and the IMF among others, the MCC evaluates the state of democracy and a country's eligibility for poverty-reduction assistance. The indicators are grouped in three larger categories: ruling justly, investing in people, and economic freedom. The eligibility of a country has depended upon its above-median performance on "at least half of the indicators in all three categories, and above the median on the Control of Corruption indicator" (Mandaville 2007, p. 1). Although the MCC does provide an important insight into its recipients and creates certain conditionality, its activities do not directly address democracy promotion.

The US and the others: major actor, swinging pendulum, and shaky bridges

US interests in the South Caucasus have followed three sets of strategic preferences: energy, traditional security, and market reform (Bryza 2006). In pursuit of these interests, the US launched developmental, democracy promotion, and reconstruction projects in the South Caucasus despite the lack of consensus between observers on whether it should be involved in the region (Nichol 2010). Proponents of US engagement in the South Caucasus have argued that conflict-resolution efforts will help to restrain warfare, smuggling, and Islamic extremism, and may contain Russian and Iranian influences over the region. Azerbaijan as a supplier with Armenia and Georgia as transit countries are important actors for US counterterrorism actions and for the energy-supply diversification plans of the US's "European allies" (Gordon 2009). New transit routes depend on the resolution of frozen conflicts and opening the borders between Armenia and Azerbaijan. Otherwise, more time and financial resources would be spent, as in the case of the US-supported Baku–Tbilisi–Jeyhan crude oil pipeline, which connected Azerbaijan to Turkey through Georgia instead of directly through Armenia. Through Azerbaijan, the South Caucasus also provides the US with access to Central Asia and Afghanistan, making the presence of conflicts undesirable for US security interests (Cornell 2005).

By the mid-1990s the local missions were provided with bigger budgetary authority and an opportunity of implementing their own grant programs within a budget appropriated by Congress for each country (Pishchikova 2010). The US government's activities in Armenia and Azerbaijan have followed roughly the same pattern: humanitarian assistance (1992–1998) focusing on provision of food, fuel, medicine, clothing, and especially internally displaced persons in Azerbaijan. Serving each year over 200,000 households and 1200 schools in Armenia, USAID provided heating fuel through its Winter Kerosene Program, which covered the years of the war with Azerbaijan and the consequent blockade. The humanitarian assistance also included the US wheat programs that supplied Armenia with half of its total requirements for bread consumption. After 1998, USAID both in Armenia and Azerbaijan turned from entirely humanitarian activities to programs targeting political development and democratic institutions. A similar path was adopted in Georgia, where projects focused on democratic institutions, economic growth, energy security, health, and education. USAID projects have been divided within thematic areas of democracy and governance, healthcare, the private sector, social protection, and water and energy. The focus of the 2009–2013 strategy is on peace and security, economic growth, democracy and governance—the alternative media, civil society, rule of law, parliamentary assistance, and political processes—and a social and health portfolio.

Despite criticisms of low budgets for democracy promotion, a rather large share of US assistance to the South Caucasus has been allocated to democracy promotion. As if reflecting the importance assigned by the US to elections, the budget for democratic reforms increased almost by 240 percent from US$9.45 million in 2002 to US$22.40 million in the elections year of 2003 in Armenia only. The budget for democratic reforms in Armenia was increased by 155 percent from US$13.41 million in 2007 to US$20.77 million in the presidential election year of 2008. However, there was no similar increase for the 2007—the year of parliamentary elections—underlining the importance of presidential elections over parliamentary ones, at least in Armenia. Georgia has even appeared in the top five of US economic assistance in 2011, while the US has donated US$1.76 billion throughout 1992–2006, becoming the largest bilateral donor.

In Armenia, democracy promotion funding had been channeled through USAID's Strategic Objectives of Increased Citizen Participation in the Political, Economic and Social Decision-making Process, later renamed into Improved Democratic Governance, and aimed to consolidate "the achievements of past democracy objectives … to improve democratic governance by both expanding civic participation and governance institutions" (USAID 2004, p. 29). In Azerbaijan, USAID started out with the Strategic Objective of Civil Society Better Organized and Represented (USAID 2000). For the 2009–2013 Strategic Plan for Armenia, the strategic objectives were renamed into priority goals, and democracy promotion has fallen under Priority Goal 2 of "bolstering those institutions that effectively promote democracy" (USAID 2009, p. 11). Under this priority goal, USAID has de-emphasized "direct support to [government] entities that have been chronically resistant to good-faith cooperation and meaningful rather than superficial reforms," albeit without ruling out "new opportunities to engage" (USAID 2009, p. 11). Country Development Cooperation Strategies for the periods of 2011–2016 and 2013–2017 elaborate on developmental objectives: democratic checks and balances, accountable governance in Georgia, more participatory, effective, and accountable governance for Armenia, and effective participation of diverse actors and institutions in Azerbaijan. Changing of objectives and their wording in strategic plans may indicate USAID's efforts to build on its previous activities and conviction that the established institutions need to be prepared for democratic consolidation. In addition, the language for the development objective of Georgia indicates USAID's inclination that democracy has taken hold in Georgia and currently requires further consolidation.

After 2004's positive evaluation of Armenia's democratic performance, USAID efforts were further complemented by a five-year and US$235.65 million compact signed between the government and the MCC in 2006. The compact had only one goal: "the reduction of rural poverty through sustainable increase in the economic performance of the agricultural sector."[5] The program has been expected to impact 75 percent of the rural population by boosting annual incomes. The disputed 2008 presidential elections turned the MCC's attention to the status of democracy in Armenia, with a road project put on operational hold in 2009. However, other related activities proceeded as planned. But in May 2011 Armenia was classified as ineligible for a second MCC compact due to its deteriorating democratic performance (Harutyunyan 2011b). This announcement was largely attributed to the events of the 2008 elections (Harutyunyan 2011b) and came a few months after a strain in US–Armenian relations over the alleged sale of arms by the Armenian government to Iran had become public (Guardian 2010a). These arms were reported to be used in killing and wounding US soldiers in Iraq in January and March 2008 (Guardian 2010b). Given Armenia's deteriorating democratic performance, its ineligibility for MCC was not surprising. However, given previous silence on democratic violations, the cut of MCC funding seems in line with its own regulations but stimulated by motives not related to democracy.

While Azerbaijan has never qualified for MCC funding due to its low performance on MCC indicators, Georgia has become the most successful one among the South Caucasus countries. The first Georgia–MCC compact signed in 2005 for the amount of US$295.3 million aimed to stimulate rehabilitation of infrastructure to promote trade and ensure a reliable energy supply. The compact also targeted the performance of regional and municipal services and productivity in farms. Given its performance on MCC indicators, in 2011 Georgia was invited to submit a proposal for another compact (Civil.Ge 2011b), which was eventually signed in 2013 for a period of five years and the amount of US$140 million (Civil.Ge 2013). From rehabilitation of the infrastructure, MCC funding has turned to capacity building, Compact II aims to improve the quality of education and increase the earning potential of Georgians, paying special attention to students and women.

The alleged arms deal between Armenia and Iran endangered US hopes of a peaceful South Caucasus. Being a co-chairman of the OSCE Minsk Group, the US "attempts to be neutral" (Migdalovitz 2001, p. i) in the talks over Nagorno-Karabakh and other military-related issues. In its policy towards the resolution of the Nagorno-Karabakh conflict, the US has preferred OSCE peacemaking to the UN, for the possibility to exclude Iran and control Russia (Migdalovitz 2001). The Clinton administration attempted to be neutral, to keep good relations with Armenian-Americans, to access the Azerbaijani industry, and to prevent a spillover of the Nagorno-Karabakh conflict into its relations with Turkey. In addition, in an effort to be sensitive to Russian interests, the US let Russia broker the settlement of the armed conflict in 1994. The Nagorno-Karabakh conflict also underlined the divisions between the executive and legislative branches of the US government. While neither president Clinton nor president Bush agreed to the Section 907 prohibiting aid to Azerbaijan, Congress seemed to ignore their considerations and passed the regulations.

The US has stated on numerous occasions it was "deeply involved" (Danielyan 2002) in the resolution of protracted conflicts, though stopping short of explicitly marking its position (Melkumian and Kalantarian 2004) in the case of Nagorno-Karabakh. With hopes for a settlement ignited in 2006 (Danielyan 2006b), the US, as with its Minsk Group counterparts, has kept calling for a conflict resolution "only by peaceful means" (Clinton in RFE/RL 2011c). However, the "real window of opportunity" (Associated Press 2006) did not turn 2006 into the "year for a deal" (RFE/RL 2006), keeping the US and other mediators "still hopeful" (Danielyan and Saghabalian 2007) and insisting on removing the snipers from the LoC (RFE/RL 2011d).

Although the rhetorical commitment of the US to conflict resolution has not been supported by tangible progress, it has been supported by close attention to the improvement of living conditions of those affected by the conflict. Unlike the EU, which has not been involved in activities within the territory of Nagorno-Karabakh, the US Congress appropriated US$12.5 million for victims of the conflict in November 1997. In the financial year 1998, USAID allocated US$8.3 million for health, shelter, and economic aid for programs in Nagorno-Karabakh.

The aid packages started in 1998 continued and totaled to US$35.77 million for 1998–2010. The research of the Armenian National Committee of America shows that Congress intended to allocate a total of more than US$70 million instead of the spent US$35.77 million (ANCA 2010).

With the Georgian conflicts, unlike in the case of the Nagorno-Karabakh conflict, the US did not hesitate in its decision on which side to support, even if essentially the reasons for conflict voiced by involved parties are similar: territorial integrity against the right of self-determination. While the EU has been more active in looking for a resolution of the Georgian conflicts, especially after 2008, the US has nevertheless made its position on the armed conflict clear. Disagreeing with Russia on Georgia's territorial integrity, in 2011 the US called for re-establishing an OSCE mission in Georgia that would include the breakaway regions. Russia, however, disagreed, citing the proclaimed independence of Abkhazia and South Ossetia. Insisting on Georgia's territorial integrity, the US has repeatedly qualified the presence of Russian troops in the breakaway regions as occupation (Gordon 2011). By signing the US–Georgia Charter on Strategic Partnership in 2009, the US reiterated its unequivocal support for Georgia's sovereignty.

US attention on the South Caucasus has coincided with the similar interests of the EU. The transatlantic relations between the US and the EU have long shaped the course of international affairs. US involvement in European affairs started with the Marshall Plan and oversaw the creation of the European Community. After the end of the Cold War, the Bush Senior administration saw the European Community as playing a special role in the stabilization of Eastern Europe (Treverton 1992; Smith and Woolcock 1993). Thus, not only did the EU seek a global role for itself but it was also encouraged by the US. Then Secretary of State James Baker called for an imminent enlargement of the EC/EU to the East (Smith 2008), which would have encouraged transformation to democracy and contained Russia's ambitions of "re-winning" Eastern Europe. Clinton's policy of "engagement and enlargement" had assigned a key role to the EU (Smith 2008), which however disappointed Washington by preferring its long process of accession through harmonization rather than US-advocated mass enlargement. However, the promise of the enlargement or the so-called "rhetorical entrapment" (Schimmelfennig 2001) of Europe was a guarantee of the eventual accession of the CEE, keeping US plans in force.

However, apart from the EU's activating plans on having a security policy and a heavy emphasis on environmental issues, more important tensions appeared after 9/11 attacks and the US's decision to intervene in Iraq. Although selected European member states supported the US's decision, the EU as a political entity was largely overlooked. The "warrior" US did not have time or willingness to wait for the "civilian power" Europe (Bull 1982; Smith 2002) to engage in long and consensus-requiring deliberations. Though the strong neoconservative stance of the first Bush administration had highlighted the differences with the EU, advocating for a multilateral approach, the relationship seemed to improve after 2005 (Andrews 2005; Zaborowski 2006). In addition, not only the EU but also the US can be classified as a normative power, because they both "try to project a particular identity in their foreign policy relations" (Risse 2009, p. 249). Obama's first victory in US presidential elections and his distancing from the Bush doctrine have increased the enthusiasm over strengthened transatlantic cooperation. However, after a period of "Obamamania" (Alcaro 2012), Europe seems to have fallen out of love with president Obama (Lister 2013). The transatlantic relationship is in need of a "renaissance" (Nuland 2013a), even if the US does not seem to take the EU seriously in democracy promotion even in the latter's own neighborhood (Nuland in Pilkington 2014).

While transatlantic relations have generally followed a friendly path, the ones with Russia have been swinging like a pendulum. After the break-up of the Soviet Union, Russia became the darling of the Clinton administration. The initial treatment of Russia by the US as a defeated Cold War enemy was substituted with the "Bill and Boris" friendship, which personified Russia with the seemingly reformist Yeltsin and marked US hopes for Russia's rapid democratization. The controversial re-election of Yeltsin amidst the ongoing war in Chechnya did not seem to trouble the US, as he was regarded as a better choice than a potential communist victory (Rutland and Dubinsky 2008). Regardless of the presidential friendship, Russia was worried by US plans for NATO enlargement to the extent that Yeltsin (1995) warned that the process would led to a "cold peace." The imminent enlargement was followed by Russia's rejection of the START II treaty and the aggravation of relations due to the Kosovo crisis. However, the real chill in friendly relations came with NATO's bombing of Yugoslavia despite strong Russian opposition: Russia's then Prime Minister Leonid Primakov, who was on the way to the US seeking "money and understanding" (Gazeta.RU 1999), turned his plane back to Russia while over the Atlantic Ocean after learning of the bombing (RIA News 2011). Mutual disillusionment was further aggravated due to Russia's poor economy and new fighting in Chechnya.

After the succession in presidency by Vladimir Putin and his promises to kill Chechen terrorists in the toilets,[6] Washington understood that it could hardly influence politics in Russia. While the major part of the twentieth century was spent in an arms and space race between the US and the Soviet Union, the beginning of the twenty-first century has been spent in an often-covert race for regional influence. President Bush claimed that he "looked the man [Putin] in the eye" and "was able to get a sense of his soul" (Bush in Wyatt 2001); however, even Bush's psychological maneuvers did not help the deteriorating relations. Russia heavily criticized US operations in Iraq and even called it a threat to a multipolar world. In a 2001 interview to *Le Figaro*, former Secretary of State Condoleezza Rice called Russia "a threat to the West in general and to our European allies in particular." US support for the wave of "color revolutions" was seen as a direct threat to Russia and *inter alia* was followed by a crackdown on political opposition and the 2006 law on NGOs, which restricted access to foreign funding. US plans to place missiles in Poland and a radar station in the Czech Republic, its support of Georgia's NATO aspirations,

Russia's possible financial support to Iran's nuclear program, the 2008 conflict in Georgia, and Russia's military cooperation with Venezuela have all negatively influenced US–Russia relations.

However, a much-discussed reset in relations occurred after the G20 summit in London in 2009, when two new presidents, Obama and Medvedev, promised a fresh start (Cooper 2009) and called upon Iran to allow foreign inspectors into the country (Babich 2010). Pressing a symbolic "reset" button, the US Secretary of State Hillary Clinton and Russia's foreign minister Sergey Lavrov (Shuster 2010) paved the way for a new nuclear arms reduction treaty (New START) in 2010. The reset was not reverted even by the discovery of 10 sleeping Russian spies (BBC 2010b), who were swapped with their Russian counterparts in 2010. Putin's third re-election was viewed by the US within the framework of mutual interest (RIA News 2012), but resulted in a string of mutual accusations. These included a Twitter-based attack by Russia's Ministry of Foreign Affairs on Ambassador Michael McFaul for a presumably distorted view on the reset (Elder 2012). The Magnitsky law passed in the US placing visa bans on Russian officials involved in the prosecution of a whistleblowing lawyer (Englund 2012) was followed by a Dima Yakovlev bill banning adoption of Russian children by US citizens (BBC 2012a). Civil war in Syria has added to tensions between the US and Russia due to their different positions, and has actually weakened the position of president Obama among Republicans due to a lack of military action after Syria's reported use of chemical weapons, while Putin's plan for destroying those weapons was put into action. However, US–Russian tensions reached their apogee after Russia granted asylum to NSA whistleblower Edward Snowden and Obama cancelled his scheduled travel to Russia (Carney 2013).

Conclusions

Both the EU and the US have demonstrated positive legitimacy for their promotion of democracy, despite internal disputes and some concerns over the quality of democracy. The US's image may have been damaged after the recent NSA revelations; however, these implications need additional analysis, which is beyond the scope of this book. In addition, as shown in this and the previous chapter, both the EU and the US have encountered Russia's democracy blocking, which ranged from promoting opposing policies and regional organizations, to outright counter-measures. The post-Cold War history has shown that the US highly personifies its relations with Russia, yet it enjoys greater autonomy when dealing with it than does the EU. Unlike the EU, that has preferred to encourage Russia's involvement in some aspects of international politics and "seeks friendship," the US has been more straightforward in its intentions in Russia's "backyard."

The EU and the US have, however, projected different images to the targets of democracy promotion and to pundits, mostly due to their divergent foreign-policy decision-making and historical legacies (Babayan 2010). In accordance with its image of a "freedom fighter," the US has been expected "to assertively advocate the promotion of liberal-democratic values" (Poppe *et al.* 2013, p. 52). In contrast, the EU has been perceived as a "civilian power" (Freres 2000; Telò 2007; Börzel and Risse 2009). This long-standing contrast between the EU and the US's international images (Kagan 2003; Kopstein 2006) had been expected to blur or even vanish with the election of Barack Obama. In addition, the EU has seemed eager to shake away its "soft power" image, even planning to launch its own drone program to potentially match the global leadership of the US (Croft 2013). Indeed, the subdued democracy-promotion rhetoric of the first Obama administration (Babayan 2013b) and the EU's increased democracy-promotion rhetoric after the Arab Spring (Babayan and Viviani 2013) may have fueled suggestions that the two powers have been moving towards a partnership, at least within democracy promotion.

In terms of specific strategies, the EU has not applied its conditionality and meritocratic approach similarly to candidate and non-candidate countries. In addition, the US scolded autocratic regimes depending upon its strategic interests. While the EU has granted membership to countries already complying with its criteria, it has not pursued the same exclusive strategy when including other countries in its policies. While the ENP and the EaP presume nominal conditionality, the EU often strays away from its strict criteria and extends policy coverage to countries not demonstrating democratic progress (Babayan 2009, 2011). Though both promoters have utilized all channels of democracy promotion, the EU's primary partners up until the establishment of the Civil Society Forum and the EED have been governmental structures, and the US's have been transnational and societal organizations. Often, the US has preferred to distance itself from the government and work only with civil-society representatives (Parsadanyan 2010), while the EU has considered working with civil society as interference in internal affairs. However, the US has not limited itself in the choice of instruments, using material and social reinforcement, additional support, and punishment, while the EU has chosen material reinforcement by reward for EU candidates and additional support for non-candidates.

The EU has been creating new policies to deal with its neighbors based on the changing interests of its member states. Neighborhood policies have been based on the enlargement mechanism as if ignoring the fact that no other policy offers the most appealing incentive of membership. The policymaking process in the EU has been often compromised by a lack of coordination between its institutions and sometimes outright competition, and often over-eagerness or reluctance of member states to promote democracy. The US created its toolbox and checklist for democracy promotion in the early 1990s and has since applied it to its target countries with marginal modifications. US unequivocal promotion of democracy has proceeded simultaneously with the European attempts at institutionalizing and revising its numerous regional policies, which also include democracy promotion. Even if the EU has been taking a virtual lead in its Eastern neighborhood, and the US has shifted its primary foreign-policy focus to the Middle East, US democracy-promotion efforts and budgets have barely changed, even increasing from year to year. The US has also voiced rhetorical support to the EU's EaP while meeting with EU officials and has reportedly "been aligning future US assistance with that of the EU" (Nuland 2013b). The US apparently views the EaP as "a step toward the longstanding vision of a more integrated economic space, stretching from Lisbon to Donetsk animated by market-oriented reforms, growing prosperity and deepening democracy" (Nuland 2013b), yet possible "aligned" assistance still seems to be a matter of future.

The picture is more varied in terms of their individual involvements in the national priority issues of the South Caucasus. In particular, the involvement varies in terms of EU and US positions on the regional conflicts. While both have expressed unequivocal support for Georgia as opposed to its breakaway regions, the situation is more complicated in the case of the Nagorno-Karabakh conflict. Among the factors mentioned below, this divergence can also be explained by Georgia's unconditional support for NATO enlargement and its EU ambitions, which are less outspoken in Armenia and Azerbaijan. The EU's involvement in the resolution of the Nagorno-Karabakh conflict was low until the prospects of creating the ENP and the subsequent inclusion of the South Caucasus states. Although EU member France has been co-chairing the OSCE Minsk Group, the EU's contribution to conflict resolution as a separate political entity was minimal, being limited to occasional speeches calling for peaceful conflict resolution. The launch of the ENP and later the EaP upgraded the EU's involvement to moderate due to its rhetorical efforts in regional cooperation. However, if unchanged, the EU's framework of conflict resolution within the ENP and the EaP is unlikely to achieve positive results (Babayan 2012b). On the other hand, US involvement has ranged from moderate to positive. Nevertheless, US involvement in the Nagorno-Karabakh issue has subdued since the election of Barack Obama, giving the lead to former president Medvedev. However, before and shortly after 2008, the US has demonstrated a firmer position on the peaceful resolution of the Nagorno-Karabakh conflict and more activeness in its efforts. With the comeback of Vladimir Putin to presidency, Russia-initiated efforts have also decreased, indicating that status quo on conflicts is likely to be preferable for Russia, since it keeps the South Caucasus countries divided.

It is understandable that involvement in the resolution of the Nagorno-Karabakh conflict will require substantial decisiveness from both the EU and the US. Deciding on the approach to conflict resolution may be especially difficult for the EU, not only due to the intergovernmental nature of its foreign policy decision-making but also due to its interest in Azerbaijan's energy resources. On the other hand, neither promoter would be interested in instigating Russia's negative reaction to more active involvement in regional affairs. However, the Nagorno-Karabakh problem has hindered the implementation of not only democracy promotion but also other policies, and it requires increased attention from international actors and an increased conciliatory approach from the conflicting parties. Even though, due to strategic reasons, a decisive involvement may be difficult to achieve, progress and visible EU and US involvement in negotiations are likely to increase the identification of both Armenia and Azerbaijan with the promoters, creating more favorable conditions for democracy and for intraregional projects.

Notes

1 By comparing the EU to a metrosexual man based on the example of football player David Beckham, the author argues that the EU has become more effective in spreading its message than the US because, unlike the latter, it uses both its "hard power and its sensitive side" (p. 66) of a norm generator and promoter.
2 The European Initiative for Democracy and Human Rights was renamed into European Instrument for Democracy and Human Rights in 2007.
3 The UfM was created in July 2008 as a relaunched Barcelona process. However, the 2009 and 2010 summits were not held due to the stalemate of the Arab–Israeli peace process. In addition, the Arab revolutions seem to add "the last nail in the UM coffin" (Torreblanca and Fanes 2011).
4 The efforts of Armenian-American lobby managed to exclude Azerbaijan from participation in the FSA under Section 907 due to the latter's blockade of Armenia as a result of the Nagorno-Karabakh conflict. However, in return for Azerbaijan's cooperation in the War on Terror, in 2001 the Senate granted the president with the possibility of a waiver to Section 907, which has since been used in 2002, 2003, 2004, and 2005.
5 See www.mca.am/new/enversion/overview.php
6 After his appointment as prime minister, Putin announced an unapologetic fight against terrorism and his call for "killing [terrorists] in the toilet" made on September 24, 1999 made media headlines. See www.youtube.com/watch?v=A_PdYRZSW-I

Part III
Sectoral democratic transformation

5 Elections in the South Caucasus

A Potemkin village rather than a solid construction

Election projects

Elections have become the ultimate indicator of democratization since the post-communist countries started holding general elections. The main difference with the post-Soviet elections compared with the façade elections held previously was the endeavor to make them at least look genuinely competitive, free, and fair. This general favoritism towards elections was also picked up by democracy promoters who initiated numerous election aid projects, election observation being one of the largest. Before the collapse of the Soviet Union, election assistance was an exceptional activity exercised only in the cases of UN trusteeships and US interventions in Central America and the Caribbean in the early twentieth century (Carothers 1999). However, election observation has become a norm and regular post-election OSCE reports provide an overview and assessment of elections.

This interest in election assistance is understandable as elections provide the most tangible measurement of the current state of democracy: the conduct and the process of elections clearly indicate whether political parties have the chance to be fairly and competitively represented, and civil society in general and individual citizens in particular have the chance of expressing their political preferences. Besides, the long-lasting effect of free and fair elections is the formation of a responsive and accountable government that equally addresses the needs of its citizens and parliamentarians, or political parties that effectively communicate those needs to the broader political society. However, as the practice shows, mere conduct of elections does not immediately or even a decade or two later lead to genuine democracy, because not all elections provide competitiveness and equal participation, as can be clearly seen from the example of many post-Soviet states.

The caveat of electoral assistance can be "overdoing elections" (Carothers 1999, p. 136) by not paying enough attention to the other components of democracy, and eventually having elections that are corrupt and lack meaningful competition. According to critics of electoral assistance, transitional countries may be better off without instant elections that are not adapted to local realities and do not have the essential element of the Western liberalism, namely the rule of law (Zakaria 1997). Echoing Kaplan's (1997) argument that in poor countries without any democratic development elections might lead to chaos, Zakaria (1997) has called for more rule-of-law development projects before establishing the elections. For different reasons, they agree that before the establishment of a full-fledged democracy the country has to undergo a period of soft authoritarianism. However, the approach of soft authoritarianism can be dubious because, without targeted and meaningful democracy promotion with all of its components, the country may maintain soft authoritarianism and the final transformation to democracy may be further delayed. Nevertheless, elections should not be put off for more than three to five years, and should always follow the establishment and stabilization of authority and main institutions (Carothers 1999). Similarly, democracy promoters should not consider the mission accomplished as soon as the first elections are held, even if it fairly passed the "free and fair" standard. The examples of many post-Soviet countries show that, after fairly successful inaugural elections, following ones failed to meet democratic standards.

Nevertheless, election assistance remains the most popular democracy-promotion activity. This is also due to the relative simplicity of transferring the tools of election assistance from one democratizing country to another as "elections pose a relatively consistent set of technical challenges across very different contexts" (Carothers 1999, p. 125). Democracy promoters can transfer not only their own electoral systems but also already-tested election-assistance tools to a new democratizing country. Election assistance implies a variety of activities that include but are not limited to the design of the electoral system, good administration of elections, voter education, election observation, and election mediation (Carothers 1999). On the way to a democratic transition and willing to fully break with the past, the electoral systems already existing in a country had to be revised and changed. The assistance from the US and European countries with long-lasting elections experience has been, thus, very handy. However, despite the initial benign intentions of promoters, it can often happen that the promoted electoral system is the one that promoters themselves know and use, and it may not be fully compatible with local realities. Projects targeting design and good administration of elections, however, need to be accompanied by voter education activities to overcome the common apathy of the population toward democratic processes.

Presidential elections in the South Caucasus

In Armenia, despite the rhetorical commitment of the authorities to free and fair elections and three nominal power changes, neither presidential electoral campaigns nor voting procedures have been evaluated as democratic since the first general elections of 1991. Notwithstanding the continuous improvement of electoral legislature under the recommendations and observations of international actors, violations were reported both by local and international observers during the 1996, 1998 (extraordinary), 2003, 2008, and 2013 presidential elections. However, criticism of any Armenian elections was voiced only by the OSCE and other western missions, with the Russia-backed CIS mission fully support-ing the "democratic conduct." Such support prompted the Central Elections Commission (CEC) chairmen to claim that the fledging Armenian democracy does not have to comply with all international standards (CSCE 2011). More-over, the improvements in the conduct of parliamentary elections were never echoed by improvements in the conduct of presidential elections despite very short intervals between the two. Former president Kocharyan's June 2002 remark that parliamentarians disrupting sessions and asking for his impeachment would be grabbed by the ears and taken to a police station (RFE/RL 2002; Zaka-rian 2002) further demonstrated the perceived supremacy of the presidency. The disappointment in the possibility of power change through elections has forced some observers in Armenia to call it a dictatorship where voting would not change anything, and to call upon others to boycott general elections of 2012 (Danielyan G. 2011).

Azerbaijan has held one additional presidential election compared with Armenia. However, again the quantity of elections did not translate into their democratic quality. Presidential elections of 1991, 1992, 1993, 1998, 2003, 2008, and 2013 initially resulted in several nominal power changes, afterwards simply cementing the dominance of the Aliyev family in Azerbaijan's politics, when the presidency was passed from the outgoing president Heydar Aliyev to his son Ilham. Receiving the worst possible score from Freedom House Nations in Transit, the electoral process in Azerbaijan has been marred by fraud, voter intimidation, violations of civil liberties, and restrictions imposed on oppositional candidates. Formal abolition of censorship in advance of the 1998 elections (OSCE 1998a) added to the formal transformation of Azerbai-jan to democracy, but the abolition stayed on paper only. The power of the presidency and the Aliyev family was virtually rendered limitless after 2012 constitutional amendments, abolishing presidential term limits and introducing longer election cycles. Rampant corruption in Azerbaijan facilitated by the Aliyev family earned the family head the title of "Corruption's Person of the Year" in 2012 (Coalson 2013).

Georgia has also held seven elections which, however, seemed to have brought it closer to democracy than Armenia and Azerbaijan, even if its start was not as promising as Armenia's. Having witnessed three power changes—only one of those peaceful without uprisings—Georgia has become for a short time the poster child of democracy promoters. Even when not living up to the promise of the Rose Revolution, Georgia's commitment to liberal democracy may have been doubted, but its commitment to EU integration and NATO enlargement has always been beyond doubt, fuelled by strong anti-Russian senti-ments. Receiving best democracy scores in the region, it seems that after all trepidations Georgia has managed to straighten its path to democracy, which is supported by 2012 parliamentary and 2013 presidential election results. It goes without saying, though, that genuine democratic transformation of Georgia would be visible before the next general elections, as this interim period would be crucial for further democratization and consolidation of achieved results.

In 1991 Levon Ter-Petrosyan won the presidency in Armenia and managed to unite Armenians, subordinating "other issues and conflicts within Armenia" (Way 2009, p. 110) to a single cause of the Nagorno-Karabakh conflict. Proclaiming its adherence to democratization (Astourian 2000, p. 2) and helped by the military's success in the war with Azerbaijan, the newly elected regime established a stable rule, which further led to the organizational power of autocratic stability in Armenia (Way 2009). Both Western policy makers (Astourian 2000) and the Armenian population regarded the Armenian regime and its ruler as the best choice, especially in comparison to other former Soviet states that had practically inherited their communist leaders. Both Azerbaijan and Georgia were among those heirs of communist regimes. In 1991, Azerbaijan elected unrivalled communist party representative Ayaz Mutalibov, who stayed in power only for a year. The first multi-candidate elections were held in 1992, when a former KGB prisoner Abulfez Elchibey was elected, marking the break from the communist past. However, Elchibey lost his popularity due to continued military losses in the Nagorno-Karabakh conflict and a worsening economy (Curtis 1995). The combination of these factors led to another election, when previously barred from elections due to age and former communist leader Heydar Aliyev won the presidency with a voter turnout of 97.6 percent. Georgia followed a slightly similar path to Azerbaijan by electing a Soviet dissident intellectual Zviad Gamsakhurdia in 1991. However, the policy of "Georgia for Georgians" (Khutsishvili 1994), human rights violations (Human Rights Watch 1991), and ongoing ethnic conflicts resulted in a violent coup d'état and a military council ruling the country. Allegedly orchestrated by Russia, the coup d'état formed a military council with the former Soviet minister of foreign affairs Eduard Shevarnadze as its chairman, until the presidency was formally restored in 1995, and Shevarnadze stayed in office until 2004.

Enchantment with Ter-Petrosyan's regime started to wane, too: he "began as a democrat and gradually lost his way" (Washington Post 1998). The Nagorno-Karabakh war resulted in a blockade from Azerbaijan and Turkey, and Ter-Petrosyan was dubbed "the most spectacular victim" of the Nagorno-Karabakh conflict since "he dared to suggest that Armenia should be more flexible over Karabakh" (Economist 1998a). He was, nevertheless, re-elected in 1996 but resigned within a year without any popular uprising or resistance from the ruling party (Astourian 2000), giving way to his strongman (Economist 1998b) and Karabakh native Robert Kocharyan, elected in extraordinary elections of 1998. While several laws passed in Armenia before the 1996 presidential elections presented "a clear improvement on previous electoral legislation" (Osborn 1996, p. 2), the elections were held in the environment of a powerful presidency, weak judiciary and legislature, and a personalized party system (Astourian 2000), and "raised a wave of indignation in all sectors of the population" (UNDP 2001, p. 39). The incumbent received three times more press coverage than the other candidates combined (Osborn 1996; Grigoryan 1997), in violation of the electoral code. The elections of 1998 marked a "significant progress" for some (UNDP 2001, p. 39) and proved Armenians to be the "Soviet nation most immune to communism" (Economist 1998b). However, the immunity to communism apparently does not mean immunity to authoritarianism. Legal changes showed a formal improvement in the electoral process in Armenia (OSCE 1998b) but no behavioral changes, due to the preferential treatment of the incumbent and his virtually unlimited resources. Public opinion polls showed that the incumbent would still have had high chances for re-election, yet Ter-Petrosyan chose to build his victory with the help of security forces and consequently lost public confidence. Adhering to fully democratic conduct of elections would entail moderate utility of adaptation for the incumbent, especially taking into account the absence of united, strong, and outspoken opposition.

Meanwhile, prior to the 1998 presidential elections, Azerbaijan also amended its Law on Election of the President of the Republic, "showing significant improvements" (OSCE 1998a). However, these positive improvements were undermined by the Law on the Central Election Commission, which was disputed by major political parties in Azerbaijan. Heydar Aliyev was re-elected, defeating five other candidates in elections which were multiparty but not fair. While changes occurred in the presidency in Armenia and Azerbaijan, Georgian president Shevarnadze was re-elected in 2000. Presidential elections were characterized by "interference by State authorities in the election process; deficient election legislation; not fully representative election administration; and unreliable voter registers" (OSCE 2000, p. 1). While some legal amendments enhanced the democratic nature of the elections, others undermined these changes, in particular late adoption of some amendments causing confusion in advance of the elections. Running against five other candidates, Shevarnadze secured his second term with 79.82 percent of votes and complete dominance of his campaign on both state and private media (OSCE 2000). As in the case of Armenia, the incumbents in Azerbaijan and Georgia would have been re-elected given the course of their domestic policies. Facing only moderate danger to their re-elections, they nevertheless opted for silencing opposition and resorting to undemocratic behavior. Thus, the late 1990s showed that despite initial promise of democratization, elections in all three South Caucasus countries became not the democratic expression of the peoples' will but a farce to satisfy a democratic facade.

Under Kocharyan, Armenia showed trends of turning into a police state (Halliday 2008) with a proper dictator, rather than a democratizing country (Danielyan 2004a). Democratic progress was largely limited to the 1999 adoption of the new electoral law on presidential, parliamentary, and local elections, which, however, lacked transparency and provisions on protection of human rights. In 2000–2001 limitations were imposed on the right of holding peaceful demonstrations (UNDP 2001). The first year of Kocharyan's presidential term had witnessed an attempted coup d'état (Danielyan 2001) and a persisting reshuffle of the government. The opposition even accused Kocharyan in orchestrating the killings of the Prime Minister Vazgen Sargsyan and parliament speaker Karen Demirchyan, while in parliamentary session, out of fear of their growing popularity and power (Kalantarian and Danielyan 2001). Legislative progress due to a new elections law was undermined by illegal activities to avoid possible defeat in elections, despite warnings from the OSCE, CoE, and proclaimed EU and US aid conditionality (Danielyan 2003a; Zakarian 2003). Given lack of progress in the Nagorno-Karabakh conflict and persisting criminal allegations against the incumbent regime, the possibility of Kocharyan's defeat was not groundless and made the utility of holding free and fair elections low for the incumbent. Thus, the 2003 presidential election did not meet international standards *inter alia* due to a "lack of sufficient political determination by the authorities to ensure a fair and honest process" (OSCE 2003a, p. 2), with the second round allegedly allowed only to avoid even worse evaluations from the international monitors. "These elections were even more disgraceful" than the ones of 1998 (Avoyan 2003) and resulted in opposition protests, as a result of which many protesters were detained and subjected to police brutality (Danielyan 2004b; Kalantarian and Danielyan 2004). Detention of opposition participants persisted despite the criticism of the EU envoy (Kalantarian *et al.* 2004) and calls to end the practice of detentions in order to not face sanctions by PACE, which would "reconsider the credentials of the Armenian delegation" (PACE 2004). However, controversial arrests also took place in May (Sarkisian 2004) and June (Kalantarian and Stepanian 2004), without PACE following up on its initial threats.

The presidential elections of 2003 became the year when Azerbaijan's autocratic turn was left in no doubt and the presidency was passed from ailing Heydar Aliyev to his son Ilham, who in defeating seven candidates secured 75.38 percent of votes. Often-mild observers were this time very critical of the election's conduct, assessing it as "failed" and lacking "sufficient political commitment to implement a genuine election process" (OSCE 2003b, p. 1). The pre-election period was characterized by widespread intimidation, which negatively influenced participation in campaigning. Yet again, although the variety of candidates provided options for selection, as has already became clear from South Caucasus elections a quantitative choice in candidates did not mean competitive elections. Some formal improvements—such as a new unified Election Code passed earlier in 2003—contained a number of safeguards against fraud and expanded the rights of observers (OSCE 2003b). However, at the same time, the Law on Public Unions and Foundations prohibited observation of elections by domestic organizations with more than 30 percent of their budget coming from foreign states. Ilham Aliyev's succession to presidency was also facilitated by—perhaps unwitting—failure of the opposition to nominate a single candidate, and the overt preference of the media for his candidacy. The elections were followed by arrests of opposition activists, large-scale demonstrations, and riots that left four dead, more than 100 injured and over 600 detained (OSCE 2003b).

While authoritarian grip in Armenia and Azerbaijan became even stronger after 2003, Georgia seemed to gain democratic momentum after rigged 2003 parliamentary elections, subsequent snap 2004 presidential elections, and the victory of Mikheil Saakashvil with 96 percent of the votes. Held on the wave of the Rose Revolution, the elections were characterized by "the collective political will to conduct a more genuine democratic election process" (OSCE 2004b,

p. 1). According to the OSCE, the elections process was marked by improved legislative framework, peaceful campaigning, and improved count and tabulation processes. However, as in Armenia and Azerbaijan, one of the drawbacks in Georgia has been "lack of clear separation between State administration and political party structures" (OSCE 2004b, p. 2). Amendments introduced to the constitution in February 2004 granted the president more powers in comparison to the parliament, keeping the power within a small elite and curtailing already limited public participation (NIT 2005). However, these concerns may have been partially alleviated for international observers, given another peaceful power change in a Georgian region of Ajara. While Ajaran leader Aslan Abashidze advanced military separatism, the region's population, mobilized by Saakashvili's United National Movement and youth group Kmara, took to the streets in large-scale protests. As a result, Abashidze left for Russia in the private jet of the former Moscow mayor (Kramer 2012a) and the region was re-integrated into Georgia's public space, maintaining its autonomy.

Barred by the constitution from a third-consecutive presidential term, Kocharyan had been expected to emulate his Russian counterpart Vladimir Putin in handpicking his successor and moving to the position of prime minister. Newly appointed and also a Karabakh native with extensive connections in Armenia's oligopolic politics, Prime Minister Serzh Sargsyan seemed to be the ultimate choice to be endorsed by Kocharyan. Sargsyan's candidacy had seemed the winning bid until the largely unexpected self-nomination of the former president Levon Ter-Petrosyan came later in 2007. The pre-election atmosphere was dominated by public disbelief in free and fair elections (IRI 2008). The Electoral Code governing the 2008 presidential elections, and first adopted in 1999, was frequently amended, with the amendments most recent to the elections were added in November and December 2007. Though the amendments included some of the OSCE recommendations made after the 2003 presidential (Khachatrian 2004) and 2007 parliamentary elections, a number of recommendations were still to be addressed. However, the Law on Television and Radio Broadcasting was amended in 2007 to provide further clarity to campaigning procedures. Thus, as in the case of the 2003 presidential elections, the legal framework, though with certain shortcomings, provided for sound ground to conduct free and fair elections. However, yet again the "lack of will to implement the provisions effectively and impartially" (OSCE 2008a, p. 4) caused the elections to fall short of the committed standards and to result in numerous infringements (Bedevian 2008a). The conduct of the elections and the dramatic aftermath defied the former optimism of the OSCE that Armenia's "government is now ready to prevent widespread vote rigging in the future" (Danielyan 2003a) and is "to hold its first-ever national election judged free and fair by the international community" (Kalantarian 2007).

Nevertheless, all the monitors—including the OSCE, the EU, and the US—congratulated "the Armenian people for the conduct of a competitive presidential election in Armenia" (EU Presidency 2008). However, the events following the elections induced the OSCE to review its initial positive assessment, since "serious challenges" emerged that "devalued the overall election process" (OSCE 2008a, p. 1). The congratulated Armenian people mobilized, protesting against the results of the elections and claiming widespread electoral fraud. Feeding on the public's disappointment with the elections and large audiences during his public speeches, Ter-Petrosyan even before voting day called on his supporters to gather at the Liberty Square in Yerevan to celebrate the victory or to protest the fraud (Danielyan and Bedevian 2008) until the election results were reversed (Shoghikian *et al.* 2008). Outgoing Kocharyan warned that if demonstrations were not peaceful "the state machine will counter them with all its power" (Danielyan and Bedevian 2008). The state machine did not wait too long. Kocharyan kept his promise of arresting Ter-Petrosyan's supporters, even if the opposition did not initiate attacks (Kalantarian *et al.* 2008; Khachatrian *et al.* 2008). More of Ter-Petrosyan's allies were arrested after sleeping protesters were forcefully dispersed on the information that explosives had been found in some of the tents (Khachatrian *et al.* 2008). Dispersal was followed by clashes with police, deaths (RFE/RL 2008b), and a 20-day state of emergency in Yerevan. The CoE criticized the state of emergency, which *inter alia* imposed a ban on rallies and gatherings, and *de facto* media censorship (OSCE 2008a). Whether the following violence was caused by the protesters or provoked by the police, or was even a kind of conspiracy advanced by foreign forces as claimed by the Armenian Prosecutor-General (EurasiaNet 2008), is unclear as the sides claimed different reasons.

The presidential elections of 2008 and 2013 in Azerbaijan demonstrated that the authorities had stopped bothering with democratic pretense, although elections had become a force of habit. Prior to the 2013 elections, Azerbaijan's government tried to restrict OSCE's mandate, which would effectively deprive OSCE of its monitoring function (Lomsadze 2013). In 2008 the incumbent Ilham Aliyev reportedly received 87.34 percent of the votes, defeating another six candidates. Failing to meet international standards yet again due to numerous irregularities, fraud, and voter intimidation, the elections further downgraded Azerbaijan's democracy scores. However, an even-greater endangerment of democratization were constitutional amendments which abolished limits to presidential terms, supposedly giving Aliyev the opportunity of a life-long presidency (NIT 2009). Thus, not only did no behavioral transformation happen in that election cycle, but democratic setback became more apparent than ever. As expected, Aliyev ran for his third term and received 84.5 percent of votes against the backdrop of protests during the Eurovision song contest, which the protesters hoped would have attracted international attention to human rights abuses. Despite the ban on public gatherings and demonstrations in the capital Baku, the elections also resulted in protests where about 4000 people took to the streets (Grove 2013). Infringements were even more egregious than before, with the Central Elections Commission accidentally releasing the results a day before the elections (Fisher 2013), then claiming that those were the results of 2008, even if those did not match. The 2013 presidential elections also raised the issue of the effectiveness of short-term election observation missions (Peter 2013; Zanoni

2013) due to opposing assessments of the joint PACE and European Parliament delegation and OSCE. While the PACE/European Parliament delegation hailed the results (PACE 2013), the OSCE delegation sharply criticized them (OSCE 2013a).

The state of affairs in "top reformer" Georgia (Reuters 2007) was not as good as hoped after the Rose Revolution. Continuous large-scale protests in 2007 accused Saakashvili of corruption, abuse of power, and even intended murder (RFE/RL 2007b), since several opposition members were dismissed or arrested. While accusing Russia of orchestrating the protests (Civil.Ge 2007a), Saakashvili announced a state of emergency but eventually agreed to early elections, which were held in January instead of autumn 2008. Saakashvili defeated six candidates, receiving 53.7 percent of the votes in an election that was called by the OSCE "the first genuinely competitive post-independence presidential election" (OSCE 2008b, p. 1), despite some irregularities. The positive outlook was not shared by Georgia's ombudsman and opposition parties, who rallied in Tbilisi after the election. Despite Saakashvili's victory in his second election, large-scale demonstrations were repeated in 2009, 2011, and 2012. The demonstrators demanded Saakashvili's resignation (RFE/RL 2009; Kramer 2012b), while the latter accused Russia of backing the protesters (Barry 2011). Saakashvili did eventually leave the presidency, however, after his term had expired, and he left for the US amidst an ongoing investigation into the murder of former Prime Minister Zurab Zhvania (Interfax 2014). Supported by the ruling parliamentary coalition, the minister of education Giorgi Margvelashvili then defeated 22 candidates with 61.12 percent of the votes. Observers assessed the elections as free and well administered (Ashton and Füle 2013), resulting in the first transfer of the Georgian presidency without an overthrow.

Unlike Georgia, in Armenia the situation started heating up shortly prior to the presidential elections in February 2013. Expecting that in an atmosphere of general apathy the elections would suffer from widespread fraud, one of the candidates resorted to a hunger strike in front of the presidential palace. Understanding that fragmented opposition had little chance of victory, another candidate appealed for a single candidate and pledged to withdraw his candidacy (Armenpress 2013a). Two important candidates, Ter-Petrosyan and Tsarukyan, had already withdrawn from the elections in December 2012, leaving Sargsyan to lead the polls, even if those were often mistrusted by the other candidates and the public (Hovanissian 2013). The elections resulted in Sargsyan's victory over six candidates with 58.64 percent of the votes. International observers congratulated Sargsyan on re-election and assessed that his re-election was generally well administered and fairly covered, even if marred by misuse of administrative resources and voter pressure (OSCE 2013b). Yet, the fairly positive evaluation of the elections was not shared by the public, who rallied and clashed with security forces after the election day and with most oppositional candidates (Armenia.Now 2013a). Raffi Hovanissian, who came second in the election but led the online polls, rallied "Barevolution" demonstrations and later went on hunger strike demanding to repeal the results of elections (Armenia.Now 2013b), which never happened. Armenia's democracy and electoral process scores (Iskandaryan 2013) did not worsen after the 2013 presidential elections, yet they have not improved either, pointing to Armenia's democratic stagnation and even setback compared with the early 2000s.

The incumbents' utility of adaptation to democracy through 1991–2013 has varied from moderate to low—the chances that an incumbent would lose power as a result of democratic elections have ranged from moderate to high. Low resonance of elections and absence of prior democratic legacies have also negatively contributed to the conduct of elections, which has not improved in Armenia and Azerbaijan despite the rhetorical identification with democracy of both the incumbents and the opposition. In addition, the oppositional rhetoric has never provided a chance for free and fair elections, and the opposition cried fraud even before it was committed. The fragmentation of the opposition and its suspicious attitude towards each other and the incumbent not only weakened public trust but also allowed the incumbent to maneuver and win over the opposition by sharing stakes in power, as can be observed from the defection of several oppositional groups after 2008's elections in all three countries. Oppositional fragmentation is especially visible in Armenia against the background of coalitional—even if forced—unity of ruling parties. The events in three South Caucasus counties demonstrate that the post-election period is as important as the campaign and the election day.

Supporting elections in the South Caucasus: ticking boxes, changing laws

US involvement in democracy promotion through elections started with the establishment of the offices of the International Foundation for Electoral Systems (IFES). The non-for-profit IFES "promotes democratic stability by providing technical assistance and applying field-based research to the electoral cycle worldwide to enhance citizen participation and strengthen civil societies, governance and transparency" (IFES 2011). Describing its activities as "elections plus," IFES usually engages *inter alia* in electoral law design, political finance reform, party and candidate registration, civic and voter education, results tabulations, and training of commission and poll workers (IFES 2011). Although IFES receives occasional additional funding from the UN and the EU, its main donor is the US government. IFES commenced its activities in the South Caucasus in 1995 by dispatching election-observation missions and expert teams to evaluate administrative systems and identify feasible areas for short-term technical assistance (Edgeworth and Lansell 1996). The early 1990s precluded meaningful debate and competition between political parties and candidates, and voter education appeared to be of "paramount" necessity (Edgeworth and Lansell 1996, p. 3).

The 1995 IFES Technical Assistance Mission to Armenia was followed-up by a task-force on the request for assistance from the Chairman of Armenia's National Assembly to the US Ambassador to Armenia, to "seek for assistance in the preparation of the election laws governing the presidential and municipal elections scheduled Fall 1996" (Gardner *et al.* 1996, p. 5). IFES developed and distributed a training manual for electoral commissions, conducted seminars for election officials, conducted voter education, and produced a series of "Town Hall" forums. Besides activities targeting specifically the 1996 elections, IFES was developing a universal electoral code and other projects targeting electoral reforms. These activities may have contributed to an improved conduct of municipal elections in comparison with the presidential ones (Gardner *et al.* 1996). Despite recorded fraud during and after the 1996 presidential elections in Armenia, IFES claimed that it had "greatly improved the electoral process and the level of transparency of the 1996 presidential elections" (Vickery *et al.* 2002, p. 1).

For 1997–2002, under a USAID/IFES Cooperative Agreement, IFES provided consulting on the development of election legislation in Armenia, conducted studies on voter and election issues, and supported the CEC with overall electoral process reform (Vickery *et al.* 2002). The IFES mission in Azerbaijan, established in 1998, provided similar technical assistance to CEC and the parliament, and implemented voter education projects, underlining citizens' activity as a building block of democracy (IFES 2002). Under the USAID/IFES Cooperative Agreement, IFES Azerbaijan *inter alia* organized voter education, provided technical assistance to CEC, and organized workshops for municipalities (Svetlik *et al.* 2003). Similar activities were conducted in Georgia, one of the notable projects being the Voter Registration Pilot program which endeavored to address the issue of inaccurate voting lists (Goldsmith 2003). Though the 1998 presidential elections in Armenia were seen as flawed, IFES completed its project in 2002 "with the satisfaction that the country had enjoyed a period of relative improvement in election administration" (Vickery *et al.* 2002, p. 36). IFES initially targeted the CEC. However, by July 2000 "forward progress with the CEC ceased because of the commission's continued resistance to reform" (Vickery *et al.* 2002, p. 2). Among the resistance points of the CEC was reluctance to "provide information on complaints or to advocate transparency of election complaints," "requests for financial support falling outside of the parameters of the MOU [memorandum of understanding]" between IFES and the CEC, and the CEC's refusal to engage "in serious reform work" (Vickery *et al.* 2002, p. 13, pp. 22–23). Thus, USAID's support to the CEC was discontinued, showing rare commitment of a democracy promoter to consistency in and credibility of its rhetoric, democratic requirements, and actions.

IFES implemented a large number of activities, each grouped under six thematic groups:

- universal electoral code: election law reform;
- seminars and roundtables;
- technical support of elections;
- ongoing support and cooperative development work;
- NGO support and development;
- resource centre development.

The involvement of NGOs in training activities and activities on raising aware-ness and voter education have signaled yet again a rare initiative on behalf of a democracy promoter to engage several levels of democracy promotion into the framework of one project, with political parties being "in closer contact with IFES than ever before" during the development of the universal electoral code (Vickery *et al.* 2002, p. 31). With an attempt at cross-sectoral democracy promo-tion, IFES brought together legislators, government officials, political party leaders, NGO leaders, and public policy advocates.

Nevertheless, these activities did not succeed in diminishing "the distinct lack of political will within the CEC [which] governed its actions and limited the possibilities of cooperation" (Vickery *et al.* 2002, p. 35). The incentives offered to the CEC officials were in the form of democratic electoral reforms and capacity-building activities to ensure the democratic performance of the CEC. "IFES directly educated election officials at all levels through election adminis-tration training" (Vickery *et al.* 2002, p. 1), seemingly flawlessly paving the way to more-democratic parliamentary and presidential elections planned for 2003. However, there was virtually no cooperation with other USAID implementers working in other sectors, except a single attendance by an IFES project manager at a roundtable organized by the National Democratic Institute (NDI) in June 2001 (Vickery *et al.* 2002, p. 11). IFES project staff in Azerbaijan participated in three workshops co-organized by the CoE for municipalities and made presenta-tions for the OSCE on its activities (Svetlik *et al.* 2003).

EU election activities in the South Caucasus started in after the conclusion of Partnership and Cooperation Agreements (PCAs), when it sent observers under the framework of the OSCE to monitor elections (European Commission 2000). The EU acknowledges the observation of elections to be "an important com-ponent of the EU's policy in promoting human rights and democratization" (European Commission 2000). The EU has based its decision to send an election-observation team on achieving minimal conditions such as a universal franchise, political parties' and candidates' right to participate in elections and to have reasonable access to the media, and freedom of expression allowing for criticism of the incumbent. By applying these conditions, the EU wishes "to ascertain that its involvement in monitoring is likely to promote further demo-cratization" (European Commission 2000). Thus, the EU has attempted to serve as an example and a possible shaming tool for democratizing countries, and in its democracy-promotion actions has often relied on the OSCE and the CoE through joint assessments and projects.

European hopes for Armenia moving closer to democracy and democratic elections were boosted by Armenia's strong commitment to CoE membership and actual adoption of several corresponding laws. Further European assistance and potential punitive measures were explicitly linked to free and fair elections, since those were the only way to ensure a "place among the democracies of the world" (Melkumian 2003). After the presidential elections in 2003, the US was "deeply disappointed" with the Armenian authorities' handling of the vote (Danielyan, Khachatrian, *et al.* 2003; Danielyan, Melkumian, *et al.* 2003).

However, the poor and heavily criticized conduct of elections did not prevent the US House of Representatives from securing an additional US$30 million towards US assistance to Armenia. The budget cut sought by the Bush administration was envisaged not due to Armenia's poor democratic performance but due to the US's own economic troubles (Danielyan 2003b). The OSCE and the Venice Commission in 2004 prepared joint recommendations for electoral law and electoral administration in Armenia, yet the threatened punitive action did not follow. In its own turn, the EU had initially left the South Caucasus countries out of the ENP, but later included Armenia, Azerbaijan, and Georgia in the policy after a number of recommendations from the European Parliament (Napoletano 2003).

With the CEC being unresponsive to IFES and USAID democracy-promotion efforts, the projects were refocused on civil society and individual citizens. The project Citizens' Awareness and Participation in Armenia (CAPA) started in the autumn of 2000 and was completed in 2004, thus spanning and slightly over-running the 2003 elections cycle. The project aimed to "promote a more transparent, responsive and democratic government by building the knowledge base and organizing capabilities of community members" (Abrahamyan 2010). CAPA was followed by another three-year USAID-funded project called Strengthening Electoral Processes and Administration in Armenia (SEPA), which started in October 2005 with a budget of US$2 million. The project aimed to increase fulfillment of the international and national election commitments of the Armenian government through activities within the areas of voter registration, voter information, and election administration. SEPA considered its stakeholders, to be the CEC, police/passport and visa departments, as well as the government, the National Assembly, and civil society. Through technical support and efforts to increase civil-society surveillance of government actions, IFES aimed to induce the authorities to hold democratic elections.

Pledging to work "very intensively" for free and fair elections, then US Ambassador John Evans stated that Armenia was on the right political track (Danielyan 2005b, 2005c) despite the heavily criticized elections of 2003. The US approved US$6 million to assist Armenia in elections through training and educational programs for voters, proxies, grants for NGOs, and publication of election-related documents (Saghabalian 2005b). The EU, however, seemed to be more pessimistic about the conduct of elections or any general polls, stressing that past elections "call into question Armenia's commitment to transparency and democracy" (Danielyan 2005d) and would substantially endanger Armenia's position in the ENP (Saghabalian 2006).

The EU and the US expressed initial positive evaluations of the 2008 presidential elections in Armenia. However, large-scale demonstrations and arrests of the opposition led both actors to criticism, even if a few days later the US acknowledged Sargsyan as a "special leader" who the US wanted to succeed (RFE/RL 2008b). Several days later, the US heavily criticized the crackdown on demonstrators and threatened to cut funding unless the state of emergency was lifted (RFE/RL 2008c). However, Congress did not approve any cuts in Armenia's assistance budget. Despite poor democratic performance, Armenia was included in the EaP even though "sufficient progress" in the country's democratization compliance with "the shared values, including democracy, rule of law and human rights" (Council of the European Union 2009, pp. 18–19) of democratization was one of the main preconditions for upgrading to the EaP. Amidst popular protests and criticism of congratulatory international reactions (Stepanian 2013c), EU and US reactions to the 2013 presidential elections were positive, likely to encourage further integration of Armenia into the EaP, and possibly prevent its accession to the Eurasian Customs Union led by Russia. As was mentioned in preceding chapters, however, what turned Armenia away from the EU was not the level of its democratic performance but Russian pressure.

6 Parties in the South Caucasus

Do they really matter?

Party development projects

"Parties remain dominant in structuring the electoral process, governing, and perhaps even in 'symbolic integration' of citizens into the democratic process" (Diamond and Gunther 2001, p. xviii), especially in newly established democracies. Strong parties are essential for successful and efficient performance of democracy, enabling and ensuring the capability of the government to address national issues (Burnell 2006). Democratization of political parties has been viewed as a priority in the "efforts to restore public confidence in the democratic process as a whole" (Albright 2003, p. 1). However, even after the establishment of elections and a seemingly pluralist party system, the "problems of performance and legitimacy" (Diamond and Gunther 2001, p. xxxi) still hinder democratic processes, making these parties either pale in their performance compared with their counterparts from consolidated democracies or, even worse, making them puppets in the power games of a handful of powerful elites. Understanding this danger has induced practitioners and academics to realize the importance of stable party systems for democratizing countries and led to the acknowledgement that party-development assistance should be given more attention within democracy-promotion policies (Burnell 2004). This understanding has mainly stemmed from the failure of "Washington-consensus"-type assistance to address the issues of the political society, neglecting "the ability of party politics to channel underlying social and economic conflicts in a peaceful way" (Burnell 2006, p. 5).

US and European organizations rushed into the development of new pro-democratic parties in the CEE to prevent them falling back into a pro-communist system. US party organizations such as the National Democratic Institute (NDI) and the International Republican Institute (IRI) were the first to enter the volatile arena, and the German *Stiftungen* followed, guided "by the sense of rediscovered political solidarity" (Carothers 2006a, p. 69) with the countries that were cut off from Europe by the communist regime. The United Nations Development Program (UNDP) and the OSCE also joined in party development. The main stimulus for this expansion was the opinion that newly democratizing countries stumble over their democratic transitions mainly due to flawed party systems and weak parties (Carothers 2006b).

While interest in party development within democracy-promotion policies has grown, "sub-literature on party assistance specifically" has been "barely visible" (Burnell 2006, p. 8), with "only a handful of articles or reports ... on the subject" (Carothers 2006a, p. 14). The same concern has been voiced by practitioners, lamenting that the "academic literature on the subject is almost non-existent; there are no scholarly articles, graduate theses or books," urging filling of this lacuna to "promote sensible policies and effective programming" (Kumar 2005, p. 526). Academic accounts of party development assistance have been provided by Burnell (2006) and Carothers, aiming "to at least arrive at stocktaking of where the field is and where it is likely going" (Carothers 2006a, p. 16).

The importance for democracy of viable parties is not in the mere existence of parties. The importance is in their function as a channel for the population's participation in politics through their need "to develop consistent policies and government programs," "to pick up demands from society and bundle them," "to recruit, select and train people for positions in government and the legislature" (Catón 2007, p. 7), and "to make the elected government accountable" (Burnell 2006, p. 17). To perform these functions, parties require certain capabilities such as policy research, and attributes such as financial resources and organizational and communication skills. Parties and party systems—the number of parties and the extent of their differences—can have long-term consequences on the quality of democracy and its further consolidation (Mainwaring 1998). Problematic party development can result in flawed interest articulation and aggregation (Carothers 2006a, p. 9), hindering the representation of the voters. In addition, weak leader-centered parties without clear programming do not allocate sufficient time to voter education, establishing contact with the latter only during the electoral campaign. Damage from non-democratic parties could be in the fulfillment of their government function, when party elites used to corrupt politics come to power, selling places on the candidate lists (Carothers 2006a).

Given the variety of problems with parties, some scholars raised the possibility of skipping party development and finding other means of institutionalizing democratic politics. The favorite to replace parties in the process of democratization has always been the civil society. Indeed, many democracy promoters have launched various projects targeting civil society, which is often understood as a vibrant group of independent NGOs that can provide the function of checks and balances, ensuring "pluralistic interactions between highly empowered citizens and state" (Carothers 2006a, p. 9). No matter how appealing, this option is not feasible in the case of democratizing countries, as the idea of civil society is still embryonic in newly democratizing countries. Even if there is a handful of active NGOs in a democratizing country, they usually do not yet possess the leverage to influence the government's decisions. Moreover, being financially unsustainable, they often receive funds from governmental sources or are dependent upon donor grants, which may seem a more independent source of financing but at the same time endangers the vitality of those NGOs once the grant flow stops. Thus, it is unclear what other institutions may have the capacity of replacing parties in performing their main functions (Doherty 2001), making it "necessary for now to live with them" (Carothers 2006a, p. 11).

The sequence of the democratization process may influence the sequence of party development (van Biezen 2003), thus the timing and sequence of a party's activities may influence the nature of its impact upon democratization. Thus, when designing a party-development project, promoters and parties should keep "the optimum balance of roles and functions" (Burnell 2006, p. 20) and timing. Following this logic, party-development assistance should take into consideration the current developmental stage of a party and of democracy in a target country. This would require prior extensive knowledge and would not allow simple transition of a democracy-promotion project from one country to another. Burnell (2006) mentions that an option for more-democratic strategy shaping could be allowing locals to decide the type and timing of a party-development project. Although this may satisfy the criticism of the lack of local ownership in democracy-promotion projects, it also contains a caveat: in authoritarian or even semi-authoritarian states people would be seldom allowed to speak up (Burnell 2006). However, to keep a promoter in charge of its project and involve domestic actors, the project development can be carried out with the participation of local stakeholders and independent experts.

Party development has fuzzy borders: the projects not directly targeting parties may have influence on their functioning. Election-assistance, civil-society, and legislature-strengthening projects may influence parties (Carothers 2006a). Here, the main focus is on the projects directly targeting political parties. Direct party-development projects have the objective of party reform and strengthening. The most common party-development projects are first, assistance before or during the electoral period, helping the parties to develop an effective electoral campaign, and second, assistance to parties on improving their overall organizational capacity (Carothers 2006a). Other direct party-development projects aim to improve their roles as legislators, and instead of having training for individual parties some of newer promoters opt for advancing the regulations governing the party system or for initiating multiparty dialogue over national issues (Carothers 2006a). However, though the improvement of organizational capacities of parties has started receiving more attention, among these activities elections-related party development is the primary focus of most of the promoters, receiving the largest funds (Kumar 2005). This "electoral" bias shows that promoters still regard elections as the cornerstone of democratic processes, which is reasonable but entails the danger of neglecting the developments—sometimes negative—that happen in between elections.

Especially in newly democratizing states, the electoral period is of crucial importance not only for new parties but also for the whole democratic process of a country. This period also enables promoters to reach their targets better as the willingness of parties to get elected lowers their resistance to external influence. Electoral-period projects mainly concentrate on helping parties plan their campaigns, starting some 8–12 months before the voting day (Carothers 2006a). These include assisting target parties on selection and training of candidates, preparation of party lists, coalition building (especially among the opposition parties that have related programs), message development and delivery, fund-raising, and polling. Unlike hired consultants, democracy promoters usually do not only aim to achieve short-term results, i.e. election, but attempt to diffuse democratic norms and values to show target parties how the electoral process may influence democracy (Carothers 2006a). This type of project is the most "popular" and extensive within party development because it requires well-defined knowledge of effective campaigning, which is something democracy promoters can easily transfer to target countries from their own experiences.

There is no sharp distinction between electoral-campaign assistance and organizational development of parties because parts of the former—message development and fundraising—are important elements of party sustenance between elections. This type of party development aims to build or strengthen the organizational capacity of the party and to improve its outreach activities. These types of development aim not only *inter alia* to establish explicit lines of authority, improve internal communication and strategic planning, establish connections with social organizations, and incorporate women and youth, but also aim to make parties "more internally democratic" (Carothers 2006a, p. 95). Party strengthening within legislatures can foster more opportunities for reforms as it concentrates on skills for drafting legislation, coalition building, and party caucuses, positively influencing not only the target party but also the legislature.

Party politics in the South Caucasus: a tribute to democratic fashion

Experiences with a single communist party had made party politics centralized on the personal appeal of the party leader, without reflecting the interests of the society. Party formation and development in the early 1990s in the South Caucasus was prevailed by clientelist relationships in the society. Party leaders used their positions for their own enrichment, their establishment as the political elite, and advancement of their own business plans instead of channeling the interests of their voters to the government. Not much has changed since then. Notwithstanding inexperience with party politics, the South Caucasus countries ventured on party formation with eagerness, resulting in more than 50 parties in the mid-1990s in Armenia alone. However, despite such a large number of political parties the ideological division into right- and left-wing parties had been largely impossible (Grigoryan 1997). Hasty formation of party blocs in Armenia before the 1996 presidential election saw unions of former "seemingly irreconcilable rivals" (Grigoryan 1997). Party politics in the early 1990s in Armenia were characterized by the fallout between the Armenian Revolutionary Federation (ARF) and then president Ter-Petrosyan, who ended up banning the ARF. The first multiparty elections in Azerbaijan to the Supreme Soviet were held in 1990 and the communist party received 280 out of 320 seats. In Georgia, Gamsakhurdia's Round-Table Free Georgia won 54 percent of votes, with the communists coming second with 29.6 percent.

The first parliamentary elections to the Armenian National Assembly of 1995 were "free, but unfair" as nine opposition parties were refused registration by the CEC and the largest opposition party (the ARF) was banned (Freedom House 1998, p. 1), Ter-Petrosyan's party, Armenian National Movement (ANM), prevailed. The elections also marked a heavy defeat of the Communist party, which lost 126 seats, making communist rhetoric and potential anti-Western sentiments practically impossible. The Republic bloc, following the lead of the ANM, opted for choosing a non-alignment policy for Armenia. ANM rhetoric against Russia resulted in Russian troops joining Azerbaijani troops in driving the remaining Armenian population out of Azerbaijan in 1991 (Cox and Eibner 1993). Democratization and further consolidation of democracy in Armenia were viewed as the pre-conditions to Armenia's development (Astourian 2000). Meanwhile, in Azerbaijan, Heydar Aliyev's New Azerbaijan Party (NAP) swept through the 1995 elections, which did not correspond to international standards. The elections, however, were held against the backdrop of mutual denunciations by president Aliyev and parties that considered Elchibey as the legitimate president. In Georgia, the 1995 elections were won by Shevarnadze's Union of Citizens of Georgia, with the communist party losing all its seats in the parliament. Thus, the liberal rhetoric of South Caucasus parliaments indicated at least nominal adherence to democracy by the parliamentarians.

The parliamentary elections of 1999 in Armenia were regarded as "a step towards compliance with OSCE commitments" (OSCE 1999, p. 1). Kocharyan's re-legalization of the ARF was also regarded as a positive step. Despite similar programs, some parties gained more votes and a parliamentary majority, while others did not even pass the five-percent threshold. Such a divergence in results was mainly based on the personification of parties with their leaders (OSCE 1999). With little possibility to differentiate between pro-government and opposition parties (OSCE 1999), the campaign mainly focused on socio-economic problems and corruption, without much attention to foreign policy. Nevertheless, the OSCE distinguished four major types of parties participating in the 1999 elections: traditional parties, such as ARF and Ramkavar, following largely nationalist ideology; splits from the original Communist Party of the Soviet Armenia, such as the CPA, Union of Communist and Socialist Parties, and others following the Marxist ideology; post-independence parties, such as the ANM, Union of Self-Determination, and others; and newly created parties and alliances, such as the Unity, Right and Unity, Rule of Law, Dignified Future, and others, basing their rhetoric on democratic and economic reforms and prosperity. The new Unity alliance of the Republican Party of Armenia, under the leadership of the increasingly powerful defense minister Vazgen Sargsyan, and the People's Party, under the leadership of the former Soviet leader Karen Demirchian, called for a democratic society and rule of law, aimed to reduce dependence upon foreign aid, and targeted integration into the international community.

After the assassinations of Sargsyan and Demirchian, shrewd manipulation of personal ambitions by some parliamentarians and further fragmentation of the opposition ensured a majority support for Kocharyan's policies. Against this backdrop, the improvements in 2003 parliamentary elections "mirrored a similar development" observed during the 1998 presidential and 1999 parliamentary elections, with the authorities pledging free and fair elections but not punishing violators (OSCE 2003c, p. 1). Once again demonstrating the inferiority of parliamentary elections to presidential ones and the general weakness of political parties, the official turnout of 52.71 percent showed a significant drop in comparison with the 64.88 percent of the second round of presidential elections. This convocation was marked by major re-alignment. The ruling coalition got involved in "back-biting" during a struggle over party lists, with Rule of Law accusing the Republican Party of serving oligarchs. The victory of the Republican Party was challenged not only by opposition parties but also by those who less than in a month before formed a coalitional government with the Republicans (Zakarian and Tamrazian 2003). In June 2003, the Republican Party, the nationalist ARF, and the centre-right Rule of Law agreed to form a coalition and divided ministerial portfolios. Though in this convocation all parties rhetorically supported democracy, regular verbal attacks and accusations against each other of foul play became routine. Caught in a "zero-sum political game" (Nelson and Katulis 2005, p. vi), the government's objective had been to maintain power, and the opposition's to overthrow the government and capture power.

As in the case of the capturing of the presidency by the Aliyev family, the parliament has also been heavily dominated by the NAP of Heydar Aliyev, marking a fusion of executive and legislative branches. This domination was cemented after the elections in 2000, when NAP won 75 seats amidst irregularities. Polling of the elections, which followed Azerbaijan's accession to the CoE, "was marred by numerous violations and the vote count was completely flawed" (OSCE 2001), despite an improved legal framework. The elections of 2005 and 2010 followed the same path, resulting in overwhelming victories for the NAP, while the results of exit polls differed, giving victory to different parties (Mitofsky and Lenski 2005). The 2010 parliamentary elections brought another major victory to NAP, which won 75 seats, while 38 government-affiliated and only nominally independent candidates won another 38 seats. For the first time major oppositional parties such as Musavat and Azerbaijan Popular Front did not receive any seats. When operating within an uneven playing field (OSCE 2010), it does not matter what rhetoric the Azerbaijani parties support. Even if nominally supporting democratic structures, the Azerbaijani parliament is tightly controlled by the president and his family, rendering the parliament redundant and simply an empty tribute to global democratic rhetoric.

Armenia, however, has continued on a straighter multiparty path, even if not a significantly more democratic one. To some extent similar to Azerbaijan, the Armenian perspective on political parties has been distorted. As if emulating Russia's oligarchs, Armenian millionaires either joined political parties or founded their own. The direct involvement and influence of businessmen in party politics became more outspoken after April 2004: one of the oligarchs most extravagant and closest to the authorities (Danielyan 2006c) established his own party, Prosperous Armenia, which has often been dubbed as the brainchild of president Kocharyan (Hayrumyan 2011). The party leader, Gagik Tsarukyan, had good relations with Kocharyan and to-be president Sargsyan, but not with the media and opposition parties since they repeatedly accused him of orchestrating violence against critical reporters and peaceful demonstrators. Nevertheless, Tsarukyan's party has gained considerable success among the electorate (Nichol 2007) with claimed membership of 12 percent of the population. The 2007 elections were regarded as an improvement and "largely in accordance with OSCE commitments." However, "the stated intention by the Armenian authorities to conduct an election in line with OSCE commitments and international standards was not fully realised" (OSCE 2003c, p. 1). Nevertheless, Heritage and Rule of Law joined the Impeachment Bloc in demanding a recount of votes, and the ANM, which dropped out of the campaign, claimed that the election was rigged by sophisticated methods.

The list of parties participating in the race underlined the fluidity and volatility of Armenian party politics. The largest opposition alliance in the parliament, Justice Bloc, has failed to maintain its unity, and in 2007 its member parties either ran separately or did not participate in the elections. The emergence of two new parties—Heritage and Prosperous Armenia—which quickly gained popularity, one more than the other, also emphasized the fluidity of the population's preferences. As expected (Economist 2007), the Republican and Prosperous Armenia Parties did not clash for power but formed another ruling coalition, which included a cooperation agreement with the ARF, as the latter did not agree on a joint presidential candidate (Abrahamyan 2007, p. 200). Shortly after the elections, Heritage and Rule of Law were the only opposition parties represented in the parliament. The self-defined national conservative Republican Party stressed the importance of state participation in the advancement of democracy, mentioning that "the activity of the state must be aimed at the natural integration to the international community" (Republican Party 2007). Led by a US-born Armenian expatriate Raffi Hovanissian, Heritage stated its objectives to be "the development of Armenia as a democratic, lawful, and rights-based country that anchors its domestic and foreign policies in the nation's sovereign interest and ultimate EU accession" (Heritage 2002).

This coalitional composition did not last long. In 2008 Rule of Law went from opposition to pro-government and signed a new coalition pact with the leaders of the Republican Party, Prosperous Armenia, and ARF. However, the ARF's hardline stance on Nagorno-Karabakh made it threaten to quit the coalition if any territorial concessions were made to Azerbaijan (Bedevian 2008b). Citing "insurmountable fundamental disagreements with president Serzh Sargsyan over his conciliatory policy toward Turkey," the ARF eventually quit the coalition (Danielyan and Martirosian 2009) and joined Heritage in opposition. The opposition has remained fragmented as shown by election of the parliament's speaker, with Heritage accusing the ARF of secretly collaborating with the coalition and blocking opposition candidates (Danielyan, E. 2011). In the wake of the 2012 parliamentary elections, the coalition remained unchanged and the opposition both in and out of parliament was as divided and undecided as it always had been. After the 2007 elections, Levon Ter-Petrosyan and his ANM formed a larger alliance of Armenian National Congress (ANC) with 12 other parties, though failing to recruit Heritage (Melkumian 2008) and not even trying to recruit the ARF, which had previously been banned by Ter-Petrosyan.

The weight of parliamentary elections was mostly felt in Georgia after the admittedly rigged 2003 elections, which led to the Rose Revolution and a string of spillover color revolutions. According to the OSCE, the elections fell short of democratic standards and the oppositional Saakashvili urged Georgians to protest against the fraud. As a result, president Shevarnadze resigned and new elections were held in 2004, largely won by National Movement-Democrats, supporting Saakashvili. Saakashvili's rhetoric left no doubt about his intentions of democratizing Georgia and integrating it into European structures and NATO. While the OSCE praised the elections, Saakashvili lamented the scarcity of oppositional parties in the new parliament. However, as mentioned in the previous chapter, Saakashvili's reforms were not always met enthusiastically by the population, resulting in several demonstrations that led to snap presidential elections and earlier parliamentary elections. The Georgian parliamentary elections of 2008 marked an oppositional reshuffle, with the Republican Party leaving the nine-party coalitional opposition and running independently with hopes of targeting moderate and undecided voters (Civil.Ge 2008c). The vacant spot in the oppositional coalition was taken by Nine Rights Party, which refrained from the 2007 demonstrations (Civil.Ge 2008d). The biggest blow to the ruling UNM, however, came from the outgoing parliament speaker Nino Burjanadze (RFE/RL 2008d), who refused to run with Saakashvili's party. Nevertheless, UNM overwhelmingly won the elections and two elected parties refused to join the parliament (KyivPost 2008). While indicating a lively debate, the 2008 elections demonstrated that Georgian parties value their elections more than performing their functions.

Seemingly in the same fashion as Tsarukyan in Armenia, reclusive billionaire Bidzina Ivanishvili stormed onto the Georgian political scene in 2011 (Barry 2012a), garnering significant popular support (BBC 2012b). However, the objective of Ivanishvili's ambition to form his own party was opposition to Saakashvili's government and his long-disputed practices. Ivanishvili organized popular protests and founded the Georgian Dream party, named after his son's rap song. Stripped of his Georgian citizenship, allegedly as retaliation from Saakashvili (RIA News 2014), Ivanishvili still participated in the 2012 elections since the Georgian parliament shortly afterwards passed a law allowing EU citizens to run for parliament. Despite a vague party platform, his coalition won 85 seats as opposed to UNM's 65, while other parties did not pass the threshold. The coalition involved six parties of varied orientations, which included western liberals, nationalists, and former allies of ousted Shevarnadze. Ivanishvili assumed the position of the prime minister, from which he voluntarily resigned in late 2013 and dedicated part of his time to civil-society development (DFWatch 2014). Saakashvili, once entertaining the idea of becoming prime minister after the presidency, conceded defeat in parliamentary elections (Barry 2012b), marking the first peaceful power transfer in Georgia.

A transfer of power did not happen in Armenia after the 2012 parliamentary elections since the Republican Party secured 48.8 percent of votes. Ter-Petrosyan's ANC became a new addition to the parliamentary parties, which otherwise remained unchanged. However, the pre-election period presented a more diverse picture, emphasizing the fragmentation of opposition and the dominance of the ruling Republican Party, despite initial disagreements with its partners. Parliamentary parties Prosperous Armenia, Heritage, and ARF, joined by oppositional ANC, supported the initiative of moving to a full party-list form of proportional representation, arguing that district authorities in case of single constituencies are dominated by the Republican Party (Hakobyan 2012). Amidst demonstrations in support of the initiative (A1+ 2012), the proposal failed after the parliamentary vote (Aleqsanyan 2012). While Prosperous Armenia from the ruling coalition joined the opposition in establishing a body overseeing the conduct of the elections (Hayrumyan 2012), the oppositional Heritage withdrew from the agreement on the grounds that the main reason of that body was to support former president Kocharyan's comeback (Bulghadarian 2012). The shakiness of Armenian coalitions was further underlined by Prosperous Armenia's gradual move into opposition and sharp criticism of Sargsyan, and especially his pension policies (Martirosyan 2014). The criticism was also supported by Kocharyan (Hovhannisyan 2014a). Allegedly in retaliation, Armenia's chief prosecutor initiated inspections and criminal cases against Tsarukyan's business ventures (Hovhannisyan 2014b). Even if embryonic, these changes may indicate shifts within Armenian party politics and increased attention to the public's interests.

In the 1990s and early 2000s, most political parties in the South Caucasus lacked coherent ideologies or policy programs. Not much has changed since. The dividing lines between party platforms are so vague that even experts have difficulties in distinguishing them (USAID 2005). Political parties mushroomed after the independence of 1991 and were first created to advance certain causes. With most of the parties identifying as either pro-government or opposition, there has been a high level of intolerance to those who think differently, labeling others as "enemies rather than as democratic competitors or a loyal opposition" (Nelson and Katulis 2005, p. 15). In addition, instead of building solid voter support, political parties—especially in Armenia and Azerbaijan—prefer to resort to electoral fraud to gain control of the flawed system.

Weak party structures, often flawed organization and campaigning, and constant floor-crossing made Armenian political parties unreliable partners and fuelled the population's distrust. When asked in 2007 which party would best perform in the resolution of Nagorno-Karabakh issue, genocide recognition, security, and socio-political issues, an average of 40 percent of respondents regularly answered "none," with 52 percent being skeptical of the parties' abilities to deal with corruption (Populus 2007). Caught in a vicious cycle of flawed party formation and management, parties are created to back certain individuals, and the majority of the population chooses a party based on its leader instead of its program. Examples of parties consolidating their successes based on the popularity of their leaders are also present in consolidated democracies, such as Angela Merkel's motherly image and CDU's success in the 2013 elections in Germany (Economist 2013). However, such personifications are confined to campaigning periods rather than the establishment of parties or their platforms. Although the usual rhetoric of Armenian and Azerbaijani party constellations has been liberal, with all parties mentioning the importance of democracy and elections, constant manipulation by the executive has characterized all convocations. The functions and capacities of the Armenian and especially Azerbaijani ruling parties have been largely distorted and misinterpreted at the will of politicians; making the multiparty system an accessory required by the democratic vogue. Regardless of the party constellation and the rhetorical commitment of parties to democracy, the positive influence of external support to political parties in such systems is highly debatable. Thus, greater attention should be paid to increasing the confidence of voters in parties and ensuring increased powers of the legislature vis-à-vis the executive.

Party development: campaigning, recruiting, but not controlling

Party development has always been a more sensitive issue for democracy promoters than monitoring elections or assisting media development. Possible accusations of partisanship and interference in domestic politics make democracy promoters involved in party development more discreet in their actions and statements. Nevertheless, some democracy promoters and their implementing partners engage in party development. Among the ones with US/USAID funding are the NDI and the IRI. Maintaining "loose affiliation with the US Democratic Party" (NDI 2011a), the NDI positions itself as a "nonprofit, nonpartisan, nongovernmental organization working to support and strengthen democratic institutions worldwide" (NDI 2011a). The NDI has been active in Georgia since 1994, and in Armenia and Azerbaijan since 1995. With a goal to assist "main political parties on long-term organizational development" (NDI 2011b), the NDI has worked on political-party building, including candidate selection, polling, platform development, and public outreach. In Azerbaijan, NDI's main role has been in monitoring elections and civil-society development through community outreach. Azerbaijan's 2011 law on NGOs funded by foreign sources has put NDI's activities under question and shut down its offices (Ismayilova 2011) under the pretext of the latter's possible meddling in local affairs by efforts of organizing a "Facebook revolution" (Fatullayev 2013) and undeclared funding. However, the issues were resolved and NDI continued its initiatives (Radio Azadliq 2013).

The mission of IRI, which as with the NDI receives part of its funding from USAID, is to advance freedom and democracy worldwide by *inter alia* developing political parties (IRI 2009). However, IRI's involvement in the South

Caucasus is sporadic. Having organized several opinion polls in Armenia, IRI has been more active in Georgia, while halting its activities in Azerbaijan, which mainly addressed civil society (Asadzade 2009).

USAID began its party-development activities in 1996 within "a full-scale citizen participation program" to "build the institutions necessary for democracy" (USAID 1999c). Within its USAID-funded activities, the NDI worked with over a dozen political parties and blocs to assist them in contesting and monitoring elections. NDI has worked through consultations, multiparty training, training designed for individual parties upon their request, and election-monitoring missions. The NDI primarily focused on the Armenian People's Party (APP), the Self-Determination Union (SDU), and the National Democratic Union (NDU), but also pledged assistance to the Republican Party of Armenia and other evolving coalitions. However, none of these parties, with the exception of the executive-endorsed Republican Party, were successful in garnering a majority of votes or even passing the threshold in successive elections. Nevertheless, one of the main achievements of the NDI was the establishment of the "It's Your Choice" (IYC) coalition of NGOs, which has since provided voter education and monitored all elections in Armenia starting from 1996. Since then, the NDI has cooperated with IYC in its activities. However, the direct involvement of the NDI in the establishment of the IYC undermines the level of ownership in this case.

NDI's activities within the 1999 elections cycle in Armenia "mainly focused on addressing internal party development and long-term planning while continuing to develop party programs" (NDI 2001, p. 1). As one of the NDI (2001) reports argues, Armenia's democratic parties struggled with the decision of whether to attempt the advancement of limited reforms or to cooperate with an increasingly authoritarian government. The NDI's activities were marked by efforts to target simultaneously political parties and citizens in promoting multiparty principles. However, the involvement of the executive branch, often quoted as the obstructer to party development, was missing, as was the involvement of local stakeholders (Chobanyan 2010), thus reducing the factor of local ownership.

In its 2004–2008 strategy, USAID acknowledged that, although it had provided assistance for political party strengthening, "the very nature of the system has hindered party development" (USAID 2004, p. 31). Citing lack of progress and the environment, USAID decided to limit its political-party development efforts and concentrate on encouraging women's participation in politics (USAID 2004). Thus, USAID envisaged a change of strategy due to the lack of progress in party development, while at the same time not following-up on its limited but reported achievements. Although the effort of empowering women is praiseworthy, the efficiency and effectiveness of such an exclusive strategy in a male-dominated and generally underdeveloped sector is dubious. The reasonable doubt stems from the potential capacity of one underrepresented and loosely organized group to influence a democratic turn in Armenian party politics.

The subsequent projects within the 2007–2008 elections cycle received funding within a USAID cooperative agreement with the Consortium for

Elections and Political Process Strengthening (CEPPS), which the NDI along with the IRI and IFES is a member of. Given the already-mentioned seemingly optimistic context of the 2007–2008 elections cycle, NDI initiated activities in 2005–2008 to:

- Address targeted weaknesses in Armenian political parties and improve their ability to participate in parliamentary and presidential elections;
- Strengthen political culture by engaging voters, particularly young people, in the political process both as individuals and through NGOs;
- Promote a fairer and more transparent electoral process through voter education and monitoring and reporting by domestic and international organizations.

(NDI 2005, p. 2)

Thus, the NDI expanded the range of its activities from party development to improving electoral processes through initiatives targeting youth and women. In addition, NDI assisted parties in strengthening their abilities in competing in and monitoring elections. Unlike during the previous elections cycle, within 2007–2008 the NDI tried to focus on both opposition and government parties, prioritizing larger parties and those that were cooperating in alliances. Through targeted and party-tailored training, NDI endeavored to improve parties' communication and use of the media, youth recruitment, poll-watching capacities, and public opinion research.

The "disappointing" political-party development in Armenia has often been blamed on the unwillingness of parties and their leaders to broaden their reach beyond Yerevan or to engage women and youth (NDI 2005, p. 3). NDI representatives also acknowledge that training is often not helpful due to a lack of receptiveness from the older generation of party cadres, who are caught in between a "mixture of Soviet and contemporary mentality" (Chobanyan 2011). In addition, they have operated in a "disadvantageous environment" (NDI 2005, p. 3) where parliament had virtually become subordinated to the executive power. Though not implementing joint projects, the NDI has initiated limited cooperation with Counterpart International, the IFES, the UK Embassy, and the UNDP, such as discussion of issues and occasional joint events (Chobanyan 2011).

European organizations warned the Armenian authorities that the 2003 parliamentary "elections must be free, fair and transparent," otherwise "it would be a disaster" (Zakarian 2003). The importance of clean parliamentary elections was again stressed after the fraudulent 2003 presidential elections. However, despite "some progress … especially regarding technical preparations," "the overall elections process did not meet the international standards in a number of key aspects" (EU Presidency 2003). The EU was especially concerned with "the reoccurrence of falsification of vote counts, the unbalanced representation in the election commissions, the intimidation of proxies and the lack of transparency in the publishing of the elections results" (EU Presidency 2003), despite repeated pledges from the Armenian authorities to abide by democratic standards. However, despite poor performance in elections and concerns raised by the EU and other European organizations, no negative changes were introduced into the financial assistance. Quite the opposite: several months later, Armenia, along with Azerbaijan and Georgia, was included in the ENP.

Following the inclusion of the South Caucasus in the ENP, the Action Plans of Armenia and Georgia proposed encouraging cooperation between EU and Armenian political parties, transparent party funding, and strengthening of political parties in Georgia. Whether omission of political parties from the ENP Action Plan of Azerbaijan was an admission that working with the dominant NAP was futile is unclear. The integration of political parties into European political parties' systems started with the establishment of the EU–Armenia Parliamentary Cooperation Committee (PCC) in 2004. Meeting twice a year, the PCC reflects on the ongoing EU–Armenia cooperation and produces recommendations on further implementation of the ENP, covering areas such as internal policies, economic policies, rule of law, and the Nagorno-Karabakh conflict. However, the EU had not implemented projects targeting directly the development of political parties until March 2011. The Armenian–European Policy and Legal Advice Centre organized a seminar in cooperation with the EU Advisory Group to Armenia discussing opportunities to "implement successful reform of national parties and to increase party cohesion" (ArmTown 2011).

7   Media in the South Caucasus

The watchdog may bark but rarely bite

Media development

While the influence of civil society on the economy or democracy range from hindering (Olson 1971; Whitehead 1997) to facilitating (Putnam 1994; Foley and Edwards 1996), the entire concept has proven elusive with its definitions inspired more by the actions of donors than by academic debates (Ottaway and Carothers 2000). Civil society covers various groups and associations that include trade unions, organizations based on culture or ethnicity, informal social networks, organizations with specific political roles like advocacy groups and those that are active mainly outside of the political realm, and those that either accept the current regime or want to change it (White 1994). Civil society does not incorporate the formal political society, private business or the market, and can be defined as a:

> realm between state and family populated by organizations which are sepa-
> rate from the state, enjoy autonomy in relation to the state and are formed
> voluntarily by members of society to protect or extend their interests or
> values.
>
> (White 1994, p. 379)

This definition of civil society has largely been associated with NGOs, making the latter the representatives of the whole of civil society (Carothers 1999), which has included advocacy and civic education NGOs, labor unions, and the media.

Though civil society was not included in the initial projects on democracy promotion, since the mid-1990s it has started to acquire a stable position within the democracy-promotion policies of many promoters (Ottaway and Carothers 2000). Its increasing popularity among democracy promoters has also occurred due to the initial institutional incapacity of many target countries, the more-liberal Clinton administration, and budget cuts (Carothers 1999), since funding civil-society organizations has proven less expensive than reforming state insti-tutions. However, a major incentive for democracy promoters to concentrate on civil-society development is its usual enthusiasm to participate in new projects and general lack of the devastating resistance characteristic to state institutions and local power holders. "Funding virtue" (Ottaway and Carothers 2000) of grassroots democracy through civil-society development has become a major tool of democracy promotion, in some cases directed at breaking the resistance of reluctant political elites.

In many democratizing states, civil-society development resembles more civil-society building because the "vibrant" civil society is practically non-existent, largely due to the dependence of its organizations on state financing. Although, civil-society organizations are the ones that welcome external democracy promotion most, they are also the most vulnerable to pressures from political forces. Starting from scratch allows democracy promoters to shape the local civil society to their image and likeness, but at the same time threatens to leave it without its own voice. In many democratizing states the growing amount of NGO assistance has led to a mushrooming of NGOs: for example, in Armenia with a population of 3 million there are more than 3000 registered local NGOs that are largely dependent upon donor funding and are not self-sustainable. Financial dependence and vulnerability to state pressure is endangering the performance of civil society's functions. The ability of civil society to organize and channel the scattered interests of its members is believed to positively influence political participation (Nie *et al.* 1969). Civil society is also often viewed as the watchdog for the government, with an objective to prevent it from dominating tendencies and to ensure political pluralism (Almond and Verba 1963). In the case of a democratizing country, this function is of utmost importance (Weigle and Butterfield 1992) because it has the potential of ensuring a smooth transition to democracy without falling back into authoritarian habits.

The media has long been regarded as the best watchdog of the government and in ideal satisfies the non-partisanship requirement of civil society. It also represents the freedom of expression requirement of democracy and can act as a forum of contestation during elections, at the same time ensuring the transparency of government actions through investigative reporting and exposure of any non-democratic behavior. Democratic consolidation is problematic "if citizens and government officials do not have regular, reliable, affordable access to accurate information about public affairs. The concept of accountability is severely lacking in a context where government officials can intimidate independent media companies into self-censorship." (ARD 2002, p. 30). However, media outlets require a number of components to perform these functions. Democracy promoters involved in media development have so far mostly concentrated on developing the reporting skills of targeted media outlets (Carothers 1999; Trail 2003). They work equally with print and broadcast media outlets, recently paying more attention to so-called alternative media—online news sources, blogging, and sometimes even Twittering (Trail 2009). Assuming that media outlets do not perform their functions well because they lack the necessary professional skills, democracy promoters organize training, workshops, and study tours to transfer their own knowledge. Consultations are often backed by donation of equipment and usually by supply of grant funding. Besides the mentioned, democracy promoters also concentrate on the development of basic media law that would protect private media outlets from governmental pressures.

Although a lack of professional skills and necessary equipment, especially in the case of regional media, negatively influences the watchdog function, and may also endanger freedom of speech, these are not the only obstacles. In most of the cases the journalists do not pursue investigative reporting not because they do not possess the required knowledge and skills, but because the pressure coming from the state and the political society often threatens not only their jobs but also their lives. A relatively small funding can improve the situation of a media outlet, especially in the initial phase of political and economic transformation (Carothers 1999). Nevertheless, it does not guarantee the advancement of democracy when the other sectors of democracy promotion are not equally socialized into these democratic principles. Media assistance is an important component of democracy promotion within civil society development section. While NGOs have the potential of channeling the population's interests and bringing them to the attention of the government, their narrowly specialized character reduces their areas of population coverage. On the other hand, the media has the potential not only to voice the concerns of the population but also to expose the actions of the government, at the same time ensuring participation in the democratic process and contestation.

Article 50 of the 1977 Soviet Constitution guaranteed all Soviet citizens freedom of speech and press freedom, even if the choice of media outlets was extremely limited. The one-sided reporting by the two main newspapers in the Soviet Union, *Pravda* (truth) and *Izvestia* (news), produced the joke that there was no truth in Pravda and there was no news in Izvestia. After seven decades under Soviet censorship, Armenia, Azerbaijan, and Georgia created their own constitutions, legally embracing democratic principles and guaranteeing freedom of expression and freedom of the mass media. Unlike the Soviet Union's media scene, the South Caucasus media environment is diverse and abundant with different types of print and broadcast outlets. Whether these outlets have taken advantage of the promised freedom in reporting the "truth and news" is a different issue. In 2013 less than 15 percent of world inhabitants lived in countries with a free press, and none of the South Caucasus countries could be included in the list.

Media freedom in the South Caucasus: plurality of voices versus legal shackles

Soviet-style reporting and resistance to change in the 1990s and the first half of the 2000s were often quoted by media observers as the fundamental reasons the South Caucasus countries fell short of international standards (MSI 2003; Freedom House 2002). Loss-making newspaper businesses made newspapers closely tie with sponsors and funders (Grigoryan 1997). The low income of journalists has often forced them to publish pre-ordered material. Most newspapers have been sponsored by business entrepreneurs or political parties, and often published pleasing but rarely objective information (MSI 2001, 2002, 2003). Fearing economic—though not as often physical—retaliation, journalists have often practiced self-censorship. In Armenia, several opposition or independent newspapers, including eight newspapers affiliated with the ARF, were closed or forcibly assigned to pro-government factions by the Ministry of Justice (Freedom House 1998). Taking advantage of the criminalization of libel rather than its inclusion into the civil code, the government has fired several journalists for articles not in line with official government policy (YPC 1996). Libel law was frequently applied to the newspaper *Hayakakan Zhamanak*, which had often been critical of the government (MSI 2001). Thus, any criticism of government officials or publication of democracy-related issues was considered "too risky" (ARD 2002, p. vii). Long-awaited and Western-encouraged decriminalization of libel (Thompson 2010) resulted in a new and controversial media law, which drastically increased penalties for cases of libel (Aslanian 2011; Chilingarian 2011). Interestingly one of the authors of the new law, Karen Andreasian, had previously participated in USAID-organized media training (Sargsyan 2010).

The accession of the South Caucasus countries into the CoE raised the hopes of experts on improved media environment in the countries, as membership had come with a body of case law on free speech. However, in Armenia, prior to the 2003 elections, the parliament continued to delay a new media law, instead passing a law regulating broadcast media through a national commission appointed by the president and "empowered to issue or revoke broadcasting license" (Freedom House 2002, p. 69). Following the adoption of the new Law on Broadcasting, in January 2000 president Kocharyan appointed all nine members of the newly established National Commission on Television and Radio (NCTR). The fist decision of the commission was to award the frequency of the popular but oppositional TV channel A1+, known for its news coverage, to an entertainment channel linked to Kocharyan (Freedom House 2003). This move was internationally regarded as Kocharyan's intention to silence the opposition prior to the 2003 parliamentary elections, "blatantly abusing the frequency licensing system in an attempt to silence a critical media voice" (Committee to Protect Journalists 2002). Other media outlets interpreted the suspension of the A1+ license as a signal of the authorities' determination to take broadcast media under full control. The EU envoy, meanwhile, voiced the EU's hopes for pluralism in Armenia but stopped short of criticizing the Commission's decision, saying that the EU is still "in the process of collecting factual information," while the OSCE called for "a more liberal attitude towards freedom of expression" (Danielyan and Melkumian 2003). Among European organizations, only the CoE took a harsher stance on this matter and "accused the Armenian authorities of failing to honour their pledge to reopen A1+" (Danielyan and Melkumian 2003). Then US ambassador John Ordway expressed his disappointment with the outcome of the tender, arguing that "A1+ submitted an extremely good proposal" (Danielyan and Melkumian 2003).

Lost licenses along with incidents of intimidation by public authorities aggravated the media environment in the South Caucasus and forced some journalists and outlets to resort to self-censorship. The coverage of post-election protests was often punished, while attacks on journalists were often considered to be carried out by bodyguards of government-associated tycoons, such as Tsarukyan or Sukiasian (Avoyan and Danielyan 2004; Kalantarian and Danielyan 2004). Due to their extensive coverage of the 2007 protests in Georgia, Imedi TV and Kavkasia in Georgia had to go off the air after being raided by security forces (Civil.Ge 2007b). The subsequent state of emergency declared by then president Saakashvili effectively left only the public TV on air (Civil.Ge 2007c). And Maestro TV suffered a grenade attack in 2009 before being purchased by another pro-government businessman. In 2010, Georgia scored worse on media freedom than after the Rose Revolution.

Ignoring appeals from the EU (AFP 2008), Azerbaijan banned on its territory such broadcasters as the BBC, Voice of America, and Radio Free Europe (BBC 2008). Over the years, several reporters and bloggers have been arrested on often-bogus charges. However, the most-publicized case is one of an award-winning investigative reporter, Khadija Ismayilova, an author of several reports (Ismayilova and Fatullayeva 2012) revealing government corruption linked to the Aliyev family. After the publication of reports, Ismayilova became a target of a smear attack in 2012 and 2013 (RFE/RL 2013k), which culminated in reportedly fabricated espionage charges (RFE/RL 2014e, 2014f).

In Armenia, the much-awaited adoption of the Law on Freedom of Information in December 2003 (fining state officials who obstruct information gathering) and the new Law on Media (removing the obligation to disclose sources) improved the legal framework. Nevertheless, due to lack of proper implementation and law enforcement, in 2005 the National Press Club declared Armenia's state system as the Enemy of the Press, because it assured "the outside world of its commitment to democracy but in reality hampers the development of independent media" (Atshemian and Kalantarian 2005). One of the examples was Radio Free Europe/Radio Liberty (RFE/RL), which enjoyed nationwide coverage through its retransmission by the Public Radio (Khachatrian and Kalantarian 2007). Even though the parliament did not pass the bill restricting operation of foreign broadcasters (Khachatrian and Bedevian 2007), RFE/RL eventually lost its nationwide coverage because Armenia's Public Radio had not renewed its contract. Subsequent legislative changes gave the National Assembly the power to appoint four members of the NCTR. However, the added value of these changes is debatable, given the almost-full control of the executive over the parliament.

The state of emergency decree in 2008 imposed a blackout on independent media and allowed broadcasting or publishing only government-sanctioned news (RFE/RL 2008e). The state of emergency marked the first ever attempt in Armenia to control the Internet as several websites, including A1+, RFE/RL, and YouTube, were blocked. More than a dozen independent and opposition publications were forced to suspend their publication. The vagueness of the changes in the media ban resulted in confusion among the newspapers, and prohibition of publication of seven newspapers based on the judgment of National Security Service censors. The year 2008 was "unprecedented not only for the number of cases of violation of the rights of journalists and mass media, but also for the facts of censorship applied towards mass media" (Committee to Protect Freedom of Expression 2008). The coverage of parliamentary elections in 2012 was largely neutral, with decreased incidents of violence against journalists: seven in 2012 in comparison with 18 in 2008 (Petrosyan 2012). However, physical abuse of journalists without subsequent police investigation persisted (Hetq 2013).

Media freedom in Azerbaijan continued deteriorating, with journalists imprisoned and media outlets raided and shut down as a result of criticizing the government and the Aliyev family (Evgrashina 2013). The refusal of the authorities to decriminalize libel reached new heights when the defamation law was extended to online speech ahead of the 2013 elections, and with the first arrests (Aliyev and Sindelar 2013, Amnesty International 2013). Similarly, violence against journalists persisted and also extended to foreign journalists deemed to be working on a material offensive to the government (RFE/RL 2010b; IFEX 2012). While harassment against Ismayilova may be the most publicized example, other journalists have suffered from government-affiliated structures, as in the case of Idrak Abbasov who was beaten by the employees of state oil-company SOCAR while documenting demolition of residential buildings (Human Rights Watch 2012). Besides physical attempts to curtail freedom of speech, the Azerbaijani government has also extensively amended the legal framework to prevent media staff from investigative reporting (Sultanova 2010). In Georgia, prior to the 2012 parliamentary elections the level of violence against journalists considered sympathetic to the opposition comparatively increased (Kharebava 2012; Refworld 2012). However, these incidents have since decreased, and in Georgia the cause of concern is mostly the polarization and financial dependence of media outlets. Yet, unlike Azerbaijan and to some extent Armenia, Georgia has the most progressive media legislation in the region (FOTP 2013, p. 2013). Very few cases against journalists are brought to court, one of the reasons being decriminalization of libel in 2004.

While control over the broadcast media has been tightening, the print media and radio have been able to enjoy a degree of pluralism. However, this is mostly due to the low circulation of newspapers and the mainly entertainment-based rather than informative programming of radio stations. Given the wide coverage and high popularity of television, regular attempts by the authorities to control it are not surprising. Stations which do not openly announce their pro-government stance have exercised self-censorship to avoid full official control and the government's potential retaliation. Unlike broadcast media, print media has largely managed to avoid governmental control and maintain the plurality of opinions but, often due to financial sponsorship, failed to maintain a balance between critical opinions. Unlike the "not free" press, Freedom House classified the Internet as free in Armenia in 2013. While no bloggers were arrested or social media and apps were blocked, investigative journalism has been fostered through web-based Hetq.am and Civilnet.am. As in the case of print media, this freedom is likely to stem from comparatively low penetration of the Internet (at 39 percent in 2013). The penetration rate of the "partly free" Internet in Azerbaijan has extended mostly to the residents of the capital Baku, however, and provided a vibrant blogosphere often critical of Azerbaijan's government. Arrests and harassment of bloggers, restrictive legislation, and occasional blocking of "misbehaving" websites have earned president Aliyev his epithet of "Internet predator" by Reporters without Borders. In Georgia, netizens have become more active, especially in election periods, which was also facilitated by the free status of the Internet. In addition, the emergence of several web-based publications such as Civil.ge and Media.ge provide fact-based news in contrast to often-partial television coverage.

Developing media: can knowledge help to watchdog?

"The development and long-term viability of democracy" has been the main reason for USAID support for independent media, which "can ensure that citizens have access to a variety of important sources of news and that information is not controlled exclusively by the state or political-economic interests" (USAID 2008, p. 1). Similarly, the EU emphasizes that "a free, independent and pluralistic media becomes even more important and is needed to ensure democracy" (European Union 2011). The US government credits itself with contributing "significant resources by developing a vibrant civil society and independent media" (USAID 2009, p. 4) and naming USAID as "a lead donor in supporting the formation and development of independent media," while the involvement of other donors such as the EU/TACIS, Open Society Institute, the UNDP, and the USIS was limited (USAID 1999a). Although the input of the US government in the development of media cannot be denied, the claim on the independence of the latter in the South Caucasus is overstretched, given the limited progress in media freedom and inability to perform its watchdog function. However, what seems to be confused when discussing media is its actual freedom from external pressure and the professional skills of journalists. Lack of financial viability and a lack of willingness from the political society to allow media freedom have been the main obstacles for the emergence of a truly independent and pluralistic media.

The US government's activities in media development started in 1995, with support given to print and broadcast media to foster autonomy and independent journalism, "particularly where D/G [democracy and governance] issues and elections are concerned" (ARD 2002, p. viii). The opportunity of discussing D/G topics as the media chooses has been seen as an indispensable prerequisite for an informed choice of voters about policies, political programs, elections, and legal changes. Thus, while understanding that the media alone cannot bring democracy, the US has underlined that "without an independent, aggressive media system, reforms and improvements will be much more difficult to achieve" (ARD 2002, p. viii). The EU has also recognized freedom of expression as of "pivotal importance" and has acknowledged independent media to be "a crucial element of democracy building" (European Commission 2001, p. 28). Within its approach, the EU has adopted a broad understanding of media which includes entertainment programs, debates, and print press. However, the media was targeted not so much as the main recipient of the assistance or as the target for development, but as a vehicle for increased citizen participation in politics. The media was seen as a vehicle to promote awareness of gender, environmental, and corruption issues through projects targeting increased newspaper distribution (ARD 2002).

For its media-development activities, USAID implementers have traditionally been International Research and Exchanges Board (IREX), Eurasia Foundation, and Internews. In its earlier projects in the South Caucasus, such as ProMedia, IREX aimed to have "publishers effectively manage media enterprises" and "journalists provide citizens with objective, fact-based, and useful information" (Trail 2003, p. 5). Surprisingly, despite USAID's own research showing that populations largely refer to television as a source of information, IREX targeted exclusively the print media, which had very little role in information sharing. Although a focused attention on the underdogs that may have the potential to grow is praiseworthy, the rationale for ignoring the broadcast media and undermining efficiency is not clear. IREX/ProMedia aimed to improve the level of investigative journalism in the region and mentioned the de-politicization of newspapers (Trail 2003) as one of its main achievements, even if "neither print nor broadcast media in contemporary Armenia can be considered autonomous" (ARD 2002, p. 12). While occasionally cooperating on joint training with other NGOs, IREX/ProMedia did not include political parties or government officials, despite the acknowledgement that "the news media will continue to flounder and function as the tools of powerful political parties and personalities" (Trail 2003, p. 21).

The Broadcast Media Strengthening Program (BMSP) implemented by Internews in Armenia filled the gap for broadcast media The five-year project organized training, initiated programming, and published handbooks as a result of which "local broadcasters improved their self-sustainability, shared news, and information programming, and fought for changes to misguided media legislation" (Canter 2005, p. 3). Within the cycle of the BMSP, in 2000 the Armenian National Assembly adopted the law on television and radio. Together with media representatives and civil-society organizations, Internews initiated a series of meeting with the NTRC and the National Assembly to communicate criticisms of the law to legislators and fuse "civil society and related industry efforts aimed at amending the Law" (Canter 2005, p. 18). Though the National Assembly did not accept all the proposed changes, it still amended the law in 2001 and removed "most harmful and contradictory provisions, such as the limitation on the licensing of television and radio production" (Canter 2005, p. 18). Similar efforts by the Internews legal team and CoE criticism (Kalantarian 2002) managed to amend the draft media law proposed by the Armenian government in 2002, turning it at the time into "one of the most liberal media laws in the NIS

[Newly Independent States]" (Canter 2005, p. 18). Before the amendments, the draft media law had also been criticized by the CoE as posing a threat to the freedom of the press (Kalantarian 2002). Combined efforts by Internews and the OSCE mission in Armenia resulted in further amendments to the Television and Radio Law. Although these efforts did not prevent putting A1+ off the air and did not result in greater freedom of the media, they nevertheless showed that democracy promoters might have greater impact when bringing together different but still interconnected levels of democracy promotion. In addition, cooperation with other democracy promoters in the field helps in giving weight to the activities and arguments, and can use the comparative advantage of each promoter, thus increasing the potential of positive democratic transformation.

ProMedia II established the ground for the Core Media Support Program for Armenia (CMSPA), also implemented by IREX. As its final report claims, "as a result of ProMedia II editors are now keenly aware of the need of their newspapers to grow as independent business" (Trail 2003, p. 1). The CMSPA was a four-year project, extended to a fifth year, that aimed to "foster self-sustainability in Armenian media sector" (Canter 2005) and argued to have fulfilled its mission substantially, contributing to the self-sustainability of Armenian broadcasters. One of the CMSPA's missions was to improve the self-sustainability of broadcaster's through improved marketing and programming. This move shows that, although changing the implementers, USAID attempted to build on its experience and follow-up on previous project results. Designed solely by IREX DC office without consultations with local stakeholders or experts (Parsadanyan 2011), it was largely modeled on another IREX project, Media Innovations for Georgia. CMSPA's difference from other similar initiatives was the loan component. Unlike ProMedia II and Internews, which targeted specific sectors within media, the CMSPA targeted both print and broadcast media and, halfway through its implementation, substantially focused on internet journalism. In its five-year span, the CMSPA organized over 200 training sessions for "targeted media outlets" (Parsadanyan 2010) with the help of invited trainers, covering topics including writing stories, investigative reporting, photojournalism, print and broadcast media management, using market research, and finding new business opportunities. Efforts to make the Armenian media audience-based instead of sponsor-based were complemented by the introduction of a TV ratings system by AGB Nielsen. This was a major development for Armenian media as the advertising market "quadrupled" (Parsadanyan 2011) over the course of the project.

The CMSPA partnered with other implementing organizations by conducting joint training and disseminating training products (e.g. newspaper supplements), with media representatives remaining the main target of the project (Parsadanyan 2011). Thus, the framework of the program was "not mandated" (Parsadanyan 2011) with moving beyond the assigned level of democracy promotion, once again underlining the limited freedom for maneuver of USAID's implementing partners. Interestingly, journalists from public media (TV and radio) were rarely invited to CMSPA training events, unlike a number of small regional outlets with minimal reach. Through its supplements and partnership with ArmeniaNow online publication, the CMSPA also focused on coverage of the 2007 parliamentary and 2008 presidential elections. Election initiatives aimed "to provide comprehensive fair and balanced elections coverage" and "fostered ... elections content, supported citizen journalism, and provided the media sector and civil society with important pre- and post-election research regarding voter attitudes" (Trail 2009, p. 10). Although, several election supplements were published and distributed, those largely contained CMSPA-produced content, without further guarantees that similarly balanced content would appear in the media regardless of the CMSPA's support. The cooperation with ArmeniaNow turned the CMSPA's and USAID's attentions to the growing online media, which unlike broadcast media was left out of the government's control and, unlike print media, was not controlled by partisan sponsors. Although Internet access was still a challenge outside Yerevan, online media was viewed as having "potential for greater impact" (Trail 2009, p. 52).

For CMSPA, overcoming the grant mentality of civil society, fostered over years by international donors, and "locating media outlets which demonstrated commitment to taking loans at commercial interests rates instead of opting for grants was a particular challenge" (Trail 2009, p. 52). Ironically, this grant mentality was not a pre-CMSPA phenomenon created by other donors, but was also supported by USAID itself over the course of the CMSPA. Under USAID funding, Eurasia Foundation launched the two-year Regional Print Media project in 2006, involving 28 regional print outlets in Armenia. Six of these outlets received grants to conduct market research, create and maintain websites of their newspapers, establish distribution departments, and cover issues of local interest (Eurasia Foundation no date). Interestingly, these goals completely coincided with the ones of CMSPA; however, initially there was no cooperation envisaged in Eurasia Foundation's project description. In addition, simultaneous provision of interest-free grants that do not need to be returned, instead of commercial loans, has potentially undermined the attractiveness of the loans strategy and thus the whole concept of the CMSPA, at least for the print media.

With a growing and vibrant presence of the Internet community and increasing visibility of online media, social networking, and text messaging in Armenia, USAID picked up the initiative of Internet media development and launched another bid for a project on alternative media. In late 2010 the Alternative Resources in Media (ARM) program was awarded for joint implementation by Internews, Eurasia Partnership Foundation, and Yerevan Press Club. The program has aimed to enhance and improve access to pluralistic and unbiased information in Armenia by targeting journalists, media managers, and citizen journalists. The turn to new media was also visible in Azerbaijan, where IREX with USAID funding launched the Media Advancement Project, aiming to "defend the emerging new media information space from government encroachment." Building on this project and the dozen Internet centers that it opened, IREX launched the Azerbaijan New Media Project, aiming to develop multimedia reporting skills. In 2010 IREX launched two projects in Georgia: the

Georgian Media Enhance Democracy, Informed Citizenry and Accountability (G-MEDIA, funded by USAID), and the Georgian Media Partnership Program (GMPP, funded by the US Embassy). Both programs aimed to increase the public's trust in Georgian media through a series of training events, consultations, and exchanges with US colleagues. Projects directed at increasing the professionalism of journalists are undoubtedly welcome and necessary, especially in the atmosphere where the public distrusts media. Often these projects work on amending media–public relations, as has been the case in Georgia after Imedi TV aired a fake report of a Russian invasion in 2010, causing widespread panic (Kramer 2010). While all these projects in the South Caucasus have partnered with local and some international NGOs for specific implementation phases, no cooperation has been reported with the EU.

USAID lists the media among "those institutions that effectively promote democracy" (USAID 2009, p. 11). Given the acknowledged power of the Armenian government over political, economic, and social lives, it is surprising that for its 2009–2013 strategy USAID decided to "opportunistically focus greater attention on these institutions that effectively promote democracy and de-emphasize direct technical assistance to recalcitrant GOAM [government] entities" (USAID 2009, p. 12). Thus, even if the previous engagement of USAID in democracy promotion in Armenia without cross-sector initiatives has not resulted in greater media freedom, the decision to yet again leave out government from its projects seems shortsighted. This approach, however, resembles the ENP approach of partial conditionality, when a non-complying state is denied assistance to its institutions and the funds are transferred to civil society, regardless of how weak or government-dependent it may be.

Before its turn to civil society, the EU had relied on its cooperation with the CoE and the OSCE. However, the EU has supported freedom of expression and independent media through the EIDHR, with the objectives that "the media are enabled to operate in accordance with international standards, i.e. in carrying out a watchdog role" and "quality and coverage of human rights issues in the media [is] improved" (European Commission 2001, p. 7). Within the EIDHR (Initiative and Instrument) framework, the EU funded 49.50 percent of the two-year project Freedom of Expression and Information and Freedom of the Media in the South Caucasus and Moldova (SC-MLD-Media). To bring the legislative framework on defamation, broadcasting regulations, and media diversity into line with CoE standards, enable public authorities to apply CoE norms, and improve the independence and quality of media, 17 activities were implemented during 2008–2009 (including the ones mentioned above). This project was implemented after a two-year hiatus in EU/CoE activities in the media sector, which has seen no follow-up activities to the few ones implemented in 2002–2003. Substantial attention was paid to election coverage, yet again underlining the general focus of donors not only on elections in general but also on the likelihood of their optimism when there is an opportunity for power turnover. The 2010 law reduced the number of broadcast media operating in Armenia and increased obstacles for the emergence of new broadcasters (Kalantarian 2010). Despite the assurances of lawmakers that they had accepted the EU and OSCE criticisms (Kalantarian 2010), the bill ignored recommendations of "crucial importance" and failed "to promote broadcast pluralism in the digital era" (RFE/RL 2010c).

EU/CoE cooperation on the media proceeded with another project, the Local Self-Governance Club as Mass Media Assistance Tool, implemented within 2009–2011, and targeting journalists and local self-governance representatives through conferences and training. The two-year project Promoting Freedom, Professionalism and Pluralism in Media in the South Caucasus and Moldova, or SC-MLD-Media II, has a budget of EUR 1.1 million and plans 57 activities in the South Caucasus and Moldova. The project aims to:

> support the development of legal and institutional guarantees for freedom of expression, higher quality journalism and a pluralistic media landscape in Armenia, Azerbaijan, Georgia and Moldova, in line with the Council of Europe standards and as regards both "traditional" and "new" media.
>
> (Council of Europe and European Union 2011)

By establishing the Civil Society Forum within the EaP and the EED, the EU directly focused on the media. Among more than 100 applications, the "unsupported" Meydan TV from Azerbaijan was selected in September 2013 as the first to prepare for the coverage of presidential elections in Azerbaijan in October 2013 and to "better balance the range of information and thus help foster a constructive debate" (Pomianowski in EED 2013). Interestingly, in none of its two brief communications (EED 2013; ENPI Info 2013) does the EED mention that Meydan TV is actually an Internet television venture run by dissident Azeri bloggers from a five-square meter studio in Berlin (Dzvelishvili 2013; von der Decken 2013). The operation of Meydan TV from Germany is explained by the objective of protecting the infrastructure from the interference of the Azeri government (Mil in Dzvelishvili 2013). The effectiveness of the approach of funding media outlets outside of the target country is still to be seen, given that the 54 percent Internet penetration rate is largely due to users concentrated in the capital. However, Meydan TV has received a chance to expose the rigged elections of 2013 (Dempsey 2013b).

Conclusions to Part III

Russia's long-stated ambitions and its political and energy dominance over the South Caucasus should have signaled to international democracy promoters the need for cooperation. The interconnectedness of different sectors and their dependence upon incumbent authorities should have prompted democracy promoters to integrate local stakeholders into the development and implementation of programs, and to integrate different sectors into their projects. In addition, protracted regional conflicts have called for increased involvement by democracy promoters. However, the reality is quite different. For example, during the years of media development USAID has continuously distanced itself from political society and has not ensured local ownership of projects, which have largely been developed and implemented by foreign NGOs. While the US has cooperated with some international organizations on the ground (US Embassy cable 2006), cooperation with the EU still seems to remain a far prospect. Nor has it initiated joint large-scale projects with other democracy promoters. The EU channeled its media-development activities through its cooperation with the CoE and attempted to influence media law-making through occasional joint statements with the OSCE.

Mere ideational identification with democracy is not sufficient for a full transfer of democratic principles, as identification is often outweighed by low utility of democratic adaptation. Along with growing general discontent with the authorities, the utility of adaptation to democracy for the incumbent presidential candidate and political parties has lowered. Given tight governmental control over the media and the potential for immediate retaliation in case of criticism, the utility of adaptation to watchdog function has always been low for Armenian and especially Azerbaijani media outlets. Despite moderate or low resonance of free and fair elections, a multiparty system, and free media, identification with democracy and its promoters in all three categories has always been positive, at least on a declaratory level. However, the fear for losing the status quo—be that the executive power, a parliamentary seat, or employment in a media outlet—has restrained all three levels when actually pursuing the proclaimed democratic objectives. Those in the media who decided to counter the ruling regime have often been harshly reprimanded. The incentives offered through democracy promotion have not been high enough to outweigh the low utility level.

EU and US democracy promotion was set on the rather fertile ground of South Caucasus democratization, with different layers of society at least moderately identifying with democratic principles and democracy promoters, albeit with low resonance of promoted democratic rules. Nevertheless, the initial pace of democratization halted, with elections regularly receiving negative evaluations from international observers, political freedoms being gradually curtailed, and political parties acting as mere puppets of the executive. Stagnation, especially visible in the case of Armenia, and setback, especially visible in the case of Azerbaijan, demonstrate a range of difficulties in achieving behavioral democratic transformation. On a theoretical level, they demonstrate that, while positive values of constructivist variables and strategies are likely to achieve formal democratic transformation, behavioral outcomes of democracy promotion largely depend upon geopolitical and strategic reasoning of both promoters and their target countries.

Political parties in the South Caucasus may have fulfilled their education, participatory, and even to some extent their interest-aggregation functions, but due to their domination by the executive and their weak party platforms they have not fulfilled their control function. Lack of pro-communist rhetoric does not automatically mean pro-democratic behavior. It is evident that democratic rhetoric has taken root in all three countries of the South Caucasus; however, most of time this rhetoric simply pays lip-service to democracy and international donors. Although the rhetoric and often vague programs of political parties have been supportive of democracy and its promoters, they will have little room to maneuver unless they genuinely adhere to their own proclaimed goals and exercise control over the government. The division of political parties into "liberal" and "non-liberal" seems to be outdated given the realities of the South Caucasus. Having political parties with democratic platforms ignore their main functions and simply serve as presidential minions defeats the entire purpose of their existence. However, noticeable defragmentation of the Armenian opposition in its attempt to challenge authoritarian rule in March 2014 may eventually lead to democratization if civil society and international actors support it, and the democracy blocker does not create obstacles.

The democratization process in Armenia has failed to result in a behavioral democratic transformation within specific sectors, since elections, parties, and the media do not fulfill their respective democratic functions. At the macro level, the country has moved from post-communism to a competitive authoritarian regime. With a democratic constitution, a sound legislative framework, and a general willingness of the authorities to formally introduce democratic reforms, the democratization process in Armenia has nonetheless been marred by a general unwillingness to comply with the reforms. OSCE and CoE recommendations were regularly taken into consideration and enacted after each election cycle, thus resulting in a formal democratic transformation. However, none of general elections has so far met the international standards, with electoral abuse, an uneven electoral playing field, and regular intimidation of the opposition. This does not come as a surprise as the utility of adaptation to democratic elections has been from moderate to low, which indicates the possibility of losing elections if they are free and fair. However, the comparative freedom and fairness of parliamentary elections went into sharp contrast with the increasing pressure exercised by the authorities during presidential elections. This can be equally explained by the higher costs of losing the executive position due to the higher constitutional powers of the president, the persistent fragmentation of the opposition, and the low level of public trust in political parties. In other words, as the parliament is controlled by the executive anyway, parliamentary elections have not mattered as much as the presidential ones.

Azerbaijan did not only stagnate in its democratization, but displayed strong authoritarianism and unintended transformation in all analyzed sectors. Idolized Heydar Baba ("Grandfather") (Antelava 2005) stabilized the country, opening its energy resources to the West; however, positive accomplishments have turned into a dynastic rule of the Aliyev family (BBC 2003). Not only the political life of Azerbaijan is controlled by the Aliyev family, but also its economic and industrial fortunes are divided among Ilham Aliyev's relatives (Asadzade and Ismayilova 2010). The presidential elections of 2003 cemented authoritarian rule in Azerbaijan, which has even stopped displaying formal democratic transformation. Harshly constraining the exercise of human rights through new legislature approved by the parliament, Azerbaijan limits the functioning of civil society and deprives the media of its watchdog function. Media outlets striving to perform their professional tasks often become subjected to physical and economic harassment. Lifting of limits on presidential terms and the complete control that president Aliyev enjoys over the parliament through its ruling party virtually prevents any debate in the Azerbaijani National Assembly.

The added value of political parties has been dubious due to the often-pugnacious atmosphere and mutual distrust among the parties, frequently instigated by the controlled media outlets. Official control and sponsorship of media outlets by business tycoons with close ties to the authorities have hindered the fulfillment of the media's watchdog function both in Armenia and Georgia. With a multiplicity of laws and amendments passed to regulate the growing media sector, media personnel have kept adapting to the changing working environment, heavily influenced by hard economic situations and incessant pressure from political forces. In the early 1990s, the Armenian and Azerbaijani media were also influenced by the ongoing Nagorno-Karabakh conflict, which imposed substantial censorship. Given the regress of media freedom in 2010 also in established democracies (Karlekar 2011) and members of the EU, this part does not argue that limited media freedom in the South Caucasus is also directly responsible for its slow democratization in other areas. Rather, constraints and opportunities for media freedom are viewed in the larger picture of democratization, since especially in Georgia and to a comparatively lesser extent in Armenia legal constraints to professional journalism and investigative reporting have diminished. Due to the obvious interconnectedness of democracy promotion target-sectors, promoters should refrain from isolating their targets. For example, due to the intensive government control over the media, projects directed solely on improving writing skills of reporters will not encourage freedom of the media if watchdog reporting is followed by a potential loss of employment or even physical damage.

The state of democracy in the South Caucasus does not derive solely from domestic conditions, but is the result of the interaction between specific domestic and international factors. The foreign-policy decision-making mechanisms of the EU downgrade the assertiveness of its policies and decelerate their implementation. Structuration of foreign policy through decision-making and representation is reflected in the rhetoric and actions of democracy promoters. The apparently more-consensual nature of EU decision-making prevents it from harsh US-style statements; however, in the end the EU's mild and the US's harsh statements are accompanied by similar actions, thus undermining the credibility of the promoter. Diverging evaluations of elections by promoters may confuse the target of democracy promotion and give the latter grounds for quoting the positive feedback of one promoter against the other's reprimand.

The analyses of democracy promotion within three different sectors—elections, parties, and the media—show no variations in the values of the analyzed international conditions, demonstrating that democracy promoters follow the same strategy regardless of the sector. Even if the value of a variable/condition has changed over the course of time, it has changed for all three sectors simultaneously. While the credibility of both the EU and the US was positive in the first decade of democracy promotion, it later decreased due to unrealized threats and promises. Despite new policies and programs (especially in the case of the EU), moderate (often social or cognitive) incentives and a low level of cooperation did not add to democratization. The low involvement of the EU and the lowered (in the 2000s) involvement of the US in the Nagorno-Karabakh conflict have overridden positive values of other variables. Schimmelfennig *et al.* (2006) argued that material incentives are needed for successful norm transfer. This study argues that if incentives are not high enough and all the other conditions hold at least at moderate value, a democracy promoter should be positively involved in the resolution of a national issue and account for a democracy-blocking regional power.

Conclusions
The damsel in distress and the bully in the sandbox

Democracy has given license for the use of any method in fighting those opposed to democracy (Hassan and Ralph 2011). Even if the second president Bush has fully availed himself of this license, widespread or "domino" (Starr 1991) demo-cratization has not happened. In early 2013 the European Commission claimed that the year would be crucial for democratic transitions, particularly in the EU's neighborhood (European Commission 2013). No doubt, the year 2013 was crucial: not for democratization but for setbacks. Apart from the dubious demo-cratization impact of the Arab Spring in the Southern neighborhood and espe-cially Egypt, the Eastern neighborhood offered its own shocks. The sudden turn of Armenia in September and Ukraine in November 2013 from long-negotiated Association Agreements with the EU in favor of the Russian-led Eurasian Customs Union has demonstrated that not only European foreign policy but the entire democracy-promotion venture is in distress. Moreover, continued Russian pressure on Armenia and Ukraine through energy agreements and on Ukraine through military action in the Russian-majority region Crimea underlined that Russia would further support its regional ambitions not only by "smart" but also by "physical" bullying. These events further support the underlying arguments of this book and emphasize its timeliness.

This book has sought to examine the outcome of external democracy promo-tion and domestic democratization processes, understood as different types of democratic transformations. In this final part of the book, I bring together the main arguments from the previous chapters and discuss comparative implica-tions for a wider understanding of democratic transformations. The book started out with an empirical puzzle of extensive democracy promotion but limited democratic transformation. In addition, it underlined the lack of an applicable meta-theory to the studies of democracy promotion, even if substantial literature exists on the origins, conceptions, conflicting objectives, substance, and strat-egies of democracy promotion. Democracy promoters and some of their targets have been closely scrutinized. However, geographical attention to democracy-promotion targets has often remained within the CEE, recently extending to MENA. Moreover, besides a few notable pieces, comparison of democracy promoters has remained limited. In addition, most democracy-promotion liter-ature has joined in a chorus blaming promoters for democracy's maladies. Yet, democracy promotion is not a singular phenomenon implemented in vacuum from other domestic or international processes. Thus, with this book I aimed to broaden the scope of democracy-promotion analysis by widening its geographic scope and allowing for more nuanced understanding of democratic transformation and the factors that are likely to influence it.

This study has analyzed the actions of the most prominent democracy promoters—the EU and the US—in the South Caucasus. It has offered a two-fold contribution to democracy-promotion studies. While setting the background for an analytical framework, I have compared democratic transformations in three countries which have long been neglected by the literature. In addition, the analysis of three different target-sectors of democracy promotion—elections, parties, and the media—add to the novel character of this book, as it provides a simultaneous focus on democratic transformation at the macro level of a country and at the micro level of specific sectors. The aim of this book has not been in drawing causal conclusions to show whether one of the promoters mainly influenced transformation. Drawing such conclusions would be far-fetched in a region congested with democracy promoters, and would contradict the argument of this book that democratic transformation is an outcome of a multifaceted interaction between international and domestic factors. This last section synthesizes theoretical and empirical findings, arguing that democracy can be facilitated from outside and that sectoral projects often wield positive outcomes for the target country. However, on a macro level, the caveats are more serious than often anticipated.

Democratic transformation

The framework developed in this book may be a useful reference for both academics and practitioners, since it provides tools for identifying the outcome of democracy and democratization, and, depending upon conditions, prompts specific policy actions. The findings of this research can also be applied to competitive, full authoritarian, as well as to democratizing regimes. Although the analyzed variables are expected to be applicable to other countries regardless of regime, and to other sectors of democracy promotion and democratization, the importance of each variable and its value would be different. Nevertheless, it is expected that within the same geographic region a number of variables will have the same value. Through the application of the framework, I have argued that democracy promotion may often yield to other policy priorities but that it is not a lost cause. Democracy promotion has the potential not only to produce numerous analyses but also to lead to genuine democratic transformation, if democracy promoters base their approaches and strategies on existing domestic conditions.

The book has presented a theoretically and empirically synthetic approach to democracy promotion, which includes rationalist and constructivist elements, international democracy promotion and democratization, and democratic transformation on the levels of the target-countries and specific target-sectors. Democracy has not become the "only game in town," even in countries that welcome democracy promotion efforts, because international conditions created by democracy promoters and domestic conditions "supplied" by democratizing countries are mismatched. International and domestic conditions are not mismatched because the donors are "blind" or the locals are "wicked" (Pishchikova 2010, p. 2), but often because other strategic interests may be of higher priority for promoters, or third regional actors may block the advancement of democracy.

The chances of liberal democracy being exported from outside will increase provided the utility of domestic adaptation to democracy is at least moderate, that promoters are actively involved in resolution of pressing national issues, and that there is no regional actor that blocks democracy and receives support for its policies from the target country. While the book had no initial intention of confronting rationalist and constructivist perspectives on international socialization, it has *inter alia* demonstrated that the two should be complemented and, paraphrasing previous arguments (Schimmelfennig *et al.* 2006), that reliance on constructivist conditions is unlikely to result in successful democracy promotion. Nevertheless, the findings corroborate a rationalist approach, arguing that despite its often normative character the process and especially the outcome of democracy promotion and democratization essentially derive from strategic reasoning and constitute a bargaining process.

The findings are largely in line with the original argument of the international socialization framework (Schimmelfennig *et al.* 2006). However, given the expanded number of influencing factors, the book aimed to offer a more nuanced explanation of the outcomes of democracy promotion and observed divergent importance of international and domestic conditions. Schimmelfennig *et al.* (2006) argued that successful rule transfer was possible if there was a credible membership perspective and low domestic political costs of rule adoption (or high utility of adaptation). Going beyond the original dependent variable of compliance (versus non-compliance), this study has argued that to account for the outcome of democracy promotion and democratization, the dependent variable of democratic transformation categorized as formal, behavioral, and unintended provides a better understanding of democracy-promotion outcomes. Behavioral democratic transformation entails the fulfillment of sectoral functions ascribed by democratic rules, thus making it the ultimate goal of democracy promoters and domestic democratizees. The analysis has shown that democratic transformation could also be mixed, as in the case of the media sector within the 2003 election cycle in Armenia. Mixed transformation is a result of formal transformation and simultaneous setback in democracy. Similar "transformation" is also noticeable in the sector of political parties. This demonstrates that mere adoption of a law or a code of conduct does not guarantee the establishment of democracy nor democratic behavior by domestic stakeholders. In addition, the adoption of a law does not prevent a setback in democracy. Consequently, to upgrade a formal democratic transformation into a behavioral one, democracy promoters need to guarantee consistency in their efforts and follow-up on their activities, without assuming that a formally adopted rule or a completed project would assure rule-based behavior.

Careful consideration of the literature on democracy promotion and democratization, and empirical evidence gathered from primary and secondary written sources and cross-checked through semi-structured interviews support the arguments. The first chapter defined the concepts of democracy, democratization, and democracy promotion, arguing that the merged processes of democratization and democracy promotion produce democratic transformations. Building on the framework of international socialization introduced in the first chapter, the second chapter further elaborated on democratic transformation and potential factors that may influence its types. While the chapter further developed the factors mentioned in the original international socialization framework—legitimacy, credibility, incentives, identification, costs/utility of adaptation, and resonance—it also introduced other international and domestic factors shaping democratic transformation: cooperation, consistency, involvement, party constellation, ownership, and the democracy blocker. The democracy blocker has proved to be the crucial factor influencing democratic transformation in the South Caucasus, especially in Armenia, but also slowing down democratization in Georgia and facilitating autocracy in Azerbaijan.

The empirical chapters commenced with analyses of the democratization process in Armenia, Azerbaijan, and Georgia, outlining the extent of their democratic transformation at the macro level. Chapter 3 introduced the protracted conflicts of Nagorno-Karabakh, Abkhazia, and South Ossetia as contributing obstacles to democratization in the South Caucasus and a major area of potential promoter involvement. The chapter also argued that, due to economic and geopolitical reasons, the presence of Russia as a regional democracy blocker is supported by Armenia's regime and population, negatively influencing Armenia's democratization. However, Azerbaijan's lower identification with democracy and the country's own natural resources have allowed it to adopt a more pragmatic approach to Russia, even if often changing the course of its politics based upon Russia's "advice." Georgia in its turn has opted for bolder actions and more outspoken support for an increased Western and a diminished Russian presence in the country, and its alignment with international organizations. Chapter 4 analyzed the evolution and implementation of EU and US democracy-promotion policies, their legitimacy and credibility in promoting democracy, and adjustments to international and South Caucasus developments. Although both actors have legitimacy in promoting democracy, their credibility often suffers from their unwillingness or indecisiveness to actively engage in conflict resolution, *inter alia* and perhaps unintentionally helping Russia in sustaining its status quo in the South Caucasus conflicts.

Chapters 5, 6, and 7 analyzed democratic transformations in the target sectors of elections, parties, and the media respectively. Since the underlying argument of this book is that the presence of a democracy blocker accounts for the major part of democratic stagnation and setbacks, Armenia has received slightly more empirical attention. These chapters have argued that, despite some favorable conditions, democratic transformation has not gone beyond the formal and in some instances has even been unintended, indicating setbacks into authoritarianism.

Discovering scarce democratic transformation within sectors, especially in Armenia and Azerbaijan, the chapters have argued that it is likely to be due to the dominance of the executive power. Nevertheless, as expected, transformation levels slightly vary within the three sectors. The recurring formal transformations within elections in Armenia and Georgia have signaled the importance of elections, not only to promoters but also to domestic actors, as the one influencing their international image. However, the negative transformation in Azerbaijan is likely to be influenced by the country's energy resources and the lackadaisical approach of democracy promoters to the former's violations of democratic values. While Russia has comparatively less influence on Azerbaijan than on Armenia, Azerbaijani authorities have displayed lower identification with democracy and lower utility of adaptation. The unintended or even negative transformation within parties and the media points to their relative insignificance in showcasing to the international community. The gap between formal transformations—adoption of a democratic legal framework—and subsequent undemocratic behavior is especially noticeable within elections in Armenia and Georgia. However, comparatively free and fair parliamentary elections point to the locally perceived insignificance of parties in an executive-dominated system. This disparity should signal to promoters that increased attention is needed beyond elections and that, even if elections become free and fair, democracy would not function properly without viable political parties and civil society. Even though this is a logical and not a groundbreaking argument, it seems it has not yet received much attention from promoters.

The countries of the South Caucasus have become telling examples of how elections on their own cannot guarantee the establishment of democracy. Within more than two decades of democratization, the South Caucasus countries have developed into hybrid regimes ranging from a nourishing democracy in Georgia, competitive authoritarianism in Armenia, and consolidated authoritarianism in Azerbaijan. In the case of Armenia, competition is often real but unfair, even if legal means exist to contest the incumbent regime. In Azerbaijan, especially after 2003, competition is neither real nor fair, and increasingly greater constraints are introduced for an even playing field. In Georgia, however, the seeds of the Rose Revolution seem to have finally sprouted, with the first peaceful and successful power change in 2012 within the parliament and in 2013 within the presidency. While coming from the same region, and often treated as a whole or a singular case, the South Caucasus states display a range of important differences both within their domestic and international politics that shape their roads to democratization.

Armenia's strained relations with Azerbaijan, closed borders with Turkey, complete dependence on Russian energy and military assistance, and lack of any "attractive" resources leave little room to maneuver for democracy advocates. Russia's dominance feeds from Armenia's domestic maladies, especially the unresolved Nagorno-Karabakh conflict, and casts a shadow over the entire regional politics. Involved in the same Nagorno-Karabakh conflict, Azerbaijan, however, benefits from its energy resources, and does not even bother with democratic pretense anymore. The EU's continued, though largely futile, interest in Azerbaijani energy induces the promoter to only mildly scold the Aliyev regime for rigged elections or human rights violations. Georgia, however, while lacking energy resources, has not lacked in outspoken commitment to European integration and democracy, and through its alignment with the EU and NATO has secured amplified international attention (RFE/RL 2014g). Such EU-enthusiasm may have resulted in a number of trade sanctions from Russia and diversionary politics in South Ossetia and Abkhazia, but it also has considerably diminished the influence of Russia's democracy blocking in Georgia. These findings also demonstrate that, besides the mentioned influencing factors, domestic assets that are attractive for the promoter can serve as a bargaining chip for autocracy-prone domestic stakeholders.

The high rhetorical identification of Armenia and Georgia, and the moderate-to-high identification of Azerbaijan with democracy and the legitimacy of democracy promoters could not compensate for the low utility of adaptation to democracy. The variable of party constellation was important in the research of Schimmelfennig *et al.* (2006). Yet, due to the parties' dependence upon the executive, party constellation appeared to be a non-variable in the South Caucasus context, at least until the 2012 Georgian parliamentary elections. This dependence has not been overcome by their pro-democratic proclamations. The executive-dominated Republican Party of Armenia has created coalitional governments and has dominated parliamentary convocations of 2003, 2007, and 2012, along with the oligarch-based Prosperous Armenia and the floor-crossing Rule of Law. The NAP in Azerbaijan has held an absolute majority in parliament, while the nominally independent members of parliament have been still affiliated to the ruling party. Political parties in Armenia and Azerbaijan have so far failed in fulfilling their control functions, and their rhetorical democratic orientation is unlikely to influence democratization.

Several factors within the South Caucasus, and especially in Armenia, are conjoined in a sort of a vicious cycle, where the democracy blocker is supported by the local attitudes which are in turn fueled by the protracted conflicts, the resolution of which greatly depends on the democracy blocker. The combination of these factors has resulted in formal and unintended transformations: a number of democratic laws have been adopted but, instead of democratic behavior, democratic stagnation or setbacks have occurred. Post-conflict democratization has always been regarded as an ordeal. However, in cases like Armenia and Azerbaijan, a protracted conflict hinders democratization and justifies the anti-democratic tendencies of the regime. The persistence of the conflict has induced the incumbent regime to support the democracy-blocking activities of a powerful regional actor. In such cases, democracy promoters need to broaden their mission and also to engage in the national issues that fuel domestic support for the democracy blocker. In cases of democracy promoters with lesser leverage and breadth of activities than the EU and the US, cooperation with their counterparts would be more likely to produce positive results.

The inconsistency in pursuing specific democracy objectives and the low involvement of promoters in issues of domestic importance are aggravated by the low domestic utility of adaptation to democracy. In competitive authoritarian regimes, which are usually chosen as targets of democracy promotion, domestic actors have low utility of adaptation to democratic principles. Low utility of adaptation is closely linked to the fear of losing the status quo. An incumbent president opposes free and fair elections as these increase the possibility of losing the presidential position. Similarly, political parties do not perform their functions out of fear of not being "re-elected" or even of being suppressed by a dominating executive. And the media does not watchdog out of fear for economic or physical damage. As in the case of the South Caucasus countries, the interconnectedness of target-sectors in competitive authoritarian—and especially in full authoritarian—regimes is expected to be high, with obvious dominance by the executive. Thus, democracy promotion needs to be simultaneously cross-sectoral, offering material incentives for democratic transformation.

Cross-sectoral promotion can be achieved through cooperation between promoters regardless of their own leverage, since it will also eliminate current negligence or competition occurring between promoters and among their implementers. Occasionally leaving the impression of two differently positioned actors, the EU and the US follow approaches to democracy promotion which are characterized by shaky credibility, lackadaisical involvement in national issues, and general disinterest in cooperation with each other. What makes the EU and the US differ are their development mechanisms for democracy promotion. Effectiveness apart, the US's statehood has provided it with an opportunity to polish its mechanisms, while the EU has been torn between the strategic interests of its member states, piling policies up instead of improving them. Even if the US may also seem a divided actor, its different approaches to the same policy are often ascribed to its strategic interests rather than the incoherence of its policymaking, as is the case with the EU. Another striking difference is the sector-encompassing and widely marketed approach of the US in comparison with the EU's over-bureaucratic and low-profile image. While neither of the approaches boasts efficiency or effectiveness, the strictly normative pledge of the EU seems to have lost its appeal and influence, necessitating a more consistent and strategic approach, especially if democracy is promoted for the sake of another agenda.

Global trends and what to do?

Given the low level of democratic transformation on a global scale and notorious democratic backlashes, promotion of democracy seems to be an ungrateful and daunting task. However, international actors that have vowed to promote democracy and have launched their worldwide activities need to sooner or later show results not only to target countries but also to their own taxpayers, who sponsor these policies. Democracy promoters have often been blamed for cooperating with autocratic regimes and preferring security and stability to democracy. The

Arab Spring has induced the EU to attempt to "revolutionize" the ENP and admit that before "it has focused too much on stability at the expense of other objectives and, more problematic, at the expense of our [the EU's] values" (Füle 2011). Nevertheless, even if the values are not inseparable from interests, still democracy promoters often "do business with governments that do not respect the rights we [the US] hold most dear" (Rice 2013). However, promoting democracy for the sake of another agenda should not unconditionally render democracy promotion ineffective. Regular critiques that democracy promotion is merely a pretext for the advancement of more mercantilist interests should not obstruct improvement of the actual policy. Even if democracy promotion is a tool for achieving other objectives, such as neutralizing terrorist groups or exerting control over natural resources, democracy promoters need to show positive results; otherwise, their primary interests would also be compromised. With seemingly non-orchestrated protests having swept MENA and large-scale protests against the reversal of Ukraine from the EU, more engaged and well-planned democracy promotion may be not only timely but also promising.

Democracy blocking in one form or the other is not only the prerogative of Russia but also other states such as China and Saudi Arabia, which while not promoting certain a type of regime may still become attractive for disillusioned and underdeveloped countries. However, while economic underdevelopment is often blamed on local governments, disillusionment with democracy stems from promoters' inactiveness, reactionary strategies, or counter-democratic actions. The EU and the US currently do not match either the level of political prowess—borderline blackmail—or the type of economic pressure employed by Russia in its "near abroad." Moreover, both the EU and the US have seemed wary of engaging in open confrontation with Russia, even if some domestic actors have flamboyantly encouraged it (Boerma 2014; Seher 2014). While a far-reaching confrontation with a democracy blocker may potentially be ill-advised, the necessity of cooperation for a goal proclaimed as common seems only logical, be it for the sake of democracy or for the advancement of other common interests. Bridging transatlantic gaps, widened by NSA snooping, may facilitate cooperation and send a strong normative message to both the civil societies and oppositional political parties in transitional states. Cooperation is especially important given that potential democracy blockers often reinforce each other's actions and reward "defecting" democratizees (Armenpress 2013b). If concerted and credible democracy promotion is not feasible, and advancing of democracy is always to depend upon the fancy of local autocrats, then it may be less costly to simply abandon the venture, even if that may risk annulling more than two decades of democratic rhetoric.

This book started out by quoting Sevareid that "democracy is not a free ride. It demands more of each of us than any other arrangement." While democracy-promotion projects undoubtedly produce some positive outputs on the micro level of individual projects, though not even sectors, it is the macro result of democratization which so far seems unattainable. Expanding beyond strict sector-confined limits is likely to result in greater democratic transformation.

Local stakeholders should not be waiting for democracy to be delivered on a silver platter but should rather act, as in the case of the Rose Revolution or subsequent demonstrations in Georgia. While Georgia seems to be finally on the way to behavioral democratic transformation, this process should be further fostered by democracy promoters and checked by the civil society. However, Armenia and especially Azerbaijan still have a long and winding road, with Nagorno-Karabakh conflict as the main stumbling block. In the case of Armenia, wary of another armed conflict, increased involvement in the resolution of the Nagorno-Karabakh conflict is likely to increase local support for democracy and promoted policies, not only rhetorically but also behaviorally, at the same time swaying the mediation torch from Russia.

Bibliography

A1+, 2012. "ARF, ANC, Heritage united [HJD, HAK, Zharangutyuny miatsan]." A1+. Available from: www.a1plus.am/56017.html [accessed February 27, 2014].

Abbasov, S., 2012. "Azerbaijan: Signs Point to Russia's Departure from Gabala Radar Base." EurasiaNet, July 25.

Abkhaz Government, 2010. "Abkhaz Delegation Renounces Its Participation in Geneva Talks on Security and Stability in the Caucasus." Official Site of the President of the Republic of Abkhazia. Available from: www.abkhaziagov.org/en/news/detail.php?ID=32028 [accessed December 10, 2012].

Abrahamyan, G., 2007. "Armenia: A Coalition Government Amidst Conflict." EurasiaNet.org. Available from: www.eurasianet.org/departments/insight/articles/eav060707a.shtml [accessed April 15, 2011].

Abrahamyan, O., 2010. IFES Deputy Head of Office. Interview with author, June, Yerevan, Armenia.

Abushov, K., 2009. "Policing the Near Abroad: Russian Foreign Policy in the South Caucasus." *Australian Journal of International Affairs*, 63 (2), pp. 187–212.

Achen, C.H. and Snidal, D., 1989. "Rational Deterrence Theory and Comparative Case Studies." *World Politics*, 41 (2), pp. 143–169.

ADAM, 2010. "Public Opinion Survey On Moral And Social Stance Of Azerbaijani Youth." Open Society Institute Assistance Foundation. Available from: www.osi.az/index.php?option=com_content&task=view&id=2155&Itemid=449 [accessed December 22, 2012].

Adcock, R. and Collier, D., 2001. "Measurement Validity: A Shared Standard for Qualitative and Quantitative Research." *The American Political Science Review*, 95 (3), pp. 529–546.

AFP, 2008. "EU warns Azerbaijan over its BBC, Voice of America ban." Google News. Available from: www.google.com/hostednews/afp/article/ALeqM5h81AFsbwdZ-VF8FdHskagnY567lA?hl=en&docId=081231190409.vu8zjqc9 [accessed February 27, 2014].

Ahlin, U., Amato, G., and Azad, U., 2004. "An Open Letter to the Heads of State and Government Of the European Union and NATO." *The Moscow Times*, September 30. Available from: www.themoscowtimes.com/opinion/article/an-open-letter-to-the-heads-of-state-and-government-of-the-european-union-and-nato/228041.html [accessed May 15, 2014].

Albright, M., 2003. "A Message from NDI Chairman." Available from: www.ndi.org/files/1661_ww_ndireport_fall2003.pdf [accessed May 16, 2014].

Alcaro, R., 2012. "Vox populi, vox Dei: Europe's Obamania relies on substance, not fiction." Transworld Op-Ed. Available from: www.transworld-fp7.eu/?p=979 [accessed November 20, 2013].

Aleqsanyan, M., 2012. "The proposal of 100% proportional representation failed [Haryur tokosanots hamamasnakan yntrakargi arajarky merjvec]." Human Rights Armenia. Available from: http://hra.am/hy/events/2012/03/01/elections [accessed February 27, 2014].

Aliyev, K. and Sindelar, D., 2013. "In Azerbaijan, Bank Tied To EBRD Breaks Seal On Controversial Libel Law." Radio Free Europe/Radio Liberty. Available from: www.rferl.org/content/azerbaijan-ebrd-libel-law/25082305.html [accessed February 28, 2014].

AlJazeera, 2013. "Bolivia president expels US aid agency." AlJazeera. Available from: www.aljazeera.com/news/americas/2013/05/201351224153629879.html [accessed November 21, 2013].

Almond, G.A. and Verba, S., 1963. *The Civic Culture: Political Attitudes and Democracy in Five Nations*. Princeton, N.J.: Princeton University Press.

Ambrosio, T., 2009. *Authoritarian Backlash: Russian Resistance to Democratization in the Former Soviet Union*. Farnham: Ashgate.

Amnesty International, 2013. "Azerbaijan criminalizes free speech online ahead of elections." Amnesty International. Available from: www.amnesty.org/en/for-media/press-releases/azerbaijan-criminalizes-free-speech-online-ahead-elections-2013-05-15 [accessed February 28, 2014].

ANCA, 2010. *Legislative History of U.S. Assistance to Nagorno Karabakh*. Washington DC: Armenian National Committee of America.

Andrews, D.M., 2005. *The Atlantic Alliance Under Stress: US–European Relations after Iraq*. Cambridge: Cambridge University Press.

Annenberg School of Communication, 2007. *Measuring Press Freedom and Democracy: Methodologies, Uses, and Impact*. Philadelphia: University of Pennsylvania.

Antelava, N., 2005. "Dead leader still influences Azeris." BBC, November 1.

Arbatova, N., 2006. "Stanut li strani SNG yablokom razdora v otnosheniax Rossii i ES?" *Mirovaya ekonomika i mezhdunarodnie otnoshenia*, 1 (6), pp. 15–20.

ARD, 2002. *Democracy and Governance Assessment of Armenia*. USAID Armenia.

ARKA, 2013a. "In 2014 SCRR plans on investing AMD 7,5 bln into modernization of Armenia's infrastructure [YUKZHD planiruet investirovat v 2014 godu 7,5 mldr dramov na modernizatsiyu infrastruktur v Armenii]." *ARKA*. Available from: http://arka.am/ru/news/interview/yukzhd_planiruet_investirovat_v_2014_godu_7_5_mlrd_dramov_na_modernizatsiyu_infrastruktur_v_armenii/ [accessed September 15, 2013].

ARKA, 2013b. "RF and Armenia will work on prolonging the term of utilizaion of the Armenian NPP—Putin [RF i Armenia budut rabotat nad prodleniem sroka ekspluatatsii Armianskoi AES-Putin]." ARKA. Available from: http://arka.am/ru/news/economy/rf_i_armeniya_budut_rabotat_nad_prodleniem_sroka_ekspluatatsii_armyanskoy_aes_putin/ [accessed September 15, 2013].

Armenia.Now, 2013a. "Oskanian backs Hovannisian's protest, calls for resignation of government." ArmeniaNow.com. Available from: www.armenianow.com/vote_2013/44622/armvote13_vartan_oskanian_raffi_hovannisian [accessed February 25, 2014].

Armenia.Now, 2013b. "Hovannisian ends hunger strike, attends Easter Service." ArmeniaNow.com. Available from: www.armenianow.com/vote_2013/44905/armvote13_raffi_hovannisian_quits_hunger_strike [accessed February 25, 2014].

Armenpress, 2013a. "Paruyr Hayrikyan handed the open letter on having joint candidate to Andrias Ghukasyan." Armenpress. Available from: http://armenpress.am/eng/news/707816/paruyr-hayrikyan-handed-the-open-letter-on-having-joint-candidate-to-andrias-ghukasyan.html [accessed February 25, 2014].

Armenpress, 2013b. "China to provide 50 million yuan military aid to Armenia." Armenpress. Available from: http://armenpress.am/eng/news/745193/ [accessed March 3, 2014].

ArmTown, 2011. "Armenian Political Parties to Integrate in the EU Political Families." Available from: www.armtown.com/news/en/lra/20110318/21092/ [accessed November 23, 2011].

Asadzade, U., 2009. "Why is IRI leaving Azerbaijan? [Pochemu IRI pokidaet Azerbaijan?]." Radio Azadliq. Available from: www.radioazadlyg.org/content/article/2178336.html [accessed February 28, 2014].

Asadzade, U. and Ismayilova, K., 2010. "Aliyev's Azerbaijani Empire Grows, As Daughter Joins The Game." Radio Free Europe/Radio Liberty. Available from: www.rferl.org/content/Aliyevs_Azerbaijani_Empire_Grows_As_Daughter_Joins_The_Game/2127137.html [accessed February 26, 2014].

Ashton, C. and Füle, Š., 2013. "Statement by EU High Representative Catherine Ashton and Commissioner Štefan Füle on the results of Georgia's presidential election." European Union. Available from: http://europa.eu/rapid/press-release_MEMO-13–940_en.htm?locale=en [accessed February 25, 2014].

Aslanian, K., 2011. "Yerevan Daily Hit By Another Libel Suit." Radio Free Europe/Radio Liberty. Available from: www.azatutyun.am/content/article/24322626.html [accessed November 8, 2011].

Associated Press, 2006. "U.S. Officials Upbeat On Karabakh Peace." Radio Free Europe/Radio Liberty. Available from: www.azatutyun.am/content/article/1582028.html [accessed June 3, 2011].

Astourian, S., 2000. *From Ter-Petrosian to Kocharian: Leadership Change in Armenia.* Berkeley Program in Soviet and Post-Soviet Studies, Institute of Slavic, East European, and Eurasian Studies, Berkeley: UC Berkeley.

AtomInfo, 2012. "The issue of prolonging the utilization of the Armenian NPP will be decided in 2013 [Vopros o prodlenii sroka ekspluatatsii Armianskoi AES budet reshen v 2013]." AtomInfo. Available from: www.atominfo.ru/newsc/l0591.htm [accessed September 15, 2013].

Atshemian, N. and Kalantarian, K., 2005. "Armenian State Declared 'Enemy Of Press.'" Radio Free Europe/Radio Liberty. Available from: www.azatutyun.am/content/article/1576792.html [accessed June 22, 2011].

Averre, D., 2011. "Competing Rationalities: Russia, the EU and the 'Shared Neighbourhood'" in Gower, J. and Timmins, G. (eds), *The European Union, Russia and the Shared Neighbourhood.* London: Routledge.

Avetisian, T., 2011a. "Armenian Gas Operator Approves Price Discount For Poor." Radio Free Europe/Radio Liberty. Available from: www.azatutyun.am/content/article/16798185.html [accessed May 4, 2011].

Avetisian, T., 2011b. "Armenia, EU Hail 'Good Progress' Towards Association Accord." Radio Free Europe/Radio Liberty. Available from: www.azatutyun.am/content/article/3542117.html [accessed November 7, 2011].

Avetisian, T., 2011c. "EU Envoy Warns Of Karabakh Escalation." Radio Free Europe/Radio Liberty. Available from: www.azatutyun.am/content/article/2319998.html [accessed May 12, 2011].

Avoyan, S., 2003. "Demirchian Rallies Supporters, Claims Victory." Radio Free Europe/Radio Liberty. Available from: www.azatutyun.am/content/article/1570905.html [accessed April 8, 2011].

Avoyan, S. and Danielyan, E., 2004. "Tycoon Denies Role in Journalist Car Bombing." Radio Free Europe/Radio Liberty. Available from: www.azatutyun.am/content/article/1574858.html [accessed April 20, 2011].

Aysor, 2008. "Russia's delivery of C-300 rockets to Azerbaijan—just a bluff." Available from: www.aysor.am/en/news/2010/08/02/c300/ [accessed September 21, 2011].

Babayan, N., 2009. "European Neighbourhood Policy in Armenia: On the Road to Failure or Success." *CEU Political Science Journal*, 03, pp. 358–388.

Babayan, N., 2010. "Now Who Answers the Phone in Europe? Cooperation within the CFSP after the Enlargements and the Lisbon Treaty." *Caucasian Review of International Affairs*, 4 (4), pp. 354–367.

Babayan, N., 2011. "Armenia: Why the European Neighbourhood Policy has failed." *FRIDE Policy Brief*, 68.

Babayan, N., 2012a. *Wandering in Twilight? Democracy Promotion by the EU and the USA and Democratization in Armenia*. Trento: University of Trento.

Babayan, N., 2012b. "Fear or Love Thy Neighbour? EU Framework of Fostering Regional Cooperation in the South Caucasus." *Journal of Contemporary European Research*, 8 (1), pp. 40–56.

Babayan, N., 2013a. "The South Caucasus" in Baracani, E. and di Quirico, R. (eds), *Alternatives to Democracy: Non-Democratic Regimes and the Limits of Democracy Diffusion in Eurasia*. European Press Academic Publishing.

Babayan, N., 2013b. *Home-made Adjustments? US Human Rights and Democracy Promotion*. TRANSWORLD Working Paper No. 20.

Babayan, N. and Braghiroli, S., 2011. "Il Buono, Il Brutto, Il Cattivo? Assessing Imperialist Aspirations of the EU, Russia and the US." *Central European Journal of International and Security Studies*, 5 (2), pp. 79–104.

Babayan, N. and Huber, D., 2012. "Motioned, Debated, Agreed? Human Rights and Democracy Promotion in International Affairs." *TRANSWORLD Working Papers*, 6.

Babayan, N. and Risse, T., 2014 (forthcoming). "We Hang out but We Don't Talk: European and American Human Rights and Democracy Promotion." *TRANSWORLD Working Papers*.

Babayan, N. and Shapovalova, N., 2011. "Armenia: the Eastern Partnership's Unrequited Suitor." *FRIDE Policy Brief*, 94.

Babayan, N. and Viviani, A., 2013. "'Shocking' Adjustments? EU Human Rights and Democracy Promotion." TRANSWORLD Working Paper No. 18.

Babich, D., 2010. "Is Russia selling out Iran?" RIA News. Available from: http://en.rian.ru/analysis/20100415/158599756.html [accessed September 21, 2011].

Bader, M., 2010. "Party politics in Georgia and Ukraine and the failure of Western assistance." *Democratization*, 17, pp. 1085–1107.

Banks.am, 2013. "We should find the formula of interaction with Customs Union, Tigran Sargsyan says." banks.am. Available from: www.banks.am/en/news/newsfeed/7827/ [accessed September 9, 2013].

Baracani, E. and di Quirico, R. (eds), 2013. *Alternatives to Democracy: Non-Democratic Regimes and the Limits of Democracy Diffusion in Eurasia*. European Press Academic Publishing.

Baran, Z., 2001. "The Caucasus: Ten Years after Independence." *The Washington Quarterly*, 25 (1), pp. 221–234.

Baran, Z., 2003. "Deals Give Russian Companies Influence over Georgia's Energy Infrastructure." EurasiaNet, August 17.

Bardakçı, M., 2010. "EU Engagement in Conflict Resolution in Georgia: Towards a More Proactive Role." *Caucasian Review of International Affairs*, 4 (3), pp. 214–236.

Barroso, J.M., 2007. "Jose Manuel Barroso=Political Scientist." Interview with John Petersen. EU-CONSENT. Available from: www.eu-consent.net/library/BARROSO-transcript.pdf [accessed May 14, 2014].

Barry, E., 2011. "2 Bodies Found in Georgia Near Site of Protests." *The New York Times*, May 28.

Barry, E., 2012a. "Jump to Politics Turns Georgian Billionaire Into Public Enemy No. 1." *The New York Times*, April 5.

Barry, E., 2012b. "Georgia's President Concedes Defeat in Parliamentary Election." *The New York Times*, October 2.

Barysch, K., 2011. "The EU and Russia: All Smiles and no Action?" Center for European Reform. Available from: www.cer.org.uk/publications/archive/policy-brief/2011/eu-and-russia-all-smiles-and-no-action [accessed November 8, 2011].

BBC, 2003. "Azeri dynasty stays in power." BBC, October 16.

BBC, 2006a. "Russia Bans Georgia Mineral Water." BBC, May 5.

BBC, 2006b. "Zapret Borjomi nazvan politicheskim resheniem." BBC, May 5.

BBC, 2006c. "Putin Fury at Georgia 'Terrorism.'" BBC, October 2.

BBC, 2006d. "Georgia 'Agrees Russia Gas Bill.'" BBC, December 22.

BBC, 2008. "Azeri ban on foreign broadcasts." BBC, December 30.

BBC, 2010a. "Russia and Georgia in Visa Row." BBC, October 15.

BBC, 2010b. "US and Russia in Airport Spy Swap." BBC, July 9.

BBC, 2011. "Putin calls for 'Eurasian Union.'" BBC, October 4.

BBC, 2012a. "Putin Backs Ban on US Adoptions." BBC, December 20.

BBC, 2012b. "Mass ppposition rally in Tbilisi, Georgia." BBC News. Available from: www.bbc.co.uk/news/world-europe-18228575 [accessed February 27, 2014].

BBC, 2013. "Armenia rift fuels EU–Russia tension." BBC, September 5.

Beard, E., 2009. "Are We Doing Enough? Sustainable Democracy Promotion and the Millennium Challenge Corporation." Available from: www.thepresidency.org/storage/documents/Fellows2009/University_of_Michigan_Beard.pdf [accessed May 16, 2014].

Bedevian, A., 2005. "Armenian Speaker Warns Russia over Gas Price Hike." Radio Free Europe/Radio Liberty. Available from: www.azatutyun.am/content/article/1579831.html [accessed November 29, 2011].

Bedevian, A., 2008a. "Armenian Opposition Cries Foul Amid Reports Of Violence, Fraud." Radio Free Europe/Radio Liberty. Available from: www.azatutyun.am/content/article/1593214.html [accessed November 9, 2011].

Bedevian, A., 2008b. "Dashnaks Threaten Coalition Exit over Karabakh Concessions." Radio Free Europe/Radio Liberty. Available from: www.azatutyun.am/content/article/1598104.html [accessed April 15, 2011].

van Biezen, I., 2003. *Political Parties in New Democracies*, London and New York: Palgrave Macmillan.

Bigg, C., 2012. "A User's Guide To Georgia's 'Neutral' Passports." Radio Free Europe/Radio Liberty. Available from: www.rferl.org/content/users-guide-to-georgias-neutral-passports/24606006.html [accessed December 10, 2012].

Bildt, C., 2013. Twitter, September 9. Available from: https://twitter.com/ [accessed September 10, 2013].

Blagov, S., 2007. "Russian Ties with Azerbaijan Reach New Lows." EurasiaNet, January 24.

Blockmans, S., Kostanyan, H., and Vorobiov, I., 2012. *Towards a Eurasian Economic Union: The Challenge of Integration and Unity*. Brussels: CEPS, CEPS Special Report No. 75.

Boerma, L., 2014. "Ukraine crisis: Republicans say weak Obama policy encouraged Russia to invade." CBS. Available from: www.cbsnews.com/news/ukraine-crisis-republicans-say-weak-obama-policy-encouraged-russia-to-invade/ [accessed March 3, 2014].

Bogdanor, V., 2007. *Legitimacy, Accountability and Democracy in the European Union*. London: Federal Trust.

Boonstra, J. and Shapovalova, N., 2010. "The EU' s Eastern Partnership: One year backwards." *FRIDE Working Paper*, 99.

Börzel, T.A. and Risse, T., 2009. "Venus Approaching Mars? The EU as an Emerging Civilian World Power." *Berlin Working Paper on European Integration*, 11.

Brinkley, D., 1997. "Democratic Enlargement: The Clinton Doctrine." *Foreign Policy*, 106, pp. 111–127.

Brunnstrom, D. and Harrison, P., 2009. "Wary Of Russia, EU Works On Eastern Ties." Radio Free Europe/Radio Liberty. Available from: www.azatutyun.am/content/article/1624457.html [accessed May 13, 2011].

Bryson, J.C. and Eley, N., 2007. *Guidance: How to Compile a Success Story*. USAID.

Bryza, M., 2006. "Caucasus: US Says Aliyev, Kocharian Must Show 'Political Will.'" Radio Free Europe/Radio Liberty. Available from: www.rferl.org/content/article/1069418.html [accessed March 1, 2014].

Bulghadarian, N., 2011. "Armenia, Azerbaijan Report More Deadly Skirmishes." Radio Free Europe/Radio Liberty. Available from: www.azatutyun.am/content/article/24350911.html [accessed October 6, 2011].

Bulghadarian, N., 2012. "Heritage sees Kocharyan behind the joint headquarters [Zharangutyuny miasnakan shtabi hetevum Qocharyannin e tesnum]." Radio Free Europe/Radio Liberty. Available from: www.azatutyun.am/content/article/24553511.html [accessed February 27, 2014].

Bull, H., 1982. "Civilian Power Europe: A Contradiction in Terms?" *JCMS: Journal of Common Market Studies*, 21 (2), pp. 149–170.

Bureau of Democracy, Human Rights, and Labor, 2010. *Advancing Freedom and Democracy*. Washington DC: US Department of State.

Burnell, P., 2004. *Building Better Democracies. Why Political Parties Matter*. London: Westmisnter Foundation for Democracy.

Burnell, P. (ed.), 2006. *Globalising Democracy: Party Politics in Emerging Democracies*. London: Routledge.

Burnell, P., 2007. "Does International Democracy Promotion Work?" *Deutsches Institut für Entwicklungspolitik*, 17.

Burnell, P., 2008a. "From Evaluating Democracy Assistance to Appraising Democracy Promotion." *Political Studies*, 56, pp. 414–434.

Burnell, P., 2008b. "Promoting Democracy" in Caramani, D. (ed.) *Comparative Politics*. Oxford: Oxford University Press, pp. 625–652.

Burnell, P., 2010. "Is There a New Autocracy Promotion?" *FRIDE Working Paper*, 96.

Burnell, P. and Gerrits, A., 2010. "Promoting Party Politics in Emerging Democracies." *Democratization*, 17, pp. 1065–1084.

Burnell, P. and Youngs, R., 2009. *New Challenges to Democratization*. London: Routledge.

Bush, G.W., 2002. "President Bush's Speech at Westpoint, June." Available from: http://ics.leeds.ac.uk/papers/vp01.cfm?outfit=pmt&folder=339&paper=380 [accessed November 4, 2011].

Bush, G.W., 2004. "President Bush's 2004 State of the Union Address." *Washington Post*, January 20, 2004. Available from: www.washingtonpost.com/wp-srv/politics/transcripts/bushtext_012004.html [accessed February 18, 2013].

Bush, G.W., 2005. "Inaugural Address by George W. Bush." *The New York Times*, January 20.

Bush, G.W., 2006. *The National Security Strategy of the United States of America*. The White House. Available from: http://georgewbush-whitehouse.archives.gov/nsc/nss/2006/ [accessed May 14, 2014].

Canter, W., 2005. *Developing Civil Society in Armenia through Independent Broadcast Media*. Internews Network.

Carney, J., 2013. "Statement by the Press Secretary on the President's Travel to Russia | The White House." Available from: www.whitehouse.gov/the-press-office/2013/08/07/statement-press-secretary-president-s-travel-russia [accessed February 22, 2014].

Carothers, T., 1999. *Aiding Democracy Abroad: The Learning Curve*. Washington, DC: Carnegie Endowment for International Peace.

Carothers, T., 2000. "Clinton Record on Democracy Promotion." Available from: www.carnegieendowment.org/publications/index.cfm?fa=view&id=442&prog=zgp&proj=zdrl [accessed May 16, 2014].

Carothers, T., 2002. "The End of the Transition Paradigm." *Journal of Democracy*, 13, pp. 5–21.

Carothers, T., 2004. *Critical Mission: Essays on Democracy Promotion*. Washington, DC: Carnegie Endowment for International Peace.

Carothers, T., 2006a. *Confronting the Weakest Link: Aiding Political Parties in New Democracies*. Washington, DC: Carnegie Endowment for International Peace.

Carothers, T., 2006b. "Examining International Political Party Aid" in Burnell, P. (ed.), *Globalising Democracy: Party Politics in Emerging Democracies*. London: Routledge, pp. 69–87.

Carothers, T., 2007. "US Democracy Promotion During and After Bush." Carnegie Endowment for International Peace. Available from: http://carnegieendowment.org/2007/09/05/u.s.-democracy-promotion-during-and-after-bush/1hyj [accessed May 12, 2014].

Carothers, T., 2009. "Democracy Promotion Under Obama: Finding a Way Forward." *Carnegie Endowment for International Peace Policy Brief*.

Carothers, T., 2010. *Revitalizing US Democracy Assistance: the Challenge of USAID*. Washington, DC: House Committee on Foreign Affairs.

Carothers, T., 2012a. "Can U.S. Democracy Policy Adapt to a Changing World?" Available from: www.gmfus.org/archives/democracy-promotion-and-nation-building-in-united-states-foreign-policy-the-u-s-model-reconsidered-from-the-post-cold-war-balkans-to-the-arab-revolts/ [accessed February 23, 2013].

Carothers, T., 2012b. *Democracy Policy Under Obama: Revitalization or Retreat?* Washington, DC: Carnegie Endowment for International Peace.

Carothers, T. and Youngs, R., 2011. "Will Rising Democracies Become International Democracy Supporters?" *FRIDE, Carnegie Papers*.

Catón, M., 2007. "Effective Party Assistance: Stronger Parties for Better Democracy." International IDEA. Available from: www.idea.int/publications/effective_party_assistance/index.cfm [accessed May 16, 2014].

Caucasian Knot, 2010a. "OSCE: in 2009 19 people died in the zone of the Nagorno Karabakh conflict [ОБСЕ: за 2009 год в зоне карабахского конфликта погибли 19 человек]." Caucasian Knot. Available from: www.kavkaz-uzel.ru/articles/167132/ [accessed September 21, 2011].

Caucasian Knot, 2010b. "Azerbaijan doubled its military budget [Azerbaijan v dva raza uvelichivaet svoi voennii budzhet/Азербайджан в два раза увеличивает свой военный бюджет." Caucasian Knot. Available from: www.kavkaz-uzel.ru/articles/175937/ [accessed April 18, 2011].

Checkel, J.T., 2001. "Why Comply? Social Learning and European Identity Change." *International Organization*, 55 (3), pp. 553–588.

Cheibub, J.A., Przeworski, A., Limongi Neto, F.P., and Alvarez, M.M., 1996. "What Makes Democracies Endure?" *Journal of Democracy*, 7 (1), pp. 39–55.

Chilingarian, E., 2011. "Court Upholds Guilty Ruling On Kocharian Libel Suit." Radio Free Europe/Radio Liberty. Available from: www.azatutyun.am/content/article/24356515.html [accessed November 8, 2011].

Chobanyan, A., 2010. Civic Program Coordinator at NDI. Interview with author, June, Yerevan, Armenia.

Chobanyan, A., 2011. Civic Program Coordinator at NDI. Email interview with author.

Chryssochoou, D., 2006. "Democracy and the European Polity" in Cini, M. (ed.), *European Union Politics*. Oxford: Oxford University Press.

Civil.Ge, 2007a. "Saakashvili Makes a Statement." Available from: www.civil.ge/eng/article.php?id=16229 [accessed February 25, 2014].

Civil.Ge, 2007b. "State of Emergency Declared in Tbilisi, as Two TV Stations Off Air." Available from: www.civil.ge/eng/article.php?id=16234 [accessed February 27, 2014].

Civil.Ge, 2007c. "Emergency Rule in Georgia, News Coverage Curtailed." Available from: www.civil.ge/eng/article.php?id=16239 [accessed February 27, 2014].

Civil.Ge, 2008a. "Abkhaz FM: No Direct Meeting held with Georgian Negotiators." Available from: www.civil.ge/eng/article.php?id=19763 [accessed March 27, 2013].

Civil.Ge, 2008b. "Exact Format of Geneva Talks Remains Unclear." Available from: www.civil.ge/eng/article.php?id=19755 [accessed March 27, 2013].

Civil.Ge, 2008c. "New Opposition Configuration Emerges Ahead of Polls." Available from: www.civil.ge/eng/article.php?id=17238 [accessed February 26, 2014].

Civil.Ge, 2008d. "Three Blocs, Nine Parties Run in Parliamentary Polls." Available from: www.civil.ge/eng/article.php?id=17549 [accessed February 26, 2014].

Civil.Ge, 2010a. "Tense Talks in Eleventh Round of Geneva Discussions." Available from: www.civil.ge/eng/article.php?id=22404 [accessed December 10, 2012].

Civil.Ge, 2010b. "Interior Minister: 'More Russian Spy Networks Operate in Georgia'." Available from: www.civil.ge/eng/article.php?id=22841 [accessed November 30, 2011].

Civil.Ge, 2011a. "Some Details of Possible Russia–Georgia WTO Deal." Available from: www.civil.ge/eng/article.php?id=24087 [accessed November 30, 2011].

Civil.Ge, 2011b. "Georgia Becomes Eligible for U.S. MCC Aid Again." Available from: www.civil.ge/eng/article.php?id=23020 [accessed February 20, 2014].

Civil.Ge, 2012a. "Sokhumi Wants Geneva Talks Format Change." Available from: www.civil.ge/eng/article.php?id=25217 [accessed March 27, 2013].

Civil.Ge, 2012b. "Twentieth Round of Geneva Talks." Available from: www.civil.ge/eng/article.php?id=24866 [accessed December 10, 2012].

Civil.Ge, 2012c. "Saakashvili: 'Lifting Visa Rules for Russia Sign of Strength'." Available from: http://civil.ge/eng/article.php?id=24508 [accessed December 20, 2012].

Civil.Ge, 2012d. "Georgia Lifts Visa Rules for Russia." Available from: http://civil.ge/eng/article.php?id=24502 [accessed December 20, 2012].

Civil.Ge, 2012e. "Moscow Sets Condition for Reciprocating on Visa-Free Rules, Offers Restoring Diplomatic Ties." Available from: http://civil.ge/eng/article.php?id=24511 [accessed December 20, 2012].

Civil.Ge, 2013. "MCC Approves USD 140 mln Aid to Boost Georgia Education." Available from: www.civil.ge/eng/article.php?id=26194 [accessed February 20, 2014].

Clapper, J.R., 2012. "Unclassified Statement for the Record on the Worldwide Threat Assessment of the US Intelligence Community for the Senate Select Committee on Intelligence." Available from: www.fas.org/irp/congress/2012_hr/013112clapper.pdf [accessed May 15, 2014].

Clinton, W.J., 1994. "Statement on the National Security Strategy Report." The American Presidency Project. Available from: www.presidency.ucsb.edu/ws/index.php?pid=50525#axzz1d87NabZd [accessed November 8, 2011].

Coalson, R., 2013. "Azerbaijani President Aliyev Named Corruption's 'Person Of The Year.'" Radio Free Europe/Radio Liberty. Available from: www.rferl.org/content/azerbaijan-ilham-aliyev-corruption-person-of-the-year/24814209.html [accessed February 27, 2014].

Cohen, E., 2004. "History and the Hyperpower." *Foreign Affairs*, July/August.

Collier, D. and Levitsky, S., 1996. "Democracy with Adjectives: Conceptual Innovation in Comparative Research." University of Notre Damme, *Kellogg Working Paper* No. 230.

Collier, D. and Levitsky, S., 1997. "Democracy with Adjectives: Conceptual Innovation in Comparative Research." *World Politics*, 49 (3), pp. 430–451.

Committee to Protect Freedom of Expression, 2008. *On Violated Rights of Journalists and Media in Armenia*. Commitee to Protect Freedom of Expression, Annual Report.

Committee to Protect Journalists, 2002. "Independent TV channel forced off the air." Committee to Protect Journalists. Available from: http://cpj.org/2002/04/independent-tv-channel-forced-off-the-air.php [accessed April 20, 2011].

ComRes, 2010. *A survey of the ComRes EuroPoll Panel conducted on behalf of European Friends of Armenia*. London: ComRes.

Cooper, H., 2009. "Promises of 'Fresh Start' for U.S.–Russia Relations." *The New York Times*, April 2.

Cornell, S., 2005. "US Engagement in the Caucasus: Changing Gears." *Helsinki Monitor*, (2).

Corso, M., 2006. "To Georgia, Wine War with Russia a Question of National Security." EurasiaNet, April 12.

Cortell, A.P. and Davis Jr., J.W., 2000. "Understanding the Domestic Impact of International Norms: A Research Agenda." *International Studies Review*, 2 (1), pp. 65–87.

Corwin, J., 2006. "U.S.: Minsk Group Fails To Produce Results On Nagorno-Karabakh." Radio Free Europe/Radio Liberty. Available from: www.rferl.org/content/article/1066548.html [accessed November 8, 2011].

Council of Europe and European Union, 2011. "SC-MLD-MEDIA II Promoting freedom, professionalism and pluralism of the media in the South Caucasus and Moldova." Available from: www.jp.coe.int/CEAD/JP/Default.asp?TransID=202&SA=1&SE=0#TopOfList [accessed November 23, 2011].

Council of the European Union, 2003. "A Secure Europe in a Better World: European Security Strategy." Available from: www.consilium.europa.eu/uedocs/cmsUpload/78367.pdf [accessed May 16, 2014].

Council of the European Union, 2006. "Council Joint Action 2006/121/CFSP of 20 February 2006 appointing the European Union Special Representative for the South Caucasus." Available from: http://eur-lex.europa.eu/Notice.do?mode=dbl&lang=ga&ihmlang=ga&lng1=ga,en&lng2=bg,cs,da,de,el,en,es,et,fi,fr,hu,it,lt,lv,nl,pl,pt,ro,sk,sl,sv,&val=422309:cs&page= [accessed May 13, 2011].

Council of the European Union, 2009. "Presidency Conclusions." Available from: http://europa.eu/rapid/press-release_DOC-09-1_en.htm?locale=en [accessed May 13, 2014].

Cox, C. and Eibner, J., 1993. *Ethnic Cleansing in Progress: War in Nagorno Karabakh*. Binz: Institute for Religious Minorities in the Islamic World,Switzerland.

Cox, M., Ikenberry, G.J., and Inoguchi, T., 2000. *American Democracy Promotion: Impulses, Strategies, and Impacts*. Oxford: Oxford University Press.

Crawford, G., 2003a. "Promoting Democracy from Without—Learning from Within (Part I)." *Democratization*, 10, pp. 77–98.

Crawford, G., 2003b. "Promoting Democracy from Without—Learning from Within (Part II)." *Democratization*, 10 (2), pp. 1–20.

Cremona, M., 2004. "European Neighbourhood Policy: Legal and Institutional Issues." *CDDRL Working Papers*.

Croft, A., 2013. "EU takes step towards launching drone program." Reuters, November 19.

Croissant, A. and Merkel, W., 2004. "Introduction: democratization in the early twenty-first century." *Democratization*, 11 (5), pp. 1–9.

Crook, C., 2007. "Think Again: Europe." Foreign Policy. Available from: www.foreign-policy.com/articles/2007/06/11/think_again_europe [accessed November 8, 2011].

CSCE, 2011. *The 2003 Presidential and Parliamentary Elections in Armenia*. Washington, DC: Commission on Security and Cooperation in Europe.

Curtis, G., 1995. *Azerbaijan: Government and Politics: The Presidential Election of 1992*. Washington, DC: Library of Congress.

Dahl, R.A., 1972. *Polyarchy: Participation and Opposition*. New Haven: Yale University Press.

Dahl, R.A., 1989. *Democracy and Its Critics*. New Haven: Yale University Press.

Dahl, R.A., 1998. *On Democracy*. New Haven: Yale University Press.

Danielyan, E., 2001. "Police Brutality Main Highlight Of Amnesty Report On Armenia." Radio Free Europe/Radio Liberty. Available from: www.azatutyun.am/content/article/1566655.html [accessed April 8, 2011].

Danielyan, E., 2002. "Envoy Says U.S. To Strengthen Ties With Armenia." Radio Free Europe/Radio Liberty. Available from: www.azatutyun.am/content/article/1570577.html [accessed June 3, 2011].

Danielyan, E., 2003a. "OSCE Hopes for Clean Vote in Armenia." Radio Free Europe/Radio Liberty. Available from: www.azatutyun.am/content/article/1570692.html [accessed April 8, 2011].

Danielyan, E., 2003b. "US Congress Approves More Aid To Armenia." Radio Free Europe/Radio Liberty. Available from: www.azatutyun.am/content/article/1572737.html [accessed July 1, 2011].

Danielyan, E., 2004a. "A Dictator in the Making." Transitions Online. Available from: www.avantart.com/armenia/diktatorinthemake.htm [accessed May 16, 2014].

Danielyan, E., 2004b. "Council Of Europe Report Highlights Police Torture In Armenia." Radio Free Europe/Radio Liberty. Available from: www.azatutyun.am/content/article/1574194.html [accessed April 8, 2011].

Danielyan, E., 2005a. "Oskanian Sees Political Reasons for Surge in Russian Gas Price." Radio Free Europe/Radio Liberty. Available from: www.azatutyun.am/content/article/1579848.html [accessed November 7, 2011].

Danielyan, E., 2005b. "West Unlikely to Sanction Armenia following Another Troubled Vote." EurasiaNet.org. Available from: www.eurasianet.org/departments/insight/articles/eav121205.shtml [accessed May 15, 2014].

Danielyan, E., 2005c. "Envoy Vows US Push For Clean Elections In Armenia." Radio Free Europe/Radio Liberty. Available from: www.azatutyun.am/content/article/1578310.html [accessed July 1, 2011].

Danielyan, E., 2005d. "EU Questions Yerevan's 'Commitment To Democracy.'" Radio Free Europe/Radio Liberty. Available from: www.azatutyun.am/content/article/1579561.html [accessed July 1, 2011].

Danielyan, E., 2006a. "OSCE, EU Urge Further Progress On Karabakh." Radio Free Europe/Radio Liberty. Available from: www.azatutyun.am/content/article/1585488.html [accessed May 12, 2011].

Danielyan, E., 2006b. "U.S. Mediator Says Karabakh Peace Possible after 2006." Radio Free Europe/Radio Liberty. Available from: www.azatutyun.am/content/article/1583269.html [accessed June 3, 2011].

Danielyan, E., 2006c. "Armenia: Oligarchic Party Gaining Ground Ahead of 2007 Vote." EurasiaNet.org. Available from: www.eurasianet.org/departments/insight/articles/eav122006.shtml [accessed April 15, 2011].

Danielyan, E., 2010. "EU Likely to Stay Cautious on Political Reform in Armenia." Radio Free Europe/Radio Liberty. Available from: www.azatutyun.am/content/article/2049408.html [accessed May 17, 2011].

Danielyan, E., 2011. "Dashnaks Back New Parliament Leadership." Radio Free Europe/Radio Liberty. Available from: www.azatutyun.am/content/article/24414946.html [accessed December 9, 2011].

Danielyan, E. and Bedevian, A., 2008. "Confident Ter-Petrosian Threatens 'Lasting' Rallies." Radio Free Europe/Radio Liberty. Available from: www.azatutyun.am/content/article/1593152.html [accessed November 9, 2011].

Danielyan, E. and Martirosian, A., 2009. "Dashnaks Quit Armenia's Ruling Coalition." Radio Free Europe/Radio Liberty. Available from: www.azatutyun.am/content/article/1616799.html [accessed April 15, 2011].

Danielyan, E. and Melkumian, H., 2003. "EU Envoys 'Collecting Information' On A1+ Affair." Radio Free Europe/Radio Liberty. Available from: www.azatutyun.am/content/article/1571985.html [accessed June 22, 2011].

Danielyan, E. and Saghabalian, A., 2007. "Mediators Still Hopeful about Karabakh Deal." Radio Free Europe/Radio Liberty. Available from: www.azatutyun.am/content/article/1591174.html [accessed June 3, 2011].

Danielyan, E., Melkumian, H., and Khachatrian, R., 2003. "Kocharian Sworn In For Second Term Amid Tight Security, Opposition Protests." Radio Free Europe/Radio Liberty. Available from: www.azatutyun.am/content/article/1571237.html [accessed April 8, 2011].

Danielyan, E., Khachatrian, R., Kalantarian, K., and Avoyan, S., 2003. "Voting Ends amid Fraud Allegations." Radio Free Europe/Radio Liberty. Available from: www.azatutyun.am/content/article/1571004.html [accessed April 8, 2011].

Danielyan, G., 2011. "Sardarapat Movement will not participate in elections [Sardarapat sharzhumy chi masnakcelu yntrutyunnerin]." Radio Free Europe/Radio Liberty. Available from: www.azatutyun.am/content/article/3546321.html [accessed April 4, 2011].

von der Decken, A., 2013. "Aserbaidschanischer Exilsender in Berlin." NDR. Available from: www.ndr.de/fernsehen/sendungen/zapp/film_fernsehen_radio/meydantv101.html [accessed November 13, 2013].

Dempsey, J., 2013a. "Does Europe Need an Endowment for Democracy?" Carnegie Endowment for International Peace. Available from: http://carnegieeurope.eu/strategiceurope/?fa=50602 [accessed February 14, 2013].

Dempsey, J., 2013b. "A Different Approach to Fostering Democracy." Carnegie Europe. Available from: http://carnegieeurope.eu/strategiceurope/?fa=53893&reloadFlag=1 [accessed March 1, 2014].

Derluguian, G.M., 2005. *Bourdieu's Secret Admirer in the Caucasus: A World-System Biography.* Chicago: University of Chicago Press.

Deudney, D. and Meiser, J., 2008. "American Exceptionalism" in Cox, M. and Stokes, D. (eds), *U.S. Foreign Policy.* Oxford: Oxford University Press.

DFWatch, 2014. "Ivanishvili's new NGO 'Citizen' will help develop Georgian media." Democracy and Freedom Watch. Available from: http://dfwatch.net/ivanishvilis-new-ngo-citizen-will-help-develop-georgian-media-48987 [accessed February 27, 2014].

Diamond, L., 1999. *Developing Democracy: Toward Consolidation.* Baltimore, MD: The Johns Hopkins University Press.

Diamond, L., 2008. "How to Save Democracy." *Newsweek Magazine.*

Diamond, L. and Gunther, R., 2001. *Political Parties and Democracy.* Baltimore, MD: The Johns Hopkins University Press.

Diamond, L., Linz, J., and Lipset, S.M. (eds.), 1989. *Democracy in Developing Countries: Latin America.* London: Adamantine Press.

Diamond, L.J., 2002. "Thinking About Hybrid Regimes." *Journal of Democracy,* 13, pp. 21–35.

Doherty, I., 2001. *Democracy out of Balance, Civil Society Can't Replace Political Parties.* National Democratic Institute. Available from: www.ndi.org/node/12716 [accessed 16 May 2014]

Dumbrell, D., 2008. "America in the 1990s: Searching for Purpose" in Cox, M. and Stokes, D. (eds), *U.S. Foreign Policy.* Oxford: Oxford University Press.

Dzvelishvili, N., 2013. "Meydan TV—Azeri alternative television in Berlin. Media.ge. Available from: www.media.ge/en/portal/articles/301286/ [accessed November 13, 2013].

ECFR, 2010. "European Foreign Policy Scorecard: Russia." Available from: www.ecfr.eu/scorecard/2010/russia/ [accessed November 8, 2011].

Economist, 1998a. "Presidents Go." *The Economist,* February 5.

Economist, 1998b. "Can Armenia's New Man Deal?" *The Economist,* April 2.

Economist, 2007. "Armenia's Murky Politics." *The Economist,* April 11.

Economist, 2011a. "The Russia–Georgia conflict: Going nowhere fast." *The Economist,* April 5.

Economist, 2011b. "The Russia–Georgia War, Three Years on: Can't We All just Get Along?" *The Economist,* August 9.

Economist, 2013. "Mutti puts the lad in his place." *The Economist,* September 1.

Edgeworth, L. and Lansell, S.R., 1996. "Technical Assistance to Armenia: July 5, 1995 National Assembly Elections." IFES. Available from: www.ifes.org/~/media/Files/Publications/VRC/Reports/1995/R01517/R01517.pdf [accessed May 16, 2014.

EED, 2013. "EED Funds First Initiative." EED. Available from: http://democracyendowment.eu/ [accessed November 13, 2013].

Elder, M., 2012. "Michael McFaul, US ambassador to Moscow, victim of Kremlin 'Twitter war.'" *The Guardian,* May 29.

Elliott, S., 2010. "Russia Plays Its Cards In Armenia, Azerbaijan, Turkey 10MOSCOW60." US Embassy Moscow (Russia), US Embassy cables No. 10MOSCOW60.

Emerson, M., 2011. "Review of the Review – of the European Neighbourhood Policy." *CEPS Commentary.*

Emerson, M., Balfour, R., Corthaut, T., Wouters, J., Kaczynski, P.M., and Remard, T., 2011. *Upgrading the EU's Role as Global Actor: Institutions, Law and the Restructuring of European Diplomacy.* Brussels: Centre for European Policy Studies (CEPS).

Englund, W., 2012. "Russians say they'll name their Magnitsky-retaliation law after baby who died in a hot car in VA." *Washington Post*. Available from: www.washingtonpost. com/blogs/worldviews/wp/2012/12/11/magnitsky-retaliation-man-baby/ [accessed February 22, 2014].

ENPI Info, 2013. "Freedom on the Net: EED hosts Syrian and Azeri activists to hear their stories." enpi-info.eu. Available from: www.enpi-info.eu/eastportal/news/latest/35045/ Freedom-on-the-Net:-EED-hosts-Syrian-and-Azeri-activists-to-hear-their-stories [accessed November 13, 2013].

Epstein, S.B., Serafino, N.M., and Miko, F.T., 2007. *Democracy Promotion Cornerstone of U.S. Foreign Policy*. CRS Report for Congress No. RL34296.

EU Delegation in Azerbaijan, 2012. "European Union to support 16 new NGO projects." Available from: http://eeas.europa.eu/delegations/azerbaijan/documents/press_ releases/2012_02_07_the_eu_to_support 16 new_ngo_projects_en.pdf [accessed May 16, 2014].

EU Delegation to Armenia, 2013. "EU response to article published by www.news.am." Available from: http://eeas.europa.eu/delegations/armenia/press_corner/all_news/ news/2013/2013_09_06_en.htm [accessed September 9, 2013].

EU Presidency, 2003. "Declaration by the Presidency on behalf of the European Union regarding Armenian Parliamentary elections." Available from: www.consilium.europa. eu/uedocs/NewsWord/en/cfsp/76410.doc [accessed May 16, 2014].

EU Presidency, 2008. "Declaration by the Presidency on behalf of the European Union on the Presidential Election in Armenia on 19 February 2008." Available from: www. eu2008.si/en/News_and_Documents/CFSP_Statements/February/0222MZZ_Armenia. html [accessed September 28, 2011].

EUobserver, 2009. "EU Leaders Soothe Russia over New Eastern Club." Available from: http://euobserver.com/24/28090 [accessed August 26, 2011].

Eurasia Foundation, no date. Regional Print Media. Available from: www.epfound.am/ files/rpm_eng.pdf [accessed May 16, 2014].

EurasiaNet, 2008. "Armenia: Authorities Advance Conspiracy Theory. Eurasianet.org. Available from: www.eurasianet.org/armenia08/news/030708.shtml [accessed April 10, 2011].

European Commission, 1997. Agenda 2000 – Vol. I: For a Stronger and Wider Union – Vol. II: The Challenge of Enlargement. Available from: http://eur-lex.europa.eu/ Notice.do?val=318888:cs&lang=en&list=318888:cs,&pos=1&page=1&nbl=1&pgs=10 &hwords= [accessed November 8, 2011].

European Commission, 2000. "Communication from the Commission on EU Election Assistance and Observation." Available from: www.eueom.eu/files/dmfile/ communication-from-the-commission-on-eu-election-assistance-and-observation_en1. pdf [accessed November 8, 2011].

European Commission, 2001. "European Initiative for Democracy and Human Rights Programming Document 2002–2004." Available from: http://ec.europa.eu/europeaid/ what/human-rights/documents/programming_2002_2004_document_eidhr_en.pdf [accessed May 16, 2014].

European Commission, 2003. "Wider Europe—Neighbourhood: A New Framework for Relations with our Eastern and Southern Neighbours." Available from: http://ec.europa. eu/world/enp/pdf/com03_104_en.pdf

European Commission, 2004. "European Neighbourhood Policy: Strategy Paper." Available from: http://ec.europa.eu/world/enp/pdf/strategy/strategy_paper_en.pdf

European Commission, 2006. "Communication from the Commission of the Council and the European Parliament on Strengthening the European Neighbourhood Policy." Available from: http://ec.europa.eu/world/enp/pdf/com06_726_en.pdf

European Commission, 2007. "A Strong European Neighbourhood Policy." Available from: http://ec.europa.eu/world/enp/pdf/strategy/strategy_paper_en.pdf

European Commission, 2010. "European Instrument for Democracy and Human Rights (EIDHR) Strategy Paper 2011–2013." Available from: http://ec.europa.eu/europeaid/what/human-rights/documents/eidhr_strategy_paper_2011_2013_com_decision_21_april_2011_text_published_on_internet_en.pdf [accessed May 16, 2014].

European Commission, 2011. "A new and ambitious European Neighbourhood Policy." Available from: http://europa.eu/rapid/press-release_MEMO-11-342_en.htm?locale=fr [accessed February 21, 2014].

European Commission, 2012. "The European Endowment for Democracy – Support for the unsupported." Available from: http://europa.eu/rapid/press-release_IP-12-1199_en.htm [accessed February 14, 2013].

European Commission, 2013. "European Endowment for Democracy – additional support for democratic change." Available from: http://europa.eu/rapid/press-release_IP-13-17_en.htm [accessed February 14, 2013].

European Community, 1987. "Declaration of Foreign Ministers of the Community on Human Rights, 21 July 1986." European Foreign Policy Bulletin database.

European Parliament, 2012. *Nagorno-Karabakh Security Situation*. European Parliament. Available from: www.europarl.europa.eu/meetdocs/2009_2014/documents/sede/dv/sede-200612expertspresentations_/sede200612expertspresentations_en.pdf [accessed May 14, 2014].

European Parliament and the Council, 2006. "Regulation (EC) No. 1638/2006 of the European Parliament and of the Council of 24 October 2006 laying down general provisions establishing a European Neighbourhood and Partnership Instrument." Available from: http://eur-lex.europa.eu/LexUriServ/LexUriServ.do?uri=CELEX:32006R1638:EN:NOT [accessed November 8, 2011].

European Union, 2003. "Council appoints an EU Special Representative for the South Caucasus." EU@UN. Available from: www.europa-eu-un.org/articles/en/article_2527_en.htm [accessed May 13, 2011].

European Union, 2011. "EU Statement on Freedom of the Media in Armenia." Available from:www.delvie.ec.europa.eu/en/eu_osce/eu_statements/2011/February/PC%20no.848%20-%20EU%20media%20freedom%20in%20ARM.pdf [accessed May 16, 2014].

Evgrashina, L., 2013. "Opposition newspaper editor jailed in Azerbaijan." Reuters, March 12.

Fabbrini, S., 2005. "Madison in Brussels: the EU and the US as compound democracies." *European Political Science*, 4 (2), pp. 188–198.

Fabbrini, S., 2007. *Compound Democracies: Why the United States and Europe Are Becoming Similar*. Oxford: Oxford University Press.

Fatullayev, A., 2013. "Two million USD for a Facebook revolution in Azerbaijan [2 milliona dollarov na facebukovuyu revolutssiyu v Azerbaijane]." Haaqqin.az. Available from: http://haqqin.az/oldage/4379 [accessed February 28, 2014].

Felgenhauer, P., 2010. "The Jamestown Foundation: Russia Struggles to Establish a Viable Military Base in Abkhazia." *Eurasia Daily Monitor*, 7 (33).

Ferrero-Waldner, B., 2006. "Remarks on democracy promotion by EU Commissioner Ferrero-Waldner." EU@UN. Available from: www.eu-un.europa.eu/articles/en/article_6574_en.htm [accessed November 8, 2011].

Finnemore, M. and Sikkink, K., 1998. "International Norm Dynamics and Political Change." *International Organization*, 52 (04), pp. 887–917.

Fisher, M., 2013. "Oops: Azerbaijan released election results before voting had even started." *Washington Post*. Available at: www.washingtonpost.com/blogs/worldviews/wp/2013/10/09/oops-azerbaijan-released-election-results-before-voting-had-even-started/ [accessed February 25, 2014].

Flockhart, T., 2005. *Socializing Democratic Norms: The Role of International Organizations for the Construction of Europe*. London: Palgrave Macmillan.

Foley, M.W. and Edwards, B., 1996. "The Paradox of Civil Society." *Journal of Democracy*, 7 (3), pp. 38–52.

Fomitschev, M., 2012. "Russia In Deadlock With Azerbaijan On Radar Site." RIA News. Available from: http://en.rian.ru/world/20120524/173643426.html [accessed December 21, 2012].

Forbirg, J., 2013. "Doing business in Belarus: Beware of hostage-takers." EuObserver. com. Available from: http://euobserver.com/opinion/121285 [accessed September 15, 2013].

FOTP, 2013. *Georgia: Freedom of the Press*. Washington, DC: Freedom House.

Freedom House, 1998. *Nations in Transit 1998: Country Report of Armenia*. Washington, DC: Freedom House.

Freedom House, 2002. *Nations in Transit 2002: Country Report of Armenia*. Washington, DC: Freedom House.

Freedom House, 2003. *Nations in Transit 2003: Country Report of Armenia*. Washington, DC: Freedom House.

Freedom House, 2012. "Freedom House Slams USG Decision to Close USAID in Moscow." Freedom House. Available from: www.freedomhouse.org/article/freedom-house-slams-usg-decision-close-usaid-moscow [accessed February 24, 2013].

Frenz, A., 2007. "The European Commission's Tacis Programme 1991–2006. A Success Story." Available from: http://ec.europa.eu/europeaid/where/neighbourhood/regional-cooperation/enpi-east/documents/annual_programmes/tacis_success_story_final_en.pdf [accessed May 16, 2014].

Freres, C., 2000. "The European Union as a Global 'Civilian Power': Development Cooperation in EU–Latin American Relations." *Journal of Interamerican Studies and World Affairs*, 42 (2), pp. 63–85.

Füle, S., 2011. "Revolutionising the European Neighbourhood Policy in response to tougher Mediterranean revolutions." Available from: http://europa.eu/rapid/press-release_SPEECH-11-436_en.htm?locale=en [accessed November 25, 2013].

Füle, Š., 2013a. "Speech: European Endowment for Democracy." Available from: http://europa.eu/rapid/press-release_SPEECH-13-6_en.htm [accessed February 14, 2013].

Füle, S., 2013b. "There is not any pressure over Armenia: EU commissioner Stefan Füle." Armenpress. Available from: http://armenpress.am/eng/news/727081/ [accessed September 15, 2013].

Füle, S., 2013c. "Statement on the pressure exercised by Russia on countries of the Eastern Partnership." European Commission. Available from: http://europa.eu/rapid/press-release_SPEECH-13-687_en.htm [accessed September 15, 2013].

Fuller, L., 2008. "Geneva Talks On Georgia Get Off To Rocky Start." Radio Free Europe/Radio Liberty. Available from: www.rferl.org/content/Geneva_Talks_On_Georgia_Get_Off_To_Rocky_Start/1330658.html [accessed March 27, 2013].

Fuller, L. and Giragosian, R., 2011. "Has The Karabakh Peace Process Reached A Dead-End?" Radio Free Europe/Radio Liberty. Available from: www.rferl.org/content/has_

the_karabakh_peace_process_reached_a_dead_end/24249198.html [accessed February 5, 2014].

Gardner, A., Shields, C., and Stover, J., 1996. "Armenia: Technical Assistance November 10, 1996 Municipal Elections." IFES. Available from: www.ifes.org/~/media/Files/Publications/VRC/Reports/1996/R01514/R01514.pdf [accessed May 16, 2014].

Gazeta.RU, 1999. "Primakov Goes to Washington for Money and Understanding [Примаков едет в Вашингтон за деньгами и пониманием]." Gazeta.RU. Available from: http://gazeta.lenta.ru/daynews/22–03–1999/20primakov.htm [accessed September 21, 2011].

George, A.L. and Bennett, A., 2005. *Case Studies and Theory Development in the Social Sciences*. Cambridge, MA: MIT Press.

Gevorgyan, S., 2013. "Moscow Talks Fallout: Armenian political parties react to Yerevan's decision to join Russia-led Customs Union." ArmeniaNow. Available from: http://armenianow.com/news/48196/armenia_political_parties_reaction_customs_union [accessed September 11, 2013].

Ghazaryan, S., 2010. *Europe's options in Nagorno-Karabakh: An analysis of views of the European Parliament*. European Friends of Armenia.

Ghazinyan, A., 2011. "Gabala Radar Station: Russia and Azerbaijan Discuss Possible Lease Extension." ArmeniaNow.com. Available from: www.armenianow.com/commentary/analysis/31413/gabala_radar_station_azerbaijan_russia_control_aircrafts [accessed November 29, 2011].

Gillespie, R. and Youngs, R., 2002. *The European Union and Democracy Promotion: The Case of North Africa* (1st edition). London: Routledge.

Gilley, B., 2009. "Is Democracy Possible?" *Journal of Democracy*, 20 (1), pp. 113–127.

Giorgadze, K., 2002. "Russia: Regional Partner or Aggressor?" *The Review of International Affairs*, 2 (1), pp. 64–79.

Goldenberg, S., 1994. *Pride of Small Nations: The Caucasus and Post-Soviet Disorder*. London: Zed Books.

Goldsmith, B., 2003. "Analysis of the Voter Registration Pilot Project in Georgia." International Foundation for Election Systems. Available from: www.ifes.org/Content/Publications/Reports/2003/Analysis-of-the-Voter-Registration-Pilot-Project-in-Georgia.aspx [accessed February 28, 2014].

Gordon, P.H., 1997. "Europe's Uncommon Foreign Policy." *International Security*, 22 (3), pp. 74–100.

Gordon, P.H., 2009. "Strengthening the Transatlantic Alliance: An Overview of the Obama Administration's Policies in Europe." Available from: www.state.gov/p/eur/rls/rm/2009/124870.htm [accessed October 31, 2012].

Gordon, P.H., 2011. "The US Relationship With Central Europe Under the Obama Administration." US Department of State. Available from: www.state.gov/p/eur/rls/rm/2011/157707.htm [accessed February 22, 2014].

Gradirovski, S. and Esipova, N., 2007. "Gallup Exclusive: Conflict in the Caucasus—New Surveys on Azerbaijan–Armenia." *Harvard International Review*.

Grävingholt, J., Bader, J., Faust, J., and Kästner, A., 2011. *The Influence of China, Russia and India on the Future of Democracy in the Euro-Asian Region*. Bonn: German Development Institute, No. 2.

Grevi, G., 2007. *Pioneering Foreign Policy: The EU Special Representatives*. Paris: Institute for Security Studies, Chaillot Paper No. 106.

Grigoryan, M., 1997. "Armenia's 1996 Presidential Election Coverage in the Media." *Caucasian Regional Studies*, 2 (1).

Grigoryan, M., 2013. "Armenia: Customs Union Commitment Risks EU Cooperation Chances." EurasiaNet, September 10.

Grove, T., 2013. "Azeri police beat, detain demonstrators after vote protest rally." Reuters, October 12.

Guardian, 2010a. "US Embassy Cables: Armenian defence Minister Rebuked over Arms Sales to Iran." *The Guardian*, December 6.

Guardian, 2010b. "US Embassy Cables: US Fury at Armenia over Arms Transfers to Iran." *The Guardian*, November 28.

Guardian, 2010c. "US embassy cables: Russia 'armed' separatist rebels ahead of Georgia war." *The Guardian*, December 1.

Guttman, L., 1994. *Louis Guttman on Theory and Methodology: Selected Writings.* Sudbury, MA: Dartmouth Publishing.

Hakobyan, T., 2012. "Majoritarian-representational argument [Metsamasnakan-hamamasnakan vechy]." Report.am. Available from: http://report.am/news/politics/ntrutyunneri-patmutyunic3-tatul-hakobyan.html [accessed February 27, 2014].

Halliday, F., 2008. "Armenia's Mixed Messages." OpenDemocracy. Available from: www.opendemocracy.org.uk/article/armenia-s-mixed-messages [accessed April 7, 2011].

Harutyunyan, S., 2011a. "Sarkisian Rules Out Another Gas Price Rise." Radio Free Europe/Radio Liberty. Available from: www.azatutyun.am/content/article/2323746.html [accessed March 26, 2011].

Harutyunyan, S., 2011b. "Armenia No Longer Eligible For U.S. Aid Program." Radio Free Europe/Radio Liberty. Available from: www.azatutyun.am/content/article/4745616.html [accessed June 3, 2011].

Harutyunyan, S., 2012. "Russia will double the number of its contracter soldiers in Armenia [Rusastany kkrknapatki Hayastanum ir paimanagrayin zintsarayoghneri tivy]." Radio Free Europe/Radio Liberty. Available from: www.azatutyun.am/content/article/24619987.html [accessed June 21, 2012].

Hassan, O. and Hammond, A., 2011. "The rise and fall of American's freedom agenda in Afghanistan: counter-terrorism, nation-building and democracy." *The International Journal of Human Rights*, 15 (4), pp. 532–551.

Hassan, O. and Ralph, J., 2011. "Democracy promotion and human rights in US foreign policy." *The International Journal of Human Rights*, 15 (4), pp. 509–519.

Haukkala, H., 2011. "Lost in Translation? Why the EU has Failed to Influence Russia's Development" in Gower, J. and Timmins, G. (eds), *The European Union, Russia and the Shared Neighbourhood*. London: Routledge.

Hayrumyan, N., 2011. "Puzzle: What niche will Kocharyan take at upcoming elections?" ArmeniaNow.com. Available from: http://armenianow.com/news/politics/27570/kocharyan_tsarukyan_armenia_politics [accessed March 4, 2014].

Hayrumyan, N., 2012. "Vote 2012: Opposition, government create dual—and dueling—monitoring staffs." ArmeniaNow.com. Available from: www.armenianow.com/vote_2012/37131/may_elections_oppositional_parliamentary_electoral_headquarters [accessed February 27, 2014].

Hayrumyan, N., 2013a. "Customs Union is Ransom for Tigran Sargsyan." Lragir.am. Available from: http://lragir.am/index.php/eng/0/comments/view/30259 [accessed September 9, 2013].

Hayrumyan, N., 2013b. "Armenian leadership meets little opposition over Customs Union decision despite opinions about 'shameful decision'." ArmeniaNow. Available from: http://armenianow.com/commentary/analysis/48309/armenia_eu_customs_union_russia [accessed September 15, 2013].

Heil, A., 2013. "Sour Grapes: Russia Bans Moldovan Wine, Again." Radio Free Europe/ Radio Liberty. Available from: www.rferl.org/content/moldova-wine-russia-import-ban/25102889.html [accessed September 15, 2013].

Heritage, 2002. "Heritage Party." Available from: www.heritage.am/indexeng.htm [accessed November 23, 2011].

Heritage, T., 2013. "Russia bans Belarusian pork imports in trade war over businessman's arrest." *The Guardian*. Available from: www.theguardian.com/world/2013/aug/30/ russia-belarusian-pork-imports-arrest [accessed September 15, 2013].

Hetq, 2013. "Media Freedom in Armenia." Hetq. Available from: http://hetq.am/eng/ articles/22867/media-freedom-in-armenia.html [accessed February 28, 2014].

Hiatt, F., 2010. "Will Obama's foreign policy follow his new democracy rhetoric?" *The Washington Post*, October 4.

Hoffmann, S., 2000. "Towards a Common European Foreign and Security Policy?" *JCMS: Journal of Common Market Studies*, 38 (2), pp. 189–198.

Hook, S.W., 2003. "Domestic Obstacles to International Affairs: The State Department under Fire at Home." *Political Science and Politics*, 36 (1), pp. 23–29.

House Committee, 2007. "Full Text of H.R. 982 (110th): ADVANCE Democracy Act of 2007." Available from: www.govtrack.us/congress/bills/110/hr982/text [accessed February 24, 2013].

Hovanissian, R., 2013. "Arminfo: Raffi Hovannisian: Public opinion polls in Armenia are often far from objective reality." ArmInfo. Available from: www.arminfo.am/index. cfm?objectid=3D243FF0–66F6–11E2-B4BEF6327207157C [accessed February 25, 2014].

Hovhannisyan, I., 2014a. "Kocharian Backs Tsarukian Criticism Of Government." Radio Free Europe/Radio Liberty. Available from: www.azatutyun.am/content/article/ 25268513.html [accessed February 27, 2014].

Hovhannisyan, I., 2014b. "Tsarukian's Party Alleges Government Harassment." Radio Free Europe/Radio Liberty. Available from: www.azatutyun.am/content/article/ 25278381.html [accessed February 27, 2014].

Hughes, S., 2006. *Newsrooms in Conflict: Journalism and the Democratization of Mexico* (1st edition). Pittsburgh: University of Pittsburgh Press.

Human Rights Watch, 1991. *Conflict in Georgia: Human Rights Violations by the Government of Zviad Gamsakhurdia*. Human Rights Watch, No. 3, 16.

Human Rights Watch, 1994. *Azerbaijan: Seven years of conflict in Nagorno-Karabakh*. Human Rights Watch. Available from: www.hrw.org/sites/default/files/reports/ AZER%20Conflict%20in%20N-K%20Dec94.pdf [accessed May 15, 2014].

Human Rights Watch, 2012. "Azerbaijan: Journalist Viciously Attacked by Police." Available from: www.hrw.org/news/2012/04/19/azerbaijan-journalist-viciously-attacked-police [accessed February 28, 2014].

Human Rights Watch, 2014. *World Report*. Human Rights Watch.

Hunter, S., Thomas, J.L., and Melikishvili, A., 2004. *Islam in Russia: the Politics of Identity and Security*. Almonk, NY: M.E. Sharp.

Huntington, S., 1999. "The Lonely Superpower." *Foreign Affairs*, March/April.

Huntington, S.P., 1991. *The Third Wave: Democratization in the Late 20th Century*. University of Oklahoma Press.

Huntington, S.P., 1993. *The Third Wave: Democratization in the Late 20th Century*. Norman: University of Oklahoma Press.

ICC, 2011. *Georgia–Russia: Learn to Live like Neighbours*. International Crisis Group, Europe Briefing, No. 65.

IFES, 2002. "Citizen Activity is Basis for Democratic Society." Available from: www.ifes.org/~/media/Files/Publications/VRC/Reports/2002/R01520/R01520.pdf [accessed May 16, 2014].

IFES, 2011. "Who We Are." IFES. Available from: www.ifes.org/About/Who-We-Are.aspx [accessed November 23, 2011].

IFEX, 2012. "Norwegian journalists held and threatened at Baku airport." IFEX. Available from: www.ifex.org/azerbaijan/2012/05/29/norwegian_journalists_held/ [accessed February 28, 2014].

Ikenberry, G.J. and Kupchan, C.A., 1990. "Socialization and Hegemonic Power." *International Organization*, 44 (3), pp. 283–315.

Inbar, E. and Sheffer, G., 1997. "Introduction" in Inbar, E. and Sheffer, G. (eds), *The National Security of Small States in a Changing World (BESA Studies in International Security*. London: Routledge.

Interfax, 2009. "Yuschenko, Saakashvili open new building of Georgian Embassy in Kyiv—Ukrainian news." Interfax Ukraine. Available from: www.interfax.com.ua/eng/main/25516/ [accessed August 14, 2012].

Interfax, 2012. "Azerbaijan Again Threatens War to Retake Nagorno-Karabakh." Available from: www.interfax.com/newsinf.asp?pg=6&id=307784 [accessed May 29, 2012].

Interfax, 2013. "Chisinau says signing DCFTA with EU poses no threat to Russian–Moldovan economic ties." Interfax News Wire. Available from: www.interfax.co.uk/ukraine-news/chisinau-says-signing-dcfta-with-eu-poses-no-threat-to-russian-moldovan-economic-ties-2/ [accessed September 10, 2013].

Interfax, 2014. "Saakashvili can return home—Georgian prime minister." Interfax. Available from: www.interfax.com/newsinf.asp?id=484042 [accessed February 27, 2014].

International Crisis Group, 2006. *Abkhazia Today*. International Crisis Group, No. 176.

International Crisis Group, 2011. *Armenia and Azerbaijan: Preventing War*. Baku/Yerevan/Tbilisi/Istanbul/Brussels: International Crisis Group, Europe Briefing No. 60.

IRI, 2008. *Armenian National Study January 13–20, 2008*. International Republican Institute.

Iskandaryan, A., 2013. "Armenia." Freedom House. Available from: www.freedomhouse.org/report/nations-transit/2013/armenia#.UxXeJoUz13s [accessed March 4, 2014].

Ismayilov, R., 2006. "Baku Banks on Independent Energy Policy." EurasiaNet, December 12.

Ismayilova, K., 2011. "Azerbaijan: Government Closes Two International NGOs." EurasiaNet, April 19.

Ismayilova, K. and Fatullayeva, N., 2012. "Azerbaijan's President Awarded Family Stake in Gold Fields." Reporting Project. Available from: https://reportingproject.net/occrp/index.php/en/ccwatch/cc-watch-indepth/1495-azerbaijans-president-awarded-family-stake-in-gold-fields [accessed February 27, 2014].

Johnson, J., 2002. "In Pursuit of a Prosperous International System" in Schraeder, P.J. (ed.) *Exporting Democracy: Rhetoric Vs. Reality*. Boulder, CO: Lynne Rienner, pp. 31–52.

Jozwiak, R., 2012. "Armenia Enraged Over Nagorno-Karabakh At EU Talks." Radio Free Europe/Radio Liberty. Available from: www.rferl.org/content/eu-azerbaijan-talk-nagorno-karabakh/24800923.html [accessed December 19, 2012].

Jupille, J., Caporaso, J.A., and Checkel, J.T., 2003. "Integrating Institutions: Rationalism, Constructivism, and the Study of the European Union." *Comparative Political Studies*, 36 (1–2), pp. 7–40.

Kagan, R., 2003. *Of Paradise and Power: America and Europe in the New World Order* (1st edition). New York: Knopf.

Kalantarian, K., 2002. "Council Of Europe Joins Media Bill Criticism." Radio Free Europe/Radio Liberty. Available from: www.azatutyun.am/content/article/1567540. html [accessed June 17, 2011].

Kalantarian, K., 2006. "Yerevan Signals Frustration with Russian Stance on Gas Price." Radio Free Europe/Radio Liberty. Available from: www.azatutyun.am/content/ article/1580169.html [accessed November 7, 2011].

Kalantarian, K., 2007. "OSCE Official Discusses Armenian Elections." Radio Free Europe/ Radio Liberty. Available from: www.armtown.com/news/en/rfe/20070116/200701162 [accessed November 9, 2011].

Kalantarian, K., 2010. "Armenian Parliament Passes Controversial TV Bill." Radio Free Europe/Radio Liberty. Available from: www.azatutyun.am/content/article/2067912. html [accessed June 22, 2011].

Kalantarian, K. and Danielyan, E., 2001. "Kocharian Was Suspected of Ordering Parliament Killings, Rivals Claim." Radio Free Europe/Radio Liberty. Available from: www. azatutyun.am/content/article/1567107.html [accessed April 7, 2011].

Kalantarian, K. and Danielyan, E., 2004. "More Opposition Backers Jailed Despite International Uproar." Radio Free Europe/Radio Liberty. Available from: www.azatutyun. am/content/article/1573669.html [accessed April 8, 2011].

Kalantarian, K. and Stepanian, R., 2004. "Opposition Reports Fresh Arrests." Radio Free Europe/Radio Liberty. Available from: www.azatutyun.am/content/article/1573862. html [accessed April 8, 2011].

Kalantarian, K., Stepanian, R., and Simonyan, K., 2008. "More Oppositionists Arrested, Charged." Radio Free Europe/Radio Liberty. Available from: www.azatutyun.am/ content/article/1594079.html [accessed November 9, 2011].

Kalantarian, K., Khachatrian, R., Stamboltsian, G., and Melkumian, H., 2004. "Kocharian, EU Envoys Discuss Rising Tensions In Armenia." Radio Free Europe/Radio Liberty. Available from: www.azatutyun.am/content/article/1573404.html [accessed April 8, 2011].

Kaplan, A., 1964. *The Conduct of Inquiry: Methodology for Behavioral Science* (1st edition). San Francisco: Chandler Publishing Company.

Kaplan, R.D., 1997. "Was Democracy Just a Moment?" *The Atlantic*. Available from: www.theatlantic.com/magazine/archive/1997/12/was-democracy-just-a-moment/6022/ [accessed November 4, 2011].

Karl, T.L., 1990. "Dilemmas of Democratization in Latin America." *Comparative Politics*, 23 (1), pp. 1–21.

Karl, T.L., 1995. "The Hybrid Regimes of Central America." *Journal of Democracy*, 6 (3), pp. 72–86.

Karlekar, K.D., 2011. "Freedom of the Press 2011: Signs of Change amid Repression," Available from: www.freedomhouse.org/report/freedom-press/freedom-press-2011#. U3IMtyi8w0E [accessed May 16, 2014].

Karumidze, Z., Wertsch, J.V., and Karumize, Z., 2005. *Enough!: The Rose Revolution In The Republic Of Georgia 2003*. Hauppauge: Nova Science.

Kegley, C.W. and Hermann, M.G., 2002. "In Pursuit of a Peaceful International System" in Schraeder, P.J. (ed.) *Exporting Democracy: Rhetoric Vs. Reality*. Boulder, CO: Lynne Rienner, pp. 15–29.

Kelkitli, F.A., 2008. "Russian Foreign Policy in South Caucasus under Putin." *Perceptions*, Winter, pp. 69–86.

Kelley, J., 2006. "New Wine in Old Wineskins: Promoting Political Reforms through the New European Neighbourhood Policy." *Journal of Common Market Studies*, 44 (1), pp. 29–55.

De Keyser, V., 2011. *Democracy Support: Seizing the moment, shifting the paradigm.* Brussels: Office for Promotion of Parliamentary Democracy.

Khachatrian, R., 2004. "European Bodies Propose Electoral Reform In Armenia." Radio Free Europe/Radio Liberty. Available from: www.azatutyun.am/content/article/1573142.html [accessed April 9, 2011].

Khachatrian, R. and Bedevian, A., 2007. "Parliament Debates RFE/RL Broadcasts amid Opposition Uproar." Radio Free Europe/Radio Liberty. Available from: www.azatutyun.am/content/article/1589206.html [accessed April 20, 2011].

Khachatrian, R. and Kalantarian, K., 2007. "Government Moves To End RFE/RL Broadcasts In Armenia." Radio Free Europe/Radio Liberty. Available from: www.azatutyun.am/content/article/1589185.html [accessed April 20, 2011].

Khachatrian, R., Bedevian, A., and Danielyan, E., 2008. "Ter-Petrosian 'Under House Arrest,' Rally Broken Up." Radio Free Europe/Radio Liberty. Available from: www.azatutyun.am/content/article/1593514.html [accessed November 9, 2011].

Khanna, P., 2004. "The Metrosexual Superpower." Foreign Policy. Available at: www.foreignpolicy.com/articles/2004/07/01/the_metrosexual_superpower [accessed November 8, 2011].

Kharebava, L., 2012. "Stop the harassment of journalists, say Tbilisi protesters." Democracy and Freedom Watch. Available from: http://dfwatch.net/stop-the-harassment-of-journalists-say-tbilisi-protesters-33544 [accessed February 28, 2014].

Khutsishvili, G., 1994. "Intervention in Transcaucasus." *Perspective*, 4 (3).

King, G., Keohane, R.O., and Verba, S., 1994. *Designing Social Inquiry: Scientific Inference in Qualitative Research.* Princeton, NJ: Princeton University Press.

Kocharyan, S., 2013. "Russia is our military-security choice; DCFTA is our economic choice." Available from: http://commonspace.eu/eng/news/6/id2754 [accessed September 10, 2013].

Kolodziej, E.A. and Kanet, R.E., 2008. *From Superpower to Besieged Global Power: Restoring World Order after the Failure of the Bush Doctrine.* Athens, GA: University of Georgia Press.

Kopstein, J., 2006. "The Transatlantic Divide over Democracy Promotion." *The Washington Quarterly*, 29 (2), pp. 85–98.

Kramer, A.E., 2010. "Panic in Georgia After a Mock News Broadcast." *The New York Times*, March 14.

Kramer, A.E., 2012a. "Barvikha, Russia, Draws Embattled Leaders Like Assad." *The New York Times*, December 28.

Kramer, A.E., 2012b. "Tens of Thousands in Georgia Protest President." *The New York Times*, May 27.

Kubicek, P., 2003. *The European Union and Democratization.* London: Routledge.

Kucera, J., 2010a. "Is Russia starting to sell weapons to Azerbaijan?" Eurasianet. Available from: www.eurasianet.org/node/61673 [accessed March 26, 2011].

Kucera, J., 2010b. "Is Russia starting to sell weapons to Azerbaijan?" EurasiaNet.org Available from: www.eurasianet.org/node/61673 [accessed March 26, 2011].

Kucera, J., 2012. "Ivanishvili On NATO, Russia And Georgia's Geopolitics." EurasiaNet, October 3.

Kumar, K., 2005. "Reflections on international political party assistance." *Democratization*, 12, pp. 505–527.

Kumar, K., 2012. *Evaluating democracy assistance.* Boulder, CO: Lynne Rienner.

Kurki, M., 2012. "How the EU can adopt a new type of democracy support." *FRIDE Working Paper*, 112.

Kurowska, X., 2009. "EUJUST Themis" in Grevi, G., Helly, D., and Keohane, D. (eds), *European Security and Defence Policy: The First Ten Years (1999–2009)*. Paris: EU Institute for Security Studies, pp. 201–209.

KyivPost, 2008. "Opposition bloc to boycott Georgia's parliament to protest governing party's big election win." *Kyiv Post*. Available from: www.kyivpost.com/content/world/opposition-bloc-to-boycott-georgias-parliament-to-29008.html [accessed February 26, 2014].

Lake, A., 1993. "From Containment to Enlargement." Available from: www.mtholyoke.edu/acad/intrel/lakedoc.html [accessed May 16, 2014].

Lavnikevich, D., 2013. "Will Yerevan compete with Minks for subsidies? [Erevan budet sopernichat s Minskom za dotatsii?]." *Belarus Business Paper [Belorusskaya Delovaya Gazeta]*. Available from: http://bdg.by/news/politics/25588.html [accessed September 11, 2013].

Lavrov, S., 2008. "Interview by Minister of Foreign Affaires of the Russian Federation Sergey Lavrov to BBC," Moscow, August 9.

Lazaryan, T., 2013. "Medvedev: The Customs Union will create additional opportunities for Armenia [Medvedev. Maksayin miutyuny Hayastani hamar lratsutsich hnaravoruty-unner ksteghtsi]." Radio Free Europe/Radio Liberty. Available from: www.azatutyun.am/content/article/25100739.html [accessed September 11, 2013].

Leonard, M., 2005. *Why Europe Will Run the 21st Century*. New York: Public Affairs.

Levitsky, S. and Way, L.A., 2010. *Competitive Authoritarianism: Hybrid Regimes After the Cold War* (1st edition). Cambridge: Cambridge University Press.

Linden, R. (ed.), 2002. *Norms and Nannies: The Impact of International Organizations on the CEE States*. Oxford: Rowman and Littlefield.

Linkevicius, L., 2013. Twitter, September 9. Available from: https://twitter.com/ [accessed September 10, 2013].

Lister, T., 2013. "Europe falls out of love with Obama over NSA spying claims." CNN. Available from: www.cnn.com/2013/10/24/world/europe/europe-us-surveillance/index.html [accessed November 20, 2013].

Lobjakas, A., 2004a. "EU Commissioner Says South Caucasus Has Future in Europe, But Must Be Patient." Radio Free Europe/Radio Liberty. Available from: www.azatutyun.am/content/article/1574130.html [accessed May 6, 2011].

Lobjakas, A., 2004b. "EU Keen to Get Involved in Nagorno-Karabakh Peace Process." Radio Free Europe/Radio Liberty. Available from: www.azatutyun.am/content/article/1573763.html [accessed May 6, 2011].

Lomsadze, G., 2013. "Azerbaijan to Move against International Organizations?" EurasiaNet, March 15.

McChesney, A., Nielsen, R., and Filatova, I., 2012. "Russia Closes USAID Office." *The Moscow Times*. Available from: www.themoscowtimes.com/news/article/russia-closes-usaid-office/468408.html [accessed November 21, 2013].

Magen, A. and McFaul, M., 2009. "Introduction: American and European Strategies to Promote Democracy" in Magen, A., Risse, T., and McFaul, M. (eds), *Promoting Democracy and the Rule of Law: American and European Strategies*. Basingstoke: Palgrave Macmillan.

Magen, A., Risse, T., and McFaul, M., 2009. *Promoting Democracy and the Rule of Law: American and European Strategies*. London: Palgrave Macmillan.

Mainwaring, S., 1998. "Party Systems in the Third Wave." *Journal of Democracy*, 9 (3), pp. 67–81.

Mainwaring, S., O'Donnell, G., and Valenzuela, S.J. (eds), 1992. *Issues in Democratic Consolidation: The New South American Democracies in Comparative Perspective.* Notre Dame: University of Notre Dame Press.

Malloy, J. and Seligson, M., 1987. *Authoritarians and Democrats: Regime Transition in Latin America* (1st edition). Pittsburgh: University of Pittsburgh Press.

Mandaville, A., 2007. "MCC and the Long Term Goal of Deepening Democracy." Available from: www.mcc.gov/documents/reports/mcc-112007-paper-democracy.pdf [accessed May 16, 2014].

Manners, I., 2002. "Normative Power Europe: A Contradiction in Terms?" *Journal of Common Market Studies*, 40 (2), pp. 235–258.

Marinov, N., 2004. "Do Sanctions Help Democracy? The US and EU's Record, 1977–2004." CDDRL Working Papers, 20.

Markarian, A., 2005. "Russia's Gazprom against Iranian Gas Transit through Armenia." Radio Free Europe/Radio Liberty. Available from: www.azatutyun.am/content/article/1576191.html [accessed November 7, 2011].

Markarian, A. and Stamboltsian, G., 2004. "EU Allots More Aid to Armenia." Radio Free Europe/Radio Liberty. Available from: www.azatutyun.am/content/article/1573276.html [accessed May 6, 2011].

Marquand, D., 1979. *Parliament for Europe*. London: Jonathan Cape.

Martin, R., 2008. "Russia's Georgia Invasion May Be about Oil." ABC News. Available from: http://abcnews.go.com/Business/story?id=5595811&page=1 [accessed August 26, 2011].

Martirosyan, N., 2014. "Gagik Tsarukyan: Pension reform is the most inhumane and inefficient method of budget replenishment." AmrInfo. Available from: www.arminfo.info/index.cfm?objectid=ADC28290–9651–11E3–807A0EB7C0D21663 [accessed February 27, 2014].

Martirosyan, S. and Mir Ismail, A., 2005. "Armenia and Azerbaijan Differ Over Russian Base Pull-Out." EurasiaNet, June 27.

Medvedev, D., 2008. "Statement by President of Russia Dmitry Medvedev." Available from: http://archive.kremlin.ru/eng/speeches/2008/08/26/1543_type82912_205752.shtml [accessed August 28, 2012].

Medzhid, F., 2011. "Experts are Sceptical over the Visit of the OSCE Minsk Group Co-Chairs"/Азербайджане эксперты скептически оценивают визит сопредседателей МГ ОБСЕ. *Caucasian Knot*. Available from: http://karabakh.kavkaz-uzel.ru/articles/182520/ [accessed September 21, 2011].

Melkumian, H., 2003. "US Concerned about Foul Play in Armenian Election Campaign." Radio Free Europe/Radio Liberty. Available from: www.azatutyun.am/content/article/1570804.html [accessed July 1, 2011].

Melkumian, H., 2008. "Press Review." Radio Free Europe/Radio Liberty. Available from: www.azatutyun.am/content/article/1596528.html [accessed April 15, 2011].

Melkumian, H. and Kalantarian, K., 2004. "Envoy Vague on Reported U.S. Push for Karabakh Peace." Radio Free Europe/Radio Liberty. Available from: www.azatutyun.am/content/article/1573970.html [accessed June 3, 2011].

Melkumian, H., Lobjakas, A., and Terian, A., 2004. "European Parliament Blocks Calls for Armenian Pullout from Azeri Lands." Radio Free Europe/Radio Liberty. Available from: www.azatutyun.am/content/article/1573157.html [accessed May 6, 2011].

Melzig, R. and Sprout, R., 2007. *Divergence and Convergence in Eastern Europe and Eurasia: One Transition Path or Two?* Program Office, Bureau for Europe and Eurasia, USAID, Working Paper Series on the Transition Countries No. 8.

Migdalovitz, C., 2001. *"Armenia–Azerbaijan Conflict."* Foreigh Affairs, Defense, and Trade Division, CRS Issue Brief for Congress No. IB92109.

Migdalovitz, C., 2004. *Armenia Update.* Washington, DC: Foreign Affairs, Defense, and Trade Division, CRS Report for Congress No. RS20812.

Minasyan, S., 2005. "EU–Armenia Cooperation and the New European Neighbourhood Policy" in Arakelian, A. and Nodia, G. (eds), *Constitutional/Political Reform Process in Georgia, in Armenia and Azerbaijan: Political Elite and Voices of the People.* Tbilisi, Georgia: International Institute for Democracy and Electoral Assistance; Caucasus Institute for Peace, Democracy and Development, pp. 129–140.

Mitofsky, W. and Lenski, J., 2005. "Adventure In Baku: Exit-Polling Azerbaijan | NCPP—National Council on Public Polls." National Council on Public Polls. Available from: http://ncpp.org/?q=node/77 [accessed February 26, 2014].

Mohammed, A., 2012. "Clinton warns of wider Caucasus conflict." Reuters. Available from:http://articles.chicagotribune.com/2012–06–04/news/sns-rt-us-armenia-clintonbre 85313y-20120604_1_armenia-and-azerbaijan-armenian-soldiers-nagorno-karabakh-conflict [accessed August 17, 2012].

Moldova.org, 2013. "Russia likely to ban wines from Moldova on Wednesday. Moldova.org. Available from: http://economie.moldova.org/news/russia-likely-to-ban-wines-from-moldova-on-wednesday-238778-eng.html [accessed September 10, 2013].

Møller, J. and Skaaning, S.-E., 2013. *Democracy and democratization in comparative perspective: conceptions, conjunctures, causes and consequences.* London: Routledge.

Moravcsik, A., 2002. "Reassessing Legitimacy in the European Union." *JCMS: Journal of Common Market Studies,* 40 (4), pp. 603–624.

Moravcsik, A., 2007. "The World's Quiet Superpower." European Voice. Available from: www.europeanvoice.com/article/imported/the-world-s-quiet-superpower/57108.aspx [accessed November 8, 2011].

Morell, J.A., 2005. "Why Are There Unintended Consequences of Program Action, and What Are the Implications for Doing Evaluation?" *American Journal of Evaluation,* 26 (4), pp. 444–463.

MSI, 2001. "Armenia: Media Sustainablity Index 2001." International Research and Exchanges Board. Available from: www.irex.org/system/files/06-Armenia.pdf [accessed May 16, 2014].

MSI, 2002. "Armenia: Media Sustainablity Index 2002." International Research and Exchanges Board. Available from: www.irex.org/system/files/Armenia.pdf [accessed May 16, 2014].

MSI, 2003. "Armenia: Media Sustainablity Index 2003." International Research and Exchanges Board. Available from: www.irex.org/system/files/MSI03-Armenia.pdf [accessed May 16, 2014].

Munck, G.L. and Verkuilen, J., 2002. "Conceptualizing and Measuring Democracy." *Comparative Political Studies,* 35 (1), pp. 5–34.

Muravchik, J., 2009. "The Abandonment of Democracy." *Commentary Magazine,* July. Available from: www.commentarymagazine.com/article/the-abandonment-of-democracy/ [accessed November 8, 2011].

Musabeyov, R., 2010. "Azerbaijan–Russia Bilateral Relations: Economics Prevails Politics." *Azerbaijan Focus,* 2 (3), pp. 141–147.

Musayelian, S. and Harutyunyan, L., 2013. "Mediators Visit Karabakh, Armenia." Radio Free Europe/Radio Liberty. Available from: www.azatutyun.am/content/article/24935383.html [accessed March 24, 2013].

Myers, S.L., 2002. "Georgia Moves against Rebels and Accuses Russia of Airstrikes." *New York Times*, August 24.

Napoletano, P., 2003. "Report on Wider Europe—Neighbourhood: A New Framework for Relations with our Eastern and Southern Neighbours." Available from: www.europarl. europa.eu/sides/getDoc.do?language=EN&objRefId=31192 [accessed May 16, 2014].

Nau, H.R., 2010. "Obama's Foreign Policy." *Hoover Institution Policy Review*, (160).

NDI, 2001. *NDI Quarterly Report: April 1 to June 30, 2001. Armenia.* National Democratic Institute.

NDI, 2005. *NDI Annual Report 2005.* National Democratic Institute.

NDI, 2011a. "About NDI." Available from: www.ndi.org/about_ndi?page=0,1 [accessed November 23, 2011].

NDI, 2011b. "Armenia." Available from: www.ndi.org/content/armenia [accessed November 23, 2011].

Nelson, S. and Katulis, B., 2005. *Armenia: Political Party Assessment.* Washington, DC: USAID.

News.am, 2010. "Russia May Betray Armenia." Available from: http://news.am/eng/news/26980.html [accessed September 21, 2011].

News.am, 2013. "EU suspends Twinning Project in Armenia." NEWS.am Available from: http://news.am/eng/news/169932.html [accessed September 9, 2013].

News.am, 2014a. "The News of the Death of the Armenian Soldier is a Tragedy. Mink Group Co-chair [Hay zinvori mahvan lury voxbergutyun e. Minski xmbi hamana-khagah]." Available from: http://news.am/arm/news/191564.html [accessed February 5, 2014].

News.am, 2014b. "Our Work is Incospicuous, You Do not Hear about It [Menq annkat enq ashkhatum, duq dra masin cheq lsum]." Available from: http://news.am/arm/news/192304.html [accessed February 5, 2014].

News.az, 2014. "Armenians Violate Ceasefire 204 times." Available from: http://news.az/articles/karabakh/86035 [accessed February 5, 2014].

Nichol, J., 2007. *Armenia's Legislative Election: Outcome and Implications for U.S. Interests.* CRS Report for Congress No. RS22675.

Nichol, J., 2010. *Armenia, Azerbaijan, and Georgia: Political Developments and Implications for US Interests.* Washingston, DC: CRS Report for Congress.

Nichol, J., 2011. *Armenia, Azerbaijan, and Georgia: Political Developments and Implications for US Interests.* Washington, DC: CRS Report for Congress.

Nie, N.H., Powell, G.B., and Prewitt, K., 1969. "Social Structure and Political Participation: Developmental Relationships, II." *The American Political Science Review*, 63 (3), pp. 808–832.

Niftiyev, E., 2010. "Gazprom–SOCAR gas deal: Should Azerbaijan commit to a long-term contract?" *Today's Zaman.* Available from: www.todayszaman.com/newsDetail_getNewsById.action;jsessionid=AB83ECA7EBC13D25B15B3DB7F37252C5?newsId=207061 [accessed August 26, 2011].

Nikolski, A., 2010. "Russia's North Caucasus Presidential Envoy Slams Georgia's Visa Move." RIA News. Available from: http://en.rian.ru/russia/20101026/161097488.html [accessed November 30, 2011].

Nikolski, A., 2013. "Putin faces protests as he woos Armenia." *Reuters.*

NIT, 2005. "Georgia." Freedom House. Available from: www.freedomhouse.org/report/nations-transit/2005/georgia#.UwzBw85fri8 [accessed February 25, 2014].

NIT, 2009. "Azerbaijan." Freedom House. Available from: www.freedomhouse.org/report/nations-transit/2009/azerbaijan#.UwzKv85fri8 [accessed February 25, 2014].

Nixey, J., 2012. "The Long Goodbye: Waning Russian Influence in the South Caucasus and Central Asia." *Chatham House Briefing Paper*, June.

Nuland, V., 2013a. "Toward A Transatlantic Renaissance: Ensuring Our Shared Future." US Department of State. Available from: www.state.gov/p/eur/rls/rm/2013/nov/217560.htm [accessed November 20, 2013].

Nuland, V., 2013b. *A Pivotal Moment for the Eastern Partnership: Outlook for Ukraine, Moldova, Georgia, Belarus, Armenia, and Azerbaijan.* Washington, DC: Subcommittee on European Affairs of the Senate Foreign Relations Committee.

O'Donnell, G., Schmitter, P.C., and Whitehead, L., 1986. *Transitions from Authoritarian Rule, Vol. 4: Tentative Conclusions about Uncertain Democracies.* Baltimore, MD: The Johns Hopkins University Press.

Obama, B., 2009. "Barack Obama's Inaugural Address." *The New York Times*, January 20.

Obama, B., 2013. "Barack Obama Inaugural Address 2013: full text." *Telegraph.co.uk*, January 21.

Olsen, G., 2002. "The European Union: An Ad Hoc Policy with a Low Priority" in Schraeder, P. (ed.), *Exporting Democracy: Rhetoric vs. Reality.* Boulder, CO and London: Lynne Riener, pp. 131–146.

Olsen, J.P. and March, J.G., 2004. *The Logic of Appropriatness.* Oslo: ARENA Centre for European Studies.

Olson, M., 1971. *The Logic of Collective Action: Public Goods and the Theory of Groups, Second printing with new preface and appendix* (revised edition). Harvard: Harvard University Press.

Orudzhev, R., 2008. "New Agreements are Needed to prevent violations of ceasefire [Нужны новые соглашения, чтобы предотвратить нарушения режима прекращения огня]." Echo-az. Available from: www.echo-az.com/archive/2008_11/1929/politica05.shtml [accessed September 21, 2011].

Osborn, A., 2009. "Azerbaijan military threat to Armenia." www.telegraph.co.uk, November 22.

Osborn, S., 1996. *Armenian Presidential Elections September 24, 1996.* Yerevan: Office for Democratic Institutions and Human Rights, OSCE.

OSCE, 1990. "Charter of Paris for a New Europe." OSCE. Available from: www.osce.org/mc/39516 [accessed May 16, 2014].

OSCE, 1998a. "Presidential Elections in the Republic of Azerbaijan 11 October 1998." OSCE. Available from: www.osce.org/odihr/elections/azerbaijan/14328 [accessed May 16, 2014].

OSCE, 1998b. *Republic of Armenia Presidential Election March 16 and 30, 1998.* Yerevan: Office for Democratic Institutions and Human Rights, OSCE.

OSCE, 1999. *Republic of Armenia Parliamentary Elections 30 May 1999.* Warsaw: Office for Democratic Institutions and Human Rights, OSCE.

OSCE, 2000. *Republic of Georgia Presidential Election 9 April 2000.* Warsaw: Office for Democratic Institutions and Human Rights, OSCE.

OSCE, 2001. "Republic of Azerbaijan Parliamentary Elections 5 November 2000 and 7 January 2001." Warsaw: Office for Democratic Institutions and Human Rights, OSCE.

OSCE, 2003a. *Republic of Armenia Presidential Election 19 February and 5 March 2003.* Warsaw: Office for Democratic Institutions and Human Rights, OSCE.

OSCE, 2003b. *Republic of Azerbaijan Presidential Elections 15 October 2003.* Warsaw: Office for Democratic Institutions and Human Rights, OSCE.

OSCE, 2003c. *Republic of Armenia Parliamentary Elections 25 May 2003.* Warsaw: Office for Democratic Institutions and Human Rights, OSCE.

OSCE, 2004a. *Report of the Co-Chairs of the OSCE Minsk Group to the OSCE Ministerial Council.* OSCE.

OSCE, 2004b. *Georgia Extraordinary Presidential Election 4 January 2004.* Warsaw: Office for Democratic Institutions and Human Rights, OSCE.

OSCE, 2008a. *Republic of Armenia Presidential Election 19 February 2008.* Warsaw: Office for Democratic Institutions and Human Rights, OSCE.

OSCE, 2008b. *Georgia Extraordinary Presidential Election 5 January 2008.* Warsaw: Office for Democratic Institutions and Human Rights, OSCE.

OSCE, 2009. "Co-Chairs of OSCE Minsk Group issue statement." Organization for Security and Co-operation in Europe. Available from: www.osce.org/mg/50689 [accessed September 21, 2011].

OSCE, 2010. "Republic of Azerbaijan Parliamentary Elections 7 November 2010." Warsaw: Office for Democratic Institutions and Human Rights, OSCE.

OSCE, 2012. "OSCE Minsk Group Co-Chairs meet with the Foreign Ministers of Armenia and Azerbaijan—Minsk Group." Available from: www.osce.org/mg/93343 [accessed March 25, 2013].

OSCE, 2013a. *Republic of Azerbaijan. Presidential Election 9 October 2013.* Warsaw: Office for Democratic Institutions and Human Rights, OSCE.

OSCE, 2013b. *Republic of Armenia Presidential Election 18 February 2013.* Warsaw: Office for Democratic Institutions and Human Rights, OSCE.

Oskanian, V., 2002. "Speech by Vartan Oskanian, Minister of Foreign Affairs, Republic of Armenia to the Yale Conference on the Caucasus and Central Asia." Ministry of Foreign Affairs of the Republic of Armenia. Available from: www.www.armeniaforeignministry.com/PR/PR177.html [accessed September 21, 2011].

Ottaway, M. and Carothers, T., 2000. *Funding Virtue: Civil Society Aid and Democracy Promotion.* Washington, DC: Carnegie Endowment for International Peace.

PACE, 2004. *Resolution 1374: Honouring of Obligations and Commitments by Armenia.* Council of Europe Parliamentary Assembly.

PACE, 2013. "Presidential election in Azerbaijan: joint statement by PACE and EP delegations." Parliamentary Assembly. Available from: www.assembly.coe.int/nw/xml/News/News-View-EN.asp?newsid=4699&lang=2&cat=31 [accessed February 25, 2014].

Packer, G., 2010. "Rights and Wrongs." *The New Yorker*, May 17.

Di Palma, G., 1990. *To Craft Democracies: An Essay on Democratic Transitions.* Berkeley, CA: University of California Press.

PanArmenian.Net, 2002. "Armenian and Russian Defense Ministers Agreed on Cooperation and Information Exchange in Military Shpere." PanArmenian.NET. Available from: www.panarmenian.net/eng/politics/news/2406/ARMENIAN_AND_RUSSIAN_DEFENSE_MINISTERS_AGREED_ON_COOPERATION_AND_INFORMATION_EXCHANGE_IN_MILITARY_SPHERE [accessed September 21, 2011].

PanArmenian.Net, 2013. "NSC chief: Customs Union offers more benefits than DCFTA." PanARMENIAN.Net. Available from: www.panarmenian.net/eng/news/169665/ [accessed September 9, 2013].

Panorama, 2013. "Vigen Sargsian: Association Agreement with EU remains on political agenda of Armenia." Available from: www.panorama.am/en/politics/2013/09/04/vigen-sargsyan/ [accessed September 11, 2013].

Parsadanyan, A., 2010. Deputy Chief of Party at Core Media Support Program for Armenia Funded by USAID and Implemented by IREX. Interview with author, June, Yerevan, Armenia.

Parsadanyan, A., 2011. Deputy Chief of Party at Core Media Support Program for Armenia Funded by USAID and Implemented by IREX. Email interview with author.

Patsuria, N., 2010. "Can Georgia Find the Backdoor for Exports into Russia?" EurasiaNet, May 17.

Perovic, J., 2005. "From Disengagement to Active Economic Competition: Russia's Return to the South Caucasus and Central Asia." *Demokratizatsiya*, 13 (1), pp. 61–85.

Pesov, E., 2010. "Georgia's Move to Cancel Visas for North Caucasus Residents 'Provocation'." *RIA News*. Available from: http://en.rian.ru/russia/20101014/160951835. html [accessed November 30, 2011].

Peter, L., 2013. "European furore over Azeri election." BBC, October 17.

Petrosyan, S., 2012. "Reporters in Armenia Can't Expect Any Assistance From Law Enforcement." Hetq. Available from: http://hetq.am/eng/articles/17891/lragroxnery-chen-karox-pashtpanutyun-aknkalel-ishkhanutyunneric.html [accessed February 28, 2014].

Petrova, T., 2012. "How Poland Promotes Democracy." *Journal of Democracy*, 23 (2), pp. 133–147.

Peuch, J.-C., 2001. "Armenia: President Kocharian Visits France." Radio Free Europe/ Radio Liberty. Available from: www.rferl.org/content/article/1095721.html [accessed September 21, 2011].

Pilkington, E., 2014. "Angela Merkel: Victoria Nuland's remarks on EU are unacceptable." *The Guardian*, February 7.

Pishchikova, K., 2010. *Promoting Democracy in Postcommunist Ukraine: The Contradictory Outcomes of US Aid to Women's NGOs*. Boulder, CO: FirstForum Press.

Popov, E., 2010. "Azerbaijan–Russia Bilateral Relations: Economics Prevails Politics." *Azerbaijan Focus*, 2 (3), pp. 13–25.

Poppe, A.E., 2010. *Whither to, Obama? US Democracy Promotion after the Cold War*. Frankfurt: Peace Research Institute, No. 96.

Poppe, A.E., Woitschach, B., and Wolff, J., 2013. "Freedom Fighter versus Civilian Power: An ideal-type comparison of US and German conceptions of democracy promotion" in Wolff, J., Spanger, H.-J., and Puhle, H.-J. (eds), *The comparative international politics of democracy promotion*. Abingdon, Oxon; New York: Routledge, pp. 38–60.

Populus, 2007. "Armenian Political Attitudes." Populus. Available from: www.populus. co.uk/uploads/download_pdf-100407-Armenia-TV-Armenian-Political-Attitudes.pdf [accessed May 16, 2014].

President of Russia, 2002. "President Vladimir Putin and President Heydar Aliyev Signed an Agreement on the Status and Principles and Terms of Using the Daryal-type Radar in Gabala." President of Russia Official Web Portal. Available from: http://archive. kremlin.ru/eng/text/news/2002/01/146984.shtml [accessed November 29, 2011].

Pressley, D., 2000. *A Decade of Change: Profiles of USAID Assistance to Europe and Eurasia*. Washington, DC: USAID.

Prodi, R., 2002. "A Wider Europe—A Proximity Policy as the key to stability "Peace, Security And Stability International Dialogue and the Role of the EU." Available from: http://europa.eu/rapid/pressReleasesAction.do?reference=SPEECH/02/619 [accessed November 8, 2011].

Psaki, J., 2013. "On the Armenia–Azerbaijan Summit on Nagorno-Karabakh." US Department of State. Available from: www.state.gov/r/pa/prs/ps/2013/11/217743.htm [accessed February 5, 2014].

Puddington, A., 2013. *Freedom in the World 2013: Democratic Breakthrough in the Balance*. Washington, DC: Freedom House.

Puddington, A., 2014. *Freedom in the World 2014: The Democratic Leadership Gap.* Washington, DC: Freedom House.

Pushkov, A., 2010. "Moving From 'Boris and Bill' to a Real Reset." *The Moscow Times,* September 8.

Putin, V., 1999. "Россия на рубеже тысячелетий [Russia crossing the Millenia] [online]." *Nezavisimaya Gazeta.* Available from: www.ng.ru/politics/1999–12–30/4_ millenium.html [accessed May 13, 2010].

Putin, V., 2011. "Новый интеграционный проект для Евразии—будущее, которое рождается сегодня [New integration project for Eurasia: the future that is being born now]." *Izvestia,* October 3.

Putnam, R.D., 1994. *Making Democracy Work: Civic Traditions in Modern Italy.* Princeton, NJ: Princeton University Press.

Radio Azadliq, 2013. "We do not sacrifice democracy for oil [My ne zhertvuem demokratiei vo imia nefti]." Radio Azadliq. Available from: www.radioazadlyg.org/content/article/24961046.html [accessed February 28, 2014].

Ragin, C.C., 1989. *The Comparative Method: Moving Beyond Qualitative and Quantitative Strategies.* Berkeley, CA: University of California Press.

Ragin, C.C., 1997. "Turning the tables: how case-oriented methods challenge variable-oriented methods." *Comparative Social Research,* 16, pp. 27–42.

Raymond, G.A., 1997. "Problems and Prospects in the Study of International Norms." *Mershon International Studies Review,* 41 (2), pp. 205–245.

Razumovskaya, O., 2013. "Russia Public Health Chief: May Ban Belarus Dairy Imports Any Day—Report." *Wall Street Journal,* September 5. Available from: http://online.wsj.com/article/BT-CO-20130905-703927.html [accessed September 15, 2013].

Reagan, R., 1982. "Address to British Parliament," London. Available from: www.historyplace.com/speeches/reagan-parliament.htm [accessed September 26, 2011].

Refworld, 2012. "Georgia: Arbitrary detention and assault of journalist and human rights defender Gela Mtivlishvili." Refworld. Available from: www.refworld.org/docid/4fdb2f06a.html [accessed February 28, 2014].

Regnum, 2006. "V khode poslednikh proverok v Moskve perstitsidi obnaruzheny v 60% moldavskikh i 44% gruzinskikh vin." Regnum News. Available from: www.regnum.ru/news/622196.html [accessed November 30, 2011].

Regnum, 2010. "Na dolu Azerbadzhana prikhoditsya 75% ekonomiki Yuzhnogo Kavkaza." Available from: www.regnum.ru/news/1309575.html [accessed November 30, 2011].

Republican Party, 2007. "Program of the Republican Party of Armenia." Available from: www.hhk.am/arm/index.php?page=program [accessed November 23, 2011].

Reuters, 2007. "FACTBOX: Georgia's Saakashvili divides country." Reuters. Available from: www.reuters.com/article/2007/11/07/us-georgia-opposition-idUSL0235425420071107 [accessed February 25, 2014].

Reuters, 2013. "Bolivia expels U.S. aid agency after Kerry 'backyard' comment." Reuters. Available from: www.reuters.com/article/2013/05/01/us-bolivia-usaid-idUSBRE94013V20130501 [accessed November 21, 2013].

RFE/RL, 2002. "Press Review [Mamuli Tesutyun]." Radio Free Europe/Radio Liberty. Available from: www.azatutyun.am/content/article/1569832.html [accessed September 28, 2011].

RFE/RL, 2006. "US Top Karabakh Negotiator Says 2006 is the Year for Deal." Radio Free Europe/Radio Liberty. Available from: www.azatutyun.am/content/article/1581106.html [accessed June 3, 2011].

RFE/RL, 2007a. "Azerbaijan Halts Oil Exports to Russia." Radio Free Europe/Radio Liberty. Available from: www.rferl.org/content/article/1073867.html [accessed August 26, 2011].

RFE/RL, 2007b. "Praise, Scorn For Accusations Against Georgia President." Radio Free Europe/Radio Liberty. Available from: www.rferl.org/content/article/1078803.html [accessed February 25, 2014].

RFE/RL, 2008a. "Armenia/Azerbaijan: Deadly Fighting Erupts In Nagorno-Karabakh." Radio Free Europe/Radio Liberty. Available from: www.rferl.org/content/article/1079580.html [accessed November 7, 2011].

RFE/RL, 2008b. "US Official Discusses Post-Election Unrest In Yerevan." Radio Free Europe/Radio Liberty. Available from: www.azatutyun.am/content/article/1593697.html [accessed July 1, 2011].

RFE/RL, 2008c. "US Threatens to Freeze Aid to Armenia." Radio Free Europe/Radio Liberty. Available from: www.azatutyun.am/content/article/1593860.html [accessed July 1, 2011].

RFE/RL, 2008d. "Georgia: In Surprise Move, Burjanadze Says She Won't Seek Reelection." Radio Free Europe/Radio Liberty. Available from: www.rferl.org/content/article/1109610.html [accessed February 26, 2014].

RFE/RL, 2008e. "Armenian Media Ban Still In Force." Radio Free Europe/Radio Liberty. Available from: www.azatutyun.am/content/article/1593885.html [accessed April 20, 2011].

RFE/RL, 2009. "Opponents Vow Protests Will Last 'As Long As Needed' To Oust Georgian President." Radio Free Europe/Radio Liberty. Available from: www.rferl.org/content/Georgian_Opposition_Vows_To_Protest_As_Long_As_Needed_Until_President_Resigns/1604901.html [accessed February 25, 2014].

RFE/RL, 2010a. "Karabakh Clashes Risk Escalation—EU Envoy." Radio Free Europe/Radio Liberty. Available from: www.azatutyun.am/content/article/2152338.html [accessed May 12, 2011].

RFE/RL, 2010b. "Norwegian Journalist Gets Azeri Treatment." Radio Free Europe/Radio Liberty. Available from: www.rferl.org/content/journalists_in_trouble_norwegian_journalist_gets_Azeri_treatment/2037587.html [accessed February 28, 2014].

RFE/RL, 2010c. "OSCE Slams Armenian TV Law." Radio Free Europe/Radio Liberty. Available from: www.azatutyun.am/content/article/2072726.html [accessed June 22, 2011].

RFE/RL, 2011a. "Abkhazia, South Ossetia Alarmed By Russia–Georgia WTO Compromise." Radio Free Europe/Radio Liberty. Available from: www.rferl.org/content/abkhazia_south_ossetia_alarmed_russia_georgia_wto_compromise/24384963.html [accessed November 30, 2011].

RFE/RL, 2011b. "Russia, Georgia Sign Deal Unblocking Russia's WTO Entry." Radio Free Europe/Radio Liberty. Available from: www.rferl.org/content/russia_georgia_sign_wto_deal/24385755.html [accessed November 30, 2011].

RFE/RL, 2011c. "Clinton Discusses Karabakh, U.S.–Armenian Ties With Nalbandian." Radio Free Europe/Radio Liberty. Available from: www.azatutyun.am/content/article/24180932.html [accessed June 3, 2011].

RFE/RL, 2011d. "U.S.: Armenia, Azerbaijan 'Must Pull Out Snipers.'" Radio Free Europe/Radio Liberty. Available from: www.rferl.org/content/us_urges_armenia_azerbaijan_to_withdraw_snipers/2343653.html [Accessed March 28, 2011].

RFE/RL, 2012a. "As Armenia Protests Killer's Pardon, Azerbaijan Promotes Him." Radio Free Europe/Radio Liberty. Available from: www.rferl.org/content/armenia-protest-azerbaijani-killer-pardon-to-osce-minsk-group/24694817.html [accessed March 25, 2013].

RFE/RL, 2012b. "Rostelekom intends to invest USD 30 mnl into Armenia's broadband network [Rostelekom nameren investirovat $30 mln v shirokopolosnii internet v Armenii]." Radio Free Europe/Radio Liberty. Available from: http://rus.azatutyun.am/content/article/24802515.html [accessed December 19, 2012].

RFE/RL, 2013a. "Are Armenia, Azerbaijan Closer To Signing Basic Principles Of Karabakh Peace Agreement?" Radio Free Europe/Radio Liberty. Available from: www.rferl.org/content/armenia-azerbaijan-karabakh-agreement/25177111.html [accessed February 5, 2014].

RFE/RL, 2013b. "Minsk Co-Chair Cites Mutual Armenian, Azerbaijan 'Respect' On Karabakh." Radio Free Europe/Radio Liberty. Available from: www.rferl.org/content/nagorno-karabakh-armenia-azerbaijan-respect/25206175.html [accessed February 5, 2014].

RFE/RL, 2013c. "EU Also Hails Aliyev–Sarkisian Talks." Radio Free Europe/Radio Liberty. Available from: www.azatutyun.am/content/article/25175548.html [accessed February 5, 2014].

RFE/RL, 2013d. "Armenia Condemns Azerbaijani Cease-Fire Violations." Radio Free Europe/Radio Liberty. Available from: www.rferl.org/content/armenia-azerbaijan-karabakh-violations/25202463.html [accessed February 5, 2014].

RFE/RL, 2013e. "Azerbaijan Puts Armenian Compensation For Nagorno-Karabakh At $300 Billion." Radio Free Europe/Radio Liberty. Available from: www.rferl.org/content/azerbaijan-compensation-armenia-karabakh/25195795.html [accessed February 5, 2014].

RFE/RL, 2013f. "Yerevan Confident About Association Agreement With EU." Radio Free Europe/Radio Liberty. Available from: www.azatutyun.am/content/article/25037930.html?utm_term=%23Armenia&utm_source=twitterfeed&utm_medium=twitter [accessed September 8, 2013].

RFE/RL, 2013g. "Füle Says EU Not Abandoning Armenia." Radio Free Europe/Radio Liberty. Available from: www.rferl.org/content/armenia-european-union-/25105725.html [accessed September 15, 2013].

RFE/RL, 2013h. "China Announces Extra Aid To Armenia." Radio Free Europe/Radio Liberty. Available from: www.azatutyun.am/content/article/25101640.html [accessed September 11, 2013].

RFE/RL, 2013i. "Armenia wants an observer status to the SCO [Armenia zhelaet poluchit status nabludatelia v SHOS]." Radio Free Europe/Radio Liberty. Available from: http://rus.azatutyun.am/archive/New/20130910/3282/3282.html?id=25101908 [accessed September 11, 2013].

RFE/RL, 2013j. "Georgia aspires for Europe but does not exclude the membership in the Eurasian Union [Gruzia stremitsa k Evrope, no ne iskluchaet chlenstva v Evraziiskom soyuze]." Radio Free Europe/Radio Liberty. Available from: http://rus.azatutyun.am/content/gruzia-kurs-na-evropu-ili-tamozhenniy-soyuz/25101810.html [accessed September 11, 2013].

RFE/RL, 2013k. "International Organizations Urge Azerbaijan To Stop Harassing Journalist." Radio Free Europe/Radio Liberty. Available from: www.rferl.org/content/azerbaijan-letter-harassment-ismayilova/25075480.html [accessed February 27, 2014].

RFE/RL, 2014a. "Retired Armenian Police Officer Arrested For Spying For Azerbaijan." Radio Free Europe/Radio Liberty. Available from: www.rferl.org/content/armenia-azerbaijan-spy-arrest/25253901.html [accessed February 5, 2014].

RFE/RL, 2014b. "Azerbaijani Forces Detain Armenian 'Saboteur.'" Radio Free Europe/Radio Liberty. Available from: www.rferl.org/content/azerbaijan-armenia-espionage/25246921.html [accessed February 5, 2014].

RFE/RL, 2014c. "Baku Says Officer Killed By Armenian Snipers." Radio Free Europe/ Radio Liberty. Available from: www.rferl.org/content/karabakh-armenian-snipers/ 25244081.html [accessed February 5, 2014].

RFE/RL, 2014d. "OSCE Mediator Sees Progress In Nagorno-Karabakh Talks." Radio Free Europe/Radio Liberty. Available from: www.rferl.org/content/azerbaijan-armenia-karabakh-progress/25253225.html [accessed February 5, 2014].

RFE/RL, 2014e. "Azerbaijani Prosecutors Pursue 'Absurd' Allegations Against Ismay-ilova." Radio Free Europe/Radio Liberty. Available from: www.rferl.org/content/release-azerbaijani-prosecutors-pursue-absurd-allegations-against-ismayilova/25271551.html [accessed February 27, 2014].

RFE/RL, 2014f. "AIB Voices Concern For Journalists in Azerbaijan." Radio Free Europe/ Radio Liberty. Available from: www.rferl.org/content/journalists-in-azerbaijan-aib-voices-concern/25275139.html [accessed February 27, 2014].

RFE/RL, 2014g. "Kerry Pledges Support For Georgians' Visa-Free Travel To EU." Radio Free Europe/Radio Liberty. Available from: www.rferl.org/content/georgia-kerry-eu-travel-visa/25278328.html [accessed March 3, 2014].

RIA, 2011. "Russia Seeks Extension of Azerbaijan Eadar Lease until 2025." *RIA News*. Available from: http://en.rian.ru/world/20111118/168801283.html [accessed November 29, 2011].

RIA, 2012a. "Putin Stated Seeing Positive Signals from Georgia [Putin zayavil, chto vidit positivnie signali ot Gruzii]." *RIA News*. Available from: http://ria.ru/world/ 20121220/915585866.html [accessed December 20, 2012].

RIA, 2012b. "RF Wants to Improve Relations with Georgia but will not Change Its Deci-sions [RF khochet uluchshit otnoshenia s Gruziei, no ne izmenit svoikh reshenii]." *RIA News*. Available from: http://ria.ru/world/20121220/915587550.html [accessed Decem-ber 20, 2012].

RIA, 2012c. "United Russia Received USAID Money—U.S. State Department. *RIA News*. Available from: http://en.ria.ru/russia/20120921/176098342.html [accessed November 21, 2013].

RIA, 2012d. "Russia Rights Activists Decry USAID Closure." *RIA News*. Available from: http://en.ria.ru/politics/20120919/176066650.html [accessed November 21, 2013].

RIA News, 2007. "Abkhazia demands Georgia pay $13 bln war compensation." RIA Novosti. Available from: http://en.rian.ru/world/20070911/77972132.html [accessed December 10, 2012].

RIA News, 2011. "The U-turn over the Atlantic [Разворот над Атлантикой]." RIA News. Available from: http://ria.ru/history_comments/20110321/356280998.html [accessed September 21, 2011].

RIA News, 2012. "U.S.–Russia Cooperation Based on Interests—White House." RIA News. Available from: http://en.ria.ru/world/20120309/172012174.html [accessed Feb-ruary 22, 2014].

RIA News, 2013. "Agreements with RF will allow Armenia not to raise gas tariffs for five years [Dogovorennosti s RF pozvoliat Armenii 5 let ne povishat tarify na gaz] [online]." RIA News. Available from: http://ria.ru/economy/20131203/981696111.html [accessed February 7, 2014].

RIA News, 2014. "Billionaire Ivanishvili Gets Back His Georgian Citizenship." RIA News. Available from: http://en.ria.ru/world/20140128/186984364/Billionaire-Ivanishvili-Gets-Back-His-Georgian-Citizenship.html [accessed February 27, 2014].

Rice, C., 2005. "Remarks at the American University in Cairo." Available from: http://2001-2009.state.gov/secretary/rm/2005/48328.htm [accessed February 24, 2013].

Rice, S.E., 2013. "Human Rights: Advancing American Interests and Values." The White House. Available from: www.whitehouse.gov/the-press-office/2013/12/04/remarks-national-security-advisor-susan-e-rice-human-rights-advancing-am [accessed March 1, 2014].

De Ridder, E. and Kochenov, D., 2011. "Democratic Conditionality in the Eastern Enlargement: Ambitious Window Dressing." *European Foreign Affairs Review*, 16 (5), pp. 589–605.

Riker, W.H., 1982. *Liberalism Against Populism: A Confrontation Between the Theory of Democracy and the Theory of Social Choice.* Long Grove, IL: Waveland Press.

Risse, T., 2009. "Conclusions: Towards Transatlantic Democracy Promotion?" in Magen, A., Risse, T., and McFaul, M. (eds), *Promoting Democracy and the Rule of Law: American and European Strategies.* Basingstoke: Palgrave Macmillan.

Risse, T., 2013. *The persistent power of human rights: from commitment to compliance.* Cambridge: Cambridge University Press.

Risse, T., Ropp, S.C., and Sikkink, K., 1999. *The Power of Human Rights: International Norms and Domestic Change.* Cambridge: Cambridge University Press.

Robbins, G., 2011. "The US continues to support the Geneva Discussions on Georgia." Mission of the United States to Switzerland. Available from: http://geneva.usmission.gov/2011/10/14/geneva-discussion-georgia/ [accessed December 10, 2012].

Robinson, W.I., 1996. *Promoting Polyarchy: Globalization, US Intervention, and Hegemony.* Cambridge: Cambridge University Press.

Rosenblum, D., 2011. "Twenty Years of Democracy and Governance Programs in Europe and Eurasia." US Department of State. Available from: www.state.gov/p/eur/rls/rm/2011/187475.htm [accessed November 20, 2013].

Rosneft, 2013. "Rosneft president Igor Sechin held a business meeting with the management of Nairit factory [President Rosnefti Igor Sechin provel rabochuyu vstrechu s rukovodstvom zavoda Nairit]." Rosneft. Available from: www.rosneft.ru/news/pressrelease/03092013.html [accessed September 15, 2013].

Rozhnov, K., 2010. "Georgia and Russia Do Business Despite Tense Relations." BBC.

Runner, P., 2008. "Poland and Sweden to pitch 'Eastern Partnership' idea." EUobserver.com. Available from: http://euobserver.com/9/26194 [accessed May 12, 2011].

Rutland, P. and Dubinsky, G., 2008. "US Foreign Policy in Russia" in Cox, M. and Stokes, D. (eds), *US Foreign Policy.* Oxford: Oxford University Press.

Rywkin, M., 2003. "Russia and the Near Abroad Under Putin." *American Foreign Policy Interests*, 25 (1), pp. 3–12.

Saakashvili, M., 2006. "The Path To Energy Security." *Washington Post*, January 9.

Saat, J.H., 2005. *The Collective Security Treaty Organization.* Surrey, England: Conflict Studies Research Center, No. 05/09.

Saghabalian, A., 2005a. "Armenia, EU To Start Delayed Talks On Joint Action Plan." Radio Free Europe/Radio Liberty. Available from: www.azatutyun.am/content/article/1578659.html [accessed May 6, 2011].

Saghabalian, A., 2005b. "US Offers $6 Million Election-Related Assistance to Armenia." Radio Free Europe/Radio Liberty. Available from: www.azatutyun.am/content/article/1579016.html [accessed July 1, 2011].

Saghabalian, A., 2006. "Clean Vote 'Crucially Important' For Armenia's Ties With EU." Radio Free Europe/Radio Liberty. Available from: www.azatutyun.am/content/article/1583174.html [accessed June 28, 2011].

Sargsyan, T., 2010. Training Department Manager at Core Media Support Program for Armenia Funded by USAID and Implemented by IREX. Interview with author, June, Yerevan, Armenia.

Sarkisian, V., 2004. "Press Review." Radio Free Europe/Radio Liberty. Available from: www.azatutyun.am/content/article/1573667.html [accessed April 8, 2011].

Sartori, G., 1970. "Concept Misformation in Comparative Politics." *The American Political Science Review*, 64 (4), p. 1033.

Schimmelfennig, F., 2001. "The Community Trap: Liberal Norms, Rhetorical Action, and the Eastern Enlargement of the European Union." *International Organization*, 55 (01), pp. 47–80.

Schimmelfennig, F., 2002. "Introduction: The Impact of International Organizations on the CEE States-Conceptual and Theoretical Issues" in Linden, R. (ed.), *Norms and Nannies: The Impact of International Organizations on the CEE States*. Oxford: Rowman and Littlefield, pp. 1–32.

Schimmelfennig, F., 2003. "Strategic Action In A Community Environment: The Decision to Enlarge the European Union to the East." *Comparative Political Studies*, 36 (1–2), pp. 156–183.

Schimmelfennig, F. and Scholtz, H., 2008. "EU Democracy Promotion in the European Neighbourhood." *European Union Politics*, 9 (2), pp. 187–215.

Schimmelfennig, F. and Sedelmeier, U. (eds), 2005. "The Demand-side Politics of EU Enlargement: Democracy and the Application for EU membership" in *The Politics of European Union Enlargement: Theoretical Approaches*. London: Routledge, pp. 3–29.

Schimmelfennig, F., Engert, S., and Knobel, H., 2006. *International Socialization in Europe: European Organizations, Political Conditionality and Democratic Change*. London: Palgrave Macmillan.

Schmitter, P.C., 2000. *How to Democratize the EU … and Why Bother?* Lanham, MD: Rowman & Littlefield.

Schmitter, P.C. and Brouwer, I., 1999. "Conceptualizing, Researching and Evaluating Democracy Promotion and Protection." Available from: http://econpapers.repec.org/paper/ftheurops/99_2f9.htm [accessed October 11, 2011].

Schmitter, P.C. and Karl, T.L., 1991. "What Democracy Is … and Is Not." *Journal of Democracy*, 2 (3), pp. 75–88.

Schmitz, H.P., 2004. "Domestic and Transnational Perspectives on Democratization." *International Studies Review*, 6 (3), pp. 403–426.

Schneider, C.Q., 2009. *The consolidation of democracy: comparing Europe and Latin America*. Milton Park, Abingdon, Oxon; New York: Routledge.

Schriek, D. van der, 2002. "Moscow Hostage Crisis Encourages Closer Russian-Azerbaijani Relations." EurasiaNet. Available from: www.eurasianet.org/departments/insight/articles/eav103002.shtml [accessed August 26, 2011].

Schumpeter, J.A., 1947. *Capitalism, Socialism and Democracy* (2nd edition). New York: Harper and Brothers.

Scott-Smith, G. and Mos, M., 2009. "New Public Diplomacy and Democracy Promotion" in Parmar, I., Miller, L.B., and Ledwidge, M. (eds), *New Directions in US Foreign Policy*. London: Routledge.

Secrieru, S., 2006. "Russia's Foreign Policy Under Putin: 'CIS Project Renewed.'" *UNISCI Dicussion Papers*, 10, pp. 289–308.

Seeberg, P., 2009. "The EU as a realist actor in normative clothes: EU democracy promotion in Lebanon and the European Neighbourhood Policy." *Democratization*, 16 (1), pp. 81–99.

Seher, J., 2014. "Republicans call on Obama to act on Ukraine." CNN. Available from: http://politicalticker.blogs.cnn.com/2014/03/01/republicans-call-on-obama-to-act-in-ukraine/ [accessed March 3, 2014].

Sen, A.K., 1999. "Democracy as a Universal Value." *Journal of Democracy*, 10 (3), pp. 3–17.

Senate Appropriations Committee, 2005. *S.Rept. 109–96/ H.R. 3057, FY 2006*. Department of State, Foreign Operations, and Related Programs Appropriations,, No. 109–96.

Senate Appropriations Committee, 2006. *S.Rept. 109–277/H.R. 5522, FY2007*. Department of State, Foreign Operations, and Related Programs Appropriations, No. 109–277.

Shah, R., 2013. "Democracy, Human Rights and Governance Strategy." USAID. Available from: www.usaid.gov/democracy-human-rights-and-governance-strategy [accessed November 21, 2013].

Shakaryants, S., 2012. "Russia leaves Gabala radar station." *The Voice of Russia*. Available from: http://english.ruvr.ru/2012_12_14/Russia-leaves-Gabala-radar-station/ [accessed December 21, 2012].

Shapovalova, N., 2009. "The EU's Eastern Partnership: Still-born?" *FRIDE Policy Brief*, 11.

Shapovalova, N. and Youngs, R., 2012. "EU democracy promotion in the Eastern neighbourhood." *FRIDE Working Paper*, 115.

Shapovalova, N. and Zarembo, K., 2010. "Russia's Machiavellian Support for Democracy." *FRIDE Policy Brief*, 56.

Shoghikian, H., 2009. "EU To Fund 'Institutional Reform' in Armenia." Radio Free Europe/Radio Liberty. Available from: www.azatutyun.am/content/article/1823478.html [accessed November 8, 2011].

Shoghikian, H., Stepanian, R., and Bedevian, A., 2008. "Ter-Petrosian Claims Victory, Rallies Thousands in Yerevan." Radio Free Europe/Radio Liberty. Available from: www.azatutyun.am/content/article/1593252.html [accessed November 9, 2011].

Shuster, S., 2010. "Clinton to Visit Moscow amid Strained U.S.–Russia Relations." *Time*, March 16. Available from: www.time.com/time/world/article/0,8599,1971651,00.html [accessed September 21, 2011].

Simonyan, S., 2013. "Rosneft President Sechin came because of Nairit [Rosneft President Sechin priexal iz-za Nairita]." InoSMI. Available from: http://inosmi.ru/sng-baltia/20130409/207871543.html [accessed September 15, 2013].

Sindelar, D., 2006. "Georgia: Tbilisi Accuses Moscow Of Energy Sabotage." Radio Free Europe/Radio Liberty. Available from: www.rferl.org/content/article/1064976.html [accessed August 26, 2011].

Smbatian, H., 2010. "Armenia, Russia Sign Extended Defense Pact." Radio Free Europe/Radio Liberty. Available from: www.azatutyun.am/content/article/2132965.html [accessed November 7, 2011].

Smith, H., 2002. *European Union Foreign Policy: What It is and What It Does*. London: Pluto Press.

Smith, K.E., 2008. *European Union Foreign Policy in a Changing World* (2nd edition). Cambridge: Polity Press.

Smith, M. and Woolcock, S., 1993. *The United States and the European Community in a transformed world*. London: Pinter.

Socor, V., 2006. "Armenia'S Giveaways to Russia: From Property-for-Debt to Property-for-Gas." *Eurasia Daily Monitor*, 3 (76).

Socor, V., 2007. "Iran–Armenia Gas Pipeline: Far More than Meets the Eye. *Eurasia Daily Monitor*, March 21.

Socor, V., 2010. "The Jamestown Foundation: Russia Deploys S-300 Air Defense Systems in Abkhazia." *Eurasia Daily Monitor*, 7 (155).

Speck, U., 2011. "Pacifism unbound: Why Germany limits EU hard power." *FRIDE Policy Brief*, 75.

Stamboltsian, G., 2013. "Saakashvili: Armenia is not the best example for Georgia. [Saakashvili. Vrastani hamar Hayastany lavaguin orinaky che]." Radio Free Europe/ Radio Liberty. Available from: www.azatutyun.am/content/article/25105095.html [accessed September 15, 2013].

Starr, H., 1991. "Democratic Dominoes: Diffusion Approaches to the Spread of Democracy in the International System." *The Journal of Conflict Resolution*, 35 (2), pp. 356–381.

State Department, 2008. "Institutionalizing The Freedom Agenda: President Bush Calls On Future Presidents And Congresses To Continue Leading The Cause Of Freedom Worldwide." *US Department of State. Archive*. Available from: http://2001-2009.state. gov/r/pa/prs/ps/2008/oct/110871.htm [accessed February 24, 2013].

Stefes, C.H., 2008. "Governance, the State, and Systemic Corruption: Armenia and Georgia in Comparison." *Caucasian Review of International Affairs*, 2 (2), pp. 73–83.

Stepanian, R., 2013a. "Government Admits Secret Rise In Russian Gas Price." Radio Free Europe/Radio Liberty. Available from: www.azatutyun.am/content/article/25191414. html?utm_source=dlvr.it&utm_medium=facebook [accessed February 7, 2014].

Stepanian, R., 2013b. "Association Agreement With EU Still Possible, Says Yerevan." Radio Free Europe/Radio Liberty. Available from: www.azatutyun.am/content/ article/25095551.html [accessed September 8, 2013].

Stepanian, R., 2013c. "Hovannisian Condemns West For Congratulating Sarkisian." Radio Free Europe/Radio Liberty. Available from: www.azatutyun.am/content/ article/24913187.html [accessed February 28, 2014].

Stepanyan, R., 2013a. "The issue of gas price subsidies will be decide within the Customs Union framework [Vopros subsidirovania tseni na gaz budet reshen v ramkakh tamozhennogo soyuza]." Radio Free Europe/Radio Liberty. Available from: http://rus. azatutyun.am/content/article/25103117.html [accessed September 15, 2013].

Stepanyan, R., 2013b. "Nalbandyan finds further cooperation with the EU possible [Nalbandyan schitaet vozmozhnim dalneishee sotrudnischestvo s ES]." Radio Free Europe/ Radio Liberty. Available from: http://rus.azatutyun.am/content/article/25101493.html [accessed September 11, 2013].

Stepanyan, R., 2013c. "Füle. No agreement will be signed with Armenia in Vilnus [Füle. Vilnyusum Hayastani het pastatught chi storagrvi]." Radio Free Europe/Radio Liberty. Available from: www.azatutyun.am/content/article/25105152.html [accessed September 15, 2013].

Sultanova, A., 2010. "Azerbaijan passes law further restricting media." Boston.com, February 13.

Svetlik, M., Carlson, J., and Zaslavskaya, I., 2003. "Azerbaijan, Final Report." IFES. Available from: www.ifes.org/~/media/Files/Publications/VRC/Reports/2003/R01519/ R01519.pdf [accessed May 16, 2014].

Talbott, S., 2003. *The Russia Hand: A Memoir of Presidential Diplomacy*. New York: Random House Trade Paperbacks.

Tamrazian, H., 2013. "Füle: A number of achievements can be made if there is trust [Füle. Ete vstahytyun lini, shat bani kareli e hasnel]." Radio Free Europe/Radio Liberty. Available from: www.azatutyun.am/content/article/25105723.html [accessed September 15, 2013].

Telegraph, 2008. "Vladimir Putin Threatened to Hang Georgia Leader 'by the Balls.'" *The Telegraph*, November 13.

Telò, M., 2007. *Europe: a civilian power? : European Union, global governance, world order*. Basingstoke: Palgrave Macmillan.

Thiel, M., 2004. "The Conditionality of U.S. & E.U. Development Aid upon Democratization—A Comparison." Online Working Paper, Universidad National Autonoma Mexico. Available from: www.estudioseuropeos.unam.mx/e_working_papers/the_conditionality_us.pdf

Thompson, M., 2010. "Media Freedom in a Democratic Society. In Conference on Media Freedom." Council of Europe. Available from: https://hub.coe.int/c/document_library/ get_file?uuid=87d7ff65-f4ff-479b-8c41-0d541418def4&groupId=10227 [accessed May 16, 2014].

Tisdall, S., 2010. "Ethiopia's 'one-party democracy' is spreading." *The Guardian*. Available from: www.guardian.co.uk/commentisfree/2010/may/26/ethiopia-one-party-democracy-africa [accessed January 14, 2013].

Tocci, N., 2006. "Conflict and Reform in Eastern Europe—EU Neglect and Competing Mediation in Georgia's Conflicts." *The International Spectator: Italian Journal of International Affairs*, 41 (4), p. 69.

Tolstrup, J., 2009. "Studying a negative external actor: Russia's management of stability and instability in the 'Near Abroad.'" *Democratization*, 16 (5), pp. 922–944.

Torreblanca, J.I. and Fanes, J.V., 2011. "Are the Arab Revolutions the last nail in the UM coffin?" The European Council on Foreign Relations. Available from: http://ecfr.eu/ content/entry/commentary_are_the_arab_revolutions_the_last_nail_in_the_um_coffin [accessed May 12, 2011].

Trail, L., 2003. *Final Report: ProMedia/Armenia*. Washington, DC: International Research and Exchanges Board.

Trail, L., 2009. *Final Program Report: Core Media Support Program for Armenia*. Washington, DC: International Research and Exchanges Board.

Trend, 2012. "Georgian Interior Ministry welcomes Russian investors." trend.az. Available from: http://en.trend.az/regions/scaucasus/georgia/2019352.html [accessed December 19, 2012].

Treverton, G.F., 1992. *America, Germany, and the Future of Europe*. Princeton, NJ: Princeton University Press.

Tsereteli, M., 2005. "Russian Economic Expansion in the Caucasus: A Challenge for Georgia." *Central-Asia Caucasus Analyst*, 6 (5), pp. 5–7.

Tsereteli, M., 2009. *The Impact of the Russia-Georgia War on the South Caucasus Transportation Corridor*. Washingston, DC: The Jamestown Foundation.

Tsotniashvili, E., 2011. "Medvedev Interview Stirs Memories of August War." *The Messenger Online*. Available from: www.messenger.com.ge/issues/2415_august_8_ 2011/2415_medvedev.html [accessed November 30, 2011].

Tsygankov, A., 2006. "If not by Tanks, then by Banks? The Role of Soft Power in Putin's Foreign Policy." *Europe–Asia Studies*, 58 (7), pp. 1079–1099.

Tsygankov, A.P. and Tarver-Wahlquist, M., 2009. "Duelling Honors: Power, Identity and the Russia–Georgia Divide." *Foreign Policy Analysis*, 5 (4), pp. 307–326.

UNDP, 2001. *10 Years of Independence and Transition in Armenia*. UNDP, National Human Development Report.

United Nations News Service, 2011. "Armenia and Azerbaijan Express Views on Nagorno-Karabakh during UN debate." United Nations-DPI/NMD—UN News Service Section. Available from: www.un.org/apps/news/story.asp?NewsID=39876&Cr=Azer baijan&Cr1 [accessed May 29, 2012].

US Congress, 1996. *Freedom for Russia and Emerging Eurasian Democracies and Open Markets*.

US Embassy cable, 2006. *Azerbaijan: Ambassador Discusses Upcoming Draft with World Bank Mission*. US Embassy Baku (Azerbaijan): Wikileaks No. 06BAKU218_a.

US Embassy cable, 2008. *Georgia Not Willing To Accept Arria In Exchange For Unomig Renewal*. US Embassy Tbilisi (Georgia): Wikileaks, No. 08TBILISI1845.

US Embassy cable, 2009a. *Russian Analysts Tell A/S Gordon Anti-Americanism Pillar Of Russian Foreign Policy*. US Embassy Moscow (Russia): Wikileaks, No. 09MOSCOW2371.

US Embassy cable, 2009b. *Baku's Perspectives On Nagorno-Karabakh*. US Embassy Baku (Azerbaijan): Wikileaks, No. 09BAKU22.

US Embassy cable, 2009c. *Azerbaijan: President's Foreign Policy Advisor Discusses Regional Issues And Nabucco*. US Embassy Baku (Azerbaijan): Wikileaks, No. 09BAKU448.

US Embassy cable, 2009d. *Azerbaijan: Defense Minister On Russia Tensions*. US Embassy Baku (Azerbaijan): Wikileaks, No. 09BAKU334.

US Embassy cable, 2009e. *Eur Das Bryza Drums Up Political Party Support For Possible Turkey And/Or NK Peace Deals*. US Embassy Yerevan (Armenia): Wikileaks, No. 09YEREVAN269.

US Embassy cable, 2009f. *Azerbaijan: MPs Debate NK And Democratic Reform*. US Embassy Baku (Azerbaijan): Wikileaks, No. 09BAKU955.

US Embassy cable, 2009g. *FM Sikorski Pitches U.S.–polish Teamwork On Community Of Democracies To A/S Posner*. US Embassy Warsaw (Poland): Wikileaks, No. 09WARSAW1069.

US Embassy cable, 2009h. *Ambassador's Meeting With Community Of Democracies Coordinator Pavilionis*. US Embassy Vilnius (Lithuania): Wikileaks, No. 09VILNIUS716.

US State Department, 2009. "Democracy." US State Department. Available from: www.state.gov/j/drl/democ/ [accessed November 21, 2013].

US State Department, 2010. "FY 2010 Department of State Agency Financial Report." Available from: www.state.gov/s/d/rm/rls/perfrpt/2010/html/153536.htm [accessed November 23, 2011].

USAID, 1999a. *The Role of Media in Democracy: A Strategic Approach*. Center for Democracy and Governance Bureau for Global Programs, Field Support, and Research, USAID, Technical Publication Series.

USAID, 1999b. *Lessons in Implementation: the NGO Story. Building Civil Society in Central and Eastern Europe and the New Independent States*. USAID.

USAID, 1999c. "USAID/Armenia Strategic Plan FY 1999 – FY 2003." USAID. Available from: www.usaid.gov/locations/europe_eurasia/countries/am/strategic.plan/html/str99pub.htm [accessed November 8, 2011].

USAID, 2000. "Strategic Plan Azerbaijan." Available from: http://pdf.usaid.gov/pdf_docs/pdabs379.pdf [accessed May 16, 2014].

USAID, 2004. "USAID/Armenia Strategy for 2004–2008." Available from: www.usaid.gov/locations/europe_eurasia/countries/am/docs/strategy_2004-2008.pdf

USAID, 2005. "At Freedom's Frontiers. A Democracy and Governance Strategic Framework." Available from: http://pdf.usaid.gov/pdf_docs/PDACF999.pdf [accessed May 16, 2014]

USAID, 2008. *New Media and International Media Development Resource Guide for Europe and Eurasia*. Washington, DC: USAID.

USAID, 2009. "Country Assistance Strategy: Armenia 2009–2013." Available from: http://armenia.usaid.gov/sites/default/files/USG%20Country%20Assistance%20Strategy%20March%20Post%20Revisions%20to%20Respond%20to%20DRL-GF-%20ACE%20comments.pdf

USAID, 2013a. "USAID Strategy on Human Rights, Democracy and Governance." USAID. Available from: www.usaid.gov/democracy-human-rights-and-governance-strategy [accessed November 21, 2013].

USAID, 2013b. "USAID Mission Director for Bolivia Sworn-in." USAID. Available from: www.usaid.gov/news-information/press-releases/usaid-mission-director-bolivia-sworn [accessed November 21, 2013].

Valiyev, A., 2009a. *Finlandization or Strategy of Keeping the Balance? Azerbaijan's Foreign policy since the Russian–Georgian War.* PONARS, Eurasia Policy memo No. 112.

Valiyev, A., 2009b. "Victim of a 'War of Ideologies.'" *Demokratizatsiya: The Journal of Post-Soviet Democratization,* 17 (3), pp. 269–288.

Vanhanen, T., 1997. *Prospects of Democracy: A Study of 172 Countries* (1st edition). London: Routledge.

Vasconcelos, A. de, 2012. *ESPAS Report: 'Global Trends 2030—Citizens in an Intercon-nected and Polycentric World'.* Paris: Institute for Security Studies.

Vickery, C., Minda, M., Svetlik, M., and Kaufman, P., 2002. "Armenia Final Report." IFES. Available from: www.ifes.org/Content/Publications/Reports/2002/Armenia-Final-Report.aspx [accessed May 16, 2014].

de Waal, T., 2012. "A Crucial Election in Georgia." Carnegie Endowment for International Peace. Available from: http://carnegieendowment.org/2012/09/11/crucial-election-in-georgia/drlp [accessed December 22, 2012].

Waisbord, S., 2000. *Watchdog Journalism in South America: News, Accountability and Democracy.* New York: Columbia University Press.

Walker, S., 2012. "The New Titan of Tbilisi." *Foreign Policy.* Available from: www.foreign-policy.com/articles/2012/10/02/the_new_titan_of_tbilisi [accessed December 20, 2012].

Washington Post, 1998. "A Democracy Loses Its Way." *The Washington Post,* February 7.

Way, L.A., 2009. "State Power and Autocratic Stability: Armenia and Georgia Compared" in Wooden, A.E. and Stefes, C.H. (eds), *The Politics of Transition in Central Asia and the Caucasus: Enduring Legacies and Emerging Challenges.* Abingdon, Oxfordshire: Routledge.

Weigle, M.A. and Butterfield, J., 1992. "Civil Society in Reforming Communist Regimes: The Logic of Emergence." *Comparative Politics,* 25 (1), pp. 1–23.

Wetzel, A. and Orbie, J., 2012. "The EU's Promotion of External Democracy: In search of the plot." The Centre for European Policy Studies, *CEPS Policy Brief.*

White, G., 1994. "Civil society, democratization and development (I): Clearing the analytical ground." *Democratization,* 1, pp. 375–390.

Whitehead, L., 1997. "Bowling in the Bronx: The Uncivil Interstices between Civil and Political Society" in Fine, R. and Rai, S. (eds.), *Civil Society: Democratic Perspectives.* London: Routledge.

Whitehead, L., 2002. *Democratization: Theory and Experience.* Oxford: Oxford University Press.

Whitehead, L., 2005. *The International Dimensions of Democratization: Europe and the Americas.* Oxford: Oxford University Press.

Wilson, W., 1917. *Making the World 'Safe for Democracy'.* Washington, DC: US Congress.

Wolff, J., Spranger, H.-J., and Puhle, H.-J., 2013. *The Comparative International Politics of Democracy Promotion.* London: Routledge.

Wyatt, C., 2001. "Bush and Putin: Best of friends." BBC, June 16.

Yalowitz, K. and Cornell, S.E., 2002. The Critical but Perilous Caucasus. *Orbis,* Volume 48, No. 1 2004, pp. 105–116.

Yeltsin, B., 1995. "The poverty of diplomacy and the diplomacy of poverty [Nischeta diplomatii I diplomatiya nischety]." *Kommersant*. Available from: www.kommersant. ru/doc/104256/print [accessed September 21, 2011].

Yevgrashina, L., 2008. "Azerbaijan Halts Oil Exports from Two Georgian Ports." Reuters, August 9.

Youngs, R., 2002. *The European Union and the Promotion of Democracy: Europe's Mediterranean and Asian Policies*. Oxford: Oxford University Press.

Youngs, R., 2008a. "Overview Assessing European Democracy Support in the Neighbourhood" in Youngs, R. (ed.), *Is the European Union supporting democracy in its neighbourhood?* Madrid: FRIDE, pp. 1–8.

Youngs, R., 2008b. "Is European democracy promotion on the wane?" *CEPS Working Documents*, 292.

Youngs, R., 2009. "Dicing with Democracy." *The World Today*, 65 (7), pp. 7–9.

Youngs, R., 2011. "Misunderstanding the maladies of liberal democracy promotion." *FRIDE Working Paper*, 106.

Youngs, R. and Shapovalova, N., 2011. *EU human rights policy towards Russia*. Directorate General for External Policies of the Union, European Parliament.

YPC, 1996. *1996: A record One Was Longing For*. Yerevan: Yerevan Press Club.

Zaborowski, M. (ed.), 2006. *Friends Again? EU–US Relations after the Crisis*. Paris: EU Institute for Security Studies.

Zakaria, F., 1997. "The Rise of Illiberal Democracy." *Foreign Affairs*, 76 (6), pp. 22–43.

Zakarian, A., 2002. "The Parliament's extraordinary hearing will discuss the proposed amendments to the law on NA proceedings [Khorhdarani artahert nstashrjany kqnnarki AZH kanonakarg orenqum arajarkvox popoxutyunnery]." Radio Free Europe/Radio Liberty. Available from: www.azatutyun.am/content/article/1569845.html [accessed September 28, 2011].

Zakarian, A., 2003. "Council Of Europe Head Calls For Free Elections in Caucasus." Radio Free Europe/Radio Liberty. Available from: www.azatutyun.am/content/article/1570755.html [accessed April 8, 2011].

Zakarian, A. and Tamrazian, H., 2003. "Opposition Challenges Election Results in Armenia's Highest Court." Radio Free Europe/Radio Liberty. Available from: www.azatutyun.am/content/article/1571784.html [accessed April 13, 2011].

Zanoni, L., 2013. "Europe, Azerbaijan, and caviar." *Osservatorio Balcani e Caucaso*. Available from: www.balcanicaucaso.org/eng/Regions-and-countries/Azerbaijan/Europe-Azerbaijan-and-caviar-144030 [accessed February 25, 2014].

Zarycky, G., 2010. Director of USAID Armenia Democracy and Governance Office. Interview with author, June, Yerevan, Armenia.

Zaynalov, M., 2009. "Azerbaijan–Gazprom Agreement Puts Nabucco in Jeopardy." *Today's Zaman*, July 16.

Zeeuw, J.D. and Kumar, K., 2006. *Promoting Democracy in Postconflict Societies*. Boulder, CO: Lynne Rienner.

Ziyadov, T., 2010. "Nagorno-Karabakh Negotiations: Though the Prism of a Multi-Issue Bargaining Model." *International Negotiation*, 15 (1), pp. 107–131.

Zourabian, L., 2006. "The Nagorno-Karabakh Settlement Revisited: Is Peace Achievable?" *Demokratizatsiya*, 14 (2), pp. 252–265.

Index

For Product Safety Concerns and Information please contact our EU
representative GPSR@taylorandfrancis.com
Taylor & Francis Verlag GmbH, Kaufingerstraße 24, 80331 München, Germany